T0316492

Population, Migration, and Socioeconomic Outcomes among Island and Mainland Puerto Ricans

Population, Migration, and Socioeconomic Outcomes among Island and Mainland Puerto Ricans

La Crisis Boricua

Marie T. Mora, Alberto Dávila and
Havidán Rodríguez

Foreword by Francisco L. Rivera-Batiz

LEXINGTON BOOKS
Lanham • Boulder • New York • London

Published by Lexington Books
An imprint of The Rowman & Littlefield Publishing Group, Inc.
4501 Forbes Boulevard, Suite 200, Lanham, Maryland 20706
www.rowman.com

Unit A, Whitacre Mews, 26-34 Stannary Street, London SE11 4AB

British Library Cataloguing in Publication Information Available
The hardback edition of this book was previously catalogued by the Library of Congress
as follows:

Library of Congress Cataloging-in-Publication Data Available

ISBN 978-1-4985-1686-0 (cloth: alk. paper)
ISBN 978-1-4985-1688-4 (pbk. : alk. paper)
ISBN 978-1-4985-1687-7 (electronic)

♾ ™ The paper used in this publication meets the minimum requirements of American
National Standard for Information Sciences—Permanence of Paper for Printed Library
Materials, ANSI/NISO Z39.48-1992.

Printed in the United States of America

We dedicate this book to the millions of Puerto Ricans, on both the island and the mainland, who continue to persevere and move forward to fulfill the ever-elusive American dream; to those who have not lost hope in the midst of La Crisis Boricua and in the aftermath of Hurricane María, but continue to aspire and work hard to achieve socioeconomic success; to those who, despite decades of economic stagnation, continue to devote themselves to improving their lives and those of their families; to those who have embarked on journeys between the island and the mainland, and throughout the continental United States as a consequence, in direct response, and in defiance to La Crisis Boricua and Hurricane María. To those Puerto Rican generations, past and present, we dedicate this book to you, and we are hopeful you will be able to fulfill the Puerto Rican dream.

Table of Contents

Illustrations

Tables

Foreword

Francisco L. Rivera-Batiz

Over the past decade, Puerto Rico has suffered one of its deepest economic and social crises in recent history. News stories about the Island's fiscal collapse and huge public debt appear on a weekly basis in the *New York Times*, *Wall Street Journal*, *The Economist*, and on the financial and economic pages of newspapers worldwide. This careful and well-researched volume by three prominent social scientists analyzes the sources of the crisis and its impact on the Puerto Rican population both on the Island and in the U.S. mainland. Tracing the demographics, migration patterns and socioeconomic outcomes of Puerto Ricans, this book presents a detailed picture of the changing and ultimately worrying landscape generated by the crisis.

Puerto Rico is at a critical juncture as a result of what the authors in this book call the "perfect storm" of economic shocks and long-standing trends that has affected its economy. The first, and most immediate, challenge arises from the government's dire financial situation. Underlying the fiscal crisis is the growth of public debt from $24 billion in 2000 to $74 billion in 2017. As a result, the ratio of debt to gross national product (GNP) rose from close to 58 percent in 2000 to 104 percent in 2017. This ballooning debt, which is compounded by $49 billion in pension obligations, is linked to decades of populist government over-spending. The accumulating debt eventually became impossible to service and in May 2017, Puerto Rico's Governor Ricardo Rosselló declared his intention to start bankruptcy-style procedures under the statutes of the Puerto Rico Oversight, Management, and Economic Stability Act (PROMESA) enacted by the U.S. Congress to manage the Island's fiscal crisis.

As the book documents, the second challenge facing Puerto Rico is its collapsing economy. The economic development strategy adopted by the government since the late 1940s—initially through the initiative called Operation

Bootstrap—relied heavily on integrating Puerto Rico into the U.S. economy and attracting U.S. foreign direct investment to the Island. This development model started to break down in the 1970s, partly as a result of rising competition from emerging markets in East Asia and Latin America. However, manufacturing employment in Puerto Rico remained strong because of a federal tax law that exempted U.S. firms operating on the Island from paying federal taxes on their profits (Section 936 of the Internal Revenue Service tax code). This sustained Puerto Rico as a pharmaceutical and manufacturing powerhouse. Furthermore, profits from these mostly American companies were deposited in the Puerto Rican financial system, which allowed the banking industry to grow as well, supporting a robust construction and real estate industry.

But most of the components of the development strategy pursued since the 1940s have been drastically undermined one by one over the last ten to fifteen years. First, the phase-out of Section 936, which began under the administration of President William Clinton in the mid-1990s and ended on December 31, 2005, led to a significant reduction of manufacturing production, as many pharmaceuticals and other firms closed their operations. Manufacturing employment in the Island dropped from 120,000 in 2003 to less than 79,000 in 2015. Foreign direct investment has shrunk and shows no sign of recovery in any significant way since then.

The American financial crisis of 2007–08 had a particularly severe impact on Puerto Rico. The period since the Great Recession started has been associated with a decline in the total number of employed workers in Puerto Rico from 1.3 million in 2006 to 990,000 in 2015, both through rising unemployment rates but also because of declining labor force participation rates, which are now below 40 percent. And linked to the collapse of the real estate and construction industries in the Island has been the downfall of a number of major local financial institutions. As a result, the assets of commercial banks in Puerto Rico decreased from $101.5 billion in 2005 to $59 billion in 2015, a decline that was matched by a sharp reduction of the banking sector's loan portfolios. The lack of access to credit has had a deep impact on the Island's private sector. Investment in physical capital declined sharply from 27 percent of GNP in 2001 to 13 percent in 2015. Compounding these changes has been a demographic transition that has reduced the natural rate of population growth and increased the fiscal burden of supporting an older, retired population.

This volume provides a timely and detailed analysis of the demographic and socioeconomic consequences of La Crisis Boricua. These consequences are deep and, as detailed in this book, they constitute historical changes for both the Island and for the United States. First is the outflow of people. The authors estimate that 646,932 people migrated out of Puerto Rico on a net basis between 2006 and 2016. This represents the largest population loss of the Island in any given decade since it became a territory of the United States in 1898. The outmigration cuts across any class and income lines in Puerto Rican society. Contrary to popular belief, the authors do find that, on average, less skilled persons were more likely to abandon the Island than the rest of the population, but at the same time they also find that there has been a substantial net outflow in specific fields, such a doctors and health professionals, a trend that may have severe consequences for health care. The drop in consumer demand associated with the population decline has also had a negative, multiplier impact on the Puerto Rican economy, sponsoring a vicious cycle of declining economic and population changes.

The substantial growth of the Puerto Rican population in the United States mainland is leading to significant social, economic, and political consequences that the book identifies with great clarity. According to the estimates provided by the authors, there are now over 5 million Puerto Ricans residing in the continental United States, as compared to the 3.3 million residing on the Island. This has been accompanied by a shift from traditional migration areas, such as the New York metropolitan area, to others, such as Florida and Texas. Furthermore, there appear to be significant differences in the characteristics of migrants moving to different regions—such as in education and skills—which may compound inequalities among the different recipient areas. For instance, the authors of the volume estimate that poverty rates of recent Puerto Rican migrants in New York and Massachusetts are close to 60 percent, while in Florida they are 33 percent and in Texas, 14 percent. Notwithstanding these differentials, the overall poverty rates of Puerto Ricans in the United States remain distressingly higher than for the overall American population. The authors also find significant differences in migration patterns and socioeconomic outcomes on the basis of gender.

The consequences of the growth of Puerto Ricans on politics in the United States are examined in this volume. Puerto Ricans tend to vote Democratic and in a country where elections are closely contested, this can have a major impact. In Florida, for example, Puerto Ricans are likely to soon surpass the Cuban population—which has traditionally voted Republican. But Florida elections have been relatively close now for a number of election cycles and Florida is one of the key states involved in turning around the balance of electoral votes one way or another. In fact, the vote of stateside Puerto Ricans may very well decide who will be the next president of the United States.

Puerto Rico and Puerto Ricans are currently at a crossroads both in their economic development and in their situation as a people. A fiscal crisis and a long-term secular stagnation threaten the socioeconomic status of the Island's population and have led to migration flows with deep consequences. The economic development strategies adopted in the past are collapsing. And while the political influence of Puerto Ricans in the mainland is growing, the political status of the Island as a territory of the United States is increasingly being questioned. The authors of this book provide a fresh, rigorous, state-of-the-art look at Puerto Rico's conundrum and its socioeconomic and policy implications. This book is required reading for anyone interested on Puerto Rico, Puerto Ricans, Latinos, and American society.

Preface

At the landmark centennial anniversary of the 1917 Jones-Shafroth Act which granted Puerto Ricans U.S. citizenship, even before Hurricane María, the island confronted an unfolding humanitarian crisis that was triggered by an acute economic crisis surging for more than a decade. Consequences of what we refer to as La Crisis Boricua include massive outmigration on a scale not seen for 60 years; a shrinking and rapidly aging population; a shutdown of high-tech industries; a significant loss in public and private sector jobs; a deteriorating infrastructure, including education, health care, and public utilities; higher sales taxes than any of the states; $74 billion in public debt plus another $49 billion in pension obligations; and defaults on payments to bondholders. La Crisis Boricua exacerbated the chronic problems that already permeated the island for decades, including high rates of unemployment and widespread poverty.

If there was ever a time for scholars to analyze how the island's socioeconomic conditions affect Puerto Ricans on the island and U.S. mainland, it is now. Even though only one of us (Havidán) is Puerto Rican, all of our Puerto Rican colleagues on the island and mainland (and many other colleagues) with whom we have discussed our findings have expressed deep interest and enthusiasm for our work. One recent example as our book went to press was during an engaged panel discussion, sponsored by the American Society of Hispanic Economists (ASHE) at the 2017 Western Economic Association International (WEAI) annual meetings.

We started working on this project in 2013, "only" seven years into La Crisis Boricua, although ironically our initial focus was not about Puerto Rico. Our colleague William Vélez had invited us to write a book chapter about socioeconomic outcomes of Puerto Ricans living on the U.S. mainland. However, the more we delved into the data, the more questions we had.

For example, we noticed that the share of all island-born Puerto Ricans who resided on the mainland had been rising (due to the massive net outmigration), but their share among all mainland residents had been falling (due to the relatively high population growth of mainland-born Puerto Ricans that more than offset the migration effects). We also noticed that contrary to some of the media reports about "brain drain" from the island, the data showed that highly educated Puerto Ricans were not disproportionately represented among recent migrants from Puerto Rico. Moreover, we found that the socioeconomic characteristics of recent migrants varied considerably across the destination areas, with some of the largest disparities occurring in the more established settlement areas.

Thus, the planned book chapter soon evolved into several manuscripts, which we began presenting at a variety of conferences and workshops. At one such conference, the 2014 WEAI annual conference in Denver, Colorado, we presented a paper in an ASHE session on "The Puerto Rican Economy, Migration, and Employment Outcomes." There we had the opportunity to talk with Joseph Parry, a representative of Lexington Books, about the importance of learning more on how Puerto Rico's economic crisis was affecting Puerto Ricans on the island and mainland, including in Florida and "nontraditional" settlement areas (such as Texas). He invited us to submit a book proposal on this topic (which we did later in the year).

Of coincidental timing, Havidán spent Christmas with family in Puerto Rico that year. He was able to see firsthand some of the effects of La Crisis Boricua, such as the deteriorating infrastructure; he also gathered anecdotal evidence about its impacts through conversations with family and friends. Given his impressions, the three of us realized we would have much clearer insights and perspectives into our empirical findings by traveling to Puerto Rico as a research team to record our impressions during this historic time. As such, we took our first collaborative research trip in April 2015, which involved visiting twenty-five of the seventy-eight *municipios* within a four-day period. The book cover alone (described in Appendix C) is one of the direct outcomes of that trip.

While any intensive traveling (whether for personal or professional reasons) naturally provides opportunities for self-reflection, Havidán was able to use this particular trip to personally retrace steps taken on his own personal and professional journey by visiting some of the places he had not seen since he was a child or young adult. For Marie, this trip was her first visit to Puerto Rico; as such, beyond being struck by the warmth and hospitality (and the delicious food!), her initial impressions of the island's socioeconomic conditions and infrastructure were formed nearly a decade into La Crisis Boricua, and will forever serve as her reference point. Alberto had been in Puerto Rico several times before, but this trip was a way to solidify his interpretation what he was observing in the data versus what was happening "on the ground."

Our second collaborative research trip occurred in January 2016; by that time, we already realized we had more empirical results than what would possibly fit into one book (one colleague commented that we probably had enough results for eight books). To ensure that the topics we wanted to highlight in this book were consistent with some of the more critical issues confronting Puerto Ricans, we arranged to discuss our findings with colleagues at the Puerto Rico Institute of Statistics (including Mario Marazzi Santiago, Executive Director, and Alberto Velasquez) as well as the University of Puerto Rico at Cayey (including José Caraballo Cueto, Director of the Census Information Center, and Raúl Figueroa-Rodríguez, Demographer). These discussions were extremely productive, engaging, and insightful. Moreover, it was during this trip that we learned about the availability of the Travelers Survey (TS) (*La Encuesta de Viajeros*) dataset, which we subsequently used to provide a more complete profile of migrants leaving the island in this book.

We note that working on this book brought many challenges as we took on a critically important topic that was continually unfolding. Numerous times we had to update a significant number of estimates to account for new releases of annual datasets (including the American Community Survey [ACS] and the Puerto Rican Community Survey [PRCS]), as we wanted our book to be as current and relevant as possible when it appeared in print. (Even so, we realized we could not update everything or we would never finish.) We also had to adjust and update a number of discussions on potential policy prescriptions to account for shifting and new policy-related initiatives, mandates, and legislation, such as the Puerto Rico Oversight, Management and Economic Stability Act (PROMESA) signed into law by then-President Barack Obama on June 28, 2016.

While much of our book is data-driven and in some places rely heavily on sophisticated empirical techniques, we have stylistically attempted to avoid the use of methodological jargon. Because of the potential role and grave importance of our empirical findings to inform and shape policy at this critical time, we felt it was our responsibility to present the results in an accessible and "reader-friendly" manner. Still, for readers wishing to digest the econometric/statistical details, we encourage them to refer to the technical Appendix B.

In all we believe that, at a minimum, our account provides detailed empirical insights into the acute effects La Crisis Boricua has had on the people of Puerto Rico and on Puerto Rican communities stateside. After a century of U.S. citizenship, the island was facing a humanitarian crisis even before Hurricane María, with little signs of recovery. As concerned and committed social scientists, we have much to contribute to this discussion.

Acknowledgments

We have been fortunate to work with a number of excellent friends and colleagues who have given us invaluable insights, suggestions, and assistance that helped to shape and guide our work during the past four years (even before we had a book contract), resulting in the book we have today. We would be remiss if we did not give a special acknowledgment to the following: Mark Hugo López; Walter Díaz; Mario Marazzi Santiago; Alberto Velazquez; José Caraballo Cueto; Raúl Figueroa-Rodríguez; William Vélez; Edwin Meléndez; Kirk Birson; María Enchautegui; Alexis Santos; Luisa Blanco Raynal; Anita Alves Pena; Myriam Quispe-Agnoli; Rogelio Sáenz; Stephen Trejo; José Padín; Carlos Vargas-Silva; and participants in a variety of conference sessions during the past four years, including those organized by the American Society of Hispanic Economists and the National Economic Association. Moreover, we are extremely appreciative of Francisco Rivera-Batiz for writing such a gracious and thoughtful Foreword. We also gratefully acknowledge John Ned, Jose Yvan Vazquez, Nora Espinoza Dávila, and Xu Sun for their research assistance at various stages throughout this project; Melba Sotelo for magically finding critical meeting times in tight schedules where none initially seemed possible; and Joseph Parry for having reached out to us to submit a book proposal and encouraging us ever since. Finally, Marie Mora gives a special heartfelt thanks to Margarita Rivera for her warmth and hospitality (and delicious pasteles) in Arecibo during our April 2015 collaborative research trip.

Authors' Addendum

Hurricane María

On September 20, 2017, Hurricane María brought catastrophic devastation and suffering across the entire island of Puerto Rico, making landfall with flooding rains and 155 mile-per-hour maximum sustained winds, equivalent to an EF-3 tornado and just one mile shy of wind speeds of a Category 5 hurricane. Described by Puerto Rico Governor Ricardo Rosselló as the "most devastating storm of the century," María's aftermath left the island's 3.4 million U.S. citizens without electricity (which the media reported would take months to restore), fresh water, fuel, and telecommunications. Other critical necessities, such as food supplies and medicine, were quickly diminishing. More than a week after María's landfall, a lot of the disaster relief, including water, food, and medicine, remained in ports or in trucks without drivers, and could not be delivered to those most in need due to logistical and transportation issues, especially outside the San Juan metropolitan area. Puerto Rico's critical infrastructure (already weakened by the effects of La Crisis Boricua plus Hurricane Irma which grazed the island just two weeks before)—including the island's power grid, buildings, dams, roads, bridges, and the agricultural sector—were significantly damaged or completely destroyed, setting Puerto Rico back for decades. A CNN article by Jill Disis (2017) released eight days after María's landfall reported that cost estimates to Puerto Rico ranged between $30 billion and $95 billion. The official death toll from María stood at 16 in Puerto Rico, but as Omaya Sosa Pascual (2017) reported in The Miami Herald, María-related deaths could be in the dozens or even hundreds.

We expected that when we submitted our final manuscript to Lexington Books in the Summer of 2017, Puerto Rico, with its $74 billion in debt plus $49 billion in unfunded pensions, would continue to endure hardships for quite some time as La Crisis Boricua showed no signs of relenting. Unfortunately, we did not anticipate that the island's then-unfolding humanitarian crisis would soon become full-blown by such an unusually powerful hurricane, which made landfall literally two days before we received the page proofs for this book. Despite the fact that Puerto Rico has a larger population than 21 of the states and Washington, DC, the seemingly slow response by some U.S. government officials (such as taking eight days after María's landfall for the U.S. to temporarily waive the 1920 Jones Act restrictions that were reportedly hindering disaster-relief efforts in Puerto Rico), exemplified the complicated relationship Puerto Rico has with the United States. That said, the strong humanitarian response and support through disaster relief aid that went to Puerto Rico from many states, including New York and Florida, was commendable and raised some degree of hope. We can only hope that the sense of urgency and the delivery of disaster relief will continue, and that it will reach those in desperate need.

In terms of the lingering effects of María, we anticipate they will amplify many of the demographic shifts and socioeconomic changes we describe throughout this book, including the massive net outmigration, thus expediting the aging of the population and the population's net decline on the island, and increasing the already relatively large Puerto Rican population growth on the mainland. The most socioeconomically vulnerable groups in Puerto Rico, such as women (especially the less educated), children, and the elderly, will likely be the most affected. As such, if the geographic settlement patterns continue along the lines of socioeconomic characteristics that we report in this book, the incidence of poverty among stateside Puerto Ricans will likely be exacerbated in the traditional receiving areas. However, it is worth noting that throughout their history, Puerto Ricans have shown that in the midst of social and economic difficulties, they are a resilient community; hope is always on the horizon; hard work and perseverance has always been present; and the expectations for a better future continue to be at the forefront. These traits are greatly needed, especially in the aftermath of this historic crisis.

Chapter 1

The Elusive American Dream

La Crisis Boricua in Perspective

At the landmark centennial anniversary of the 1917 Jones-Shafroth Act, which granted Puerto Ricans U.S. citizenship, the island confronts an unfolding humanitarian crisis. Puerto Rico's decade-long (and still ongoing) economic crisis—henceforth La Crisis Boricua—has resulted in massive outmigration on a relative scale not seen for sixty years; a shrinking and rapidly aging population; a crippling shutdown of high-tech industries; a significant loss in public and private sector jobs; a deteriorating infrastructure (including the infrastructures related to education, health care, and public utilities); higher sales taxes than any of the states; $74 billion in public debt plus another $49 billion in pension obligations; defaults on payments to bondholders; and at the time this book was being finalized, the filing for bankruptcy protection. This unrelenting crisis exacerbated the chronic problems that already permeated the island for decades, including high rates of unemployment and widespread poverty. Thus, on both the island and U.S. mainland, this "perfect storm" left Puerto Ricans facing grave and unprecedented economic, social, and demographic challenges.

In this book, we provide empirical and theoretical insights into such challenges by investigating how La Crisis Boricua affected migration patterns, employment, and other socioeconomic and demographic outcomes among Puerto Ricans on the island and mainland. We anticipate that our findings and policy implications will contribute to the public discourse of identifying viable solutions to stem the crisis and improve the socioeconomic outcomes of millions of American citizens. The economic and humanitarian crisis permeating Puerto Rican society as this book goes into press, the major exodus of Puerto Ricans to the mainland, and the increasing number of Puerto Ricans throughout the U.S. mainland, including in nontraditional areas, make this a timely and policy-relevant book. We also expect that future social scientists and other scholars will find our study to be of academic and policy interest, as we provide a detailed analytical "snapshot" of issues and outcomes of particular relevance to Puerto Ricans, taken as these historic events are unfolding.

Moreover, the regional and national importance of this book goes beyond the Commonwealth of Puerto Rico and stateside Puerto Rican communities. In broader terms, La Crisis Boricua provides a natural setting to analyze the socioeconomic and demographic impacts of massive net outmigration on receiving and sending communities as well as factors related to the adjustment of migrants into their receiving communities. Consider also that Puerto Ricans represent the second largest Hispanic group (after Mexican Americans), and one of the fastest growing populations, living in the continental U.S. As Table 1.1 shows, the 5.37 million Puerto Ricans living stateside in 2015 represented nearly one out of ten Hispanics in the 50 states plus Washington, D.C.[1] When including the additional 3.33 million Puerto Ricans residing on the island in 2015,[2] Puerto Ricans represented nearly 15 percent of all Hispanics in the states plus Puerto Rico. Not surprisingly, in certain traditional settlement areas on the eastern seaboard, including New York, Pennsylvania, Massachusetts, and Connecticut, Puerto Ricans represented the largest Hispanic group.

Moreover, the geographic coverage of their regional impacts has expanded due to recent migration shifts, as we explore throughout this book. In Florida (which can be considered as an "older new" destination state),[3] there were 1.1 million Puerto Rican residents in 2015—essentially the same number as those in New York. Even Texas, a state with virtually no historical ties with the island, represented the fourth largest receiving area (6.8%) of all Puerto Rican migrants from the island between 2006 and 2015, as Table 1.1 shows. It was also the third largest (behind Florida and Pennsylvania) for adult migrants from the island between the ages of twenty-five and sixty-four.

It follows that these shifts in island-to-mainland migration patterns (and those internal to the mainland as discussed in more detail in chapter 5), along with their relatively high mainland fertility rates, have resulted in a greater role for Puerto Ricans to shape the socioeconomic and demographic outcomes in both Puerto Rico and areas on the U.S. mainland, including those in which Puerto Ricans had a negligible presence before the onset of La Crisis Boricua.

AN OVERVIEW OF PUERTO RICAN MIGRATION AND POPULATION GROWTH

As noted, the sheer magnitude of net outmigration during Puerto Rico's unrelenting economic crisis has triggered a series of additional economic, social, and demographic challenges for the island and mainland. Between 2006 and 2016 alone, we estimate that on net, 646,932 people (Puerto Rican

Table 1.1 Puerto Rican Population Size: Overall and in Selected States, 2015

State or Puerto Rico	Puerto Rican Population Size	Puerto Ricans among Total Population (%)	Receiving Area of Incoming Migrants from PR: 2006–2015 (%)	Puerto Rican Population Growth: 2006–2015 (%)	Largest Hispanic Group (% among Hispanics)	Second Largest Hispanic Group (% among Hispanics)
U.S. Mainland and Puerto Rico	8,696,208	2.7	—	—	Mexican Americans (59.7)	Puerto Ricans (14.5)
Puerto Rico	3,325,095	95.7	—	−11.1	Puerto Ricans (96.9)	Dominicans (1.9)
U.S. Mainland	5,371,113	1.7	100.0	34.8	Mexican Americans (63.3)	Puerto Ricans (9.5)
New York	1,073,024	5.4	8.4	−1.6	Puerto Ricans (28.8)	Dominicans (23.1)
Florida	1,066,737	5.3	33.7	57.3	Cubans (28.5)	Puerto Ricans (21.5)
New Jersey	502,677	5.6	5.3	26.1	Puerto Ricans (28.5)	Dominicans (16.2)
Pennsylvania	444,366	3.5	9.3	53.2	Puerto Ricans (51.2)	Mexican Americans (16.0)
Massachusetts	314,528	4.6	6.5	37.4	Puerto Ricans (41.5)	Dominicans (17.8)
Connecticut	276,275	7.7	4.4	26.9	Puerto Ricans (49.8)	Mexican Americans (9.5)
Texas	189,313	0.7	6.8	108.9	Mexican Americans (86.7)	Salvadorans (2.9)

Source: Authors' estimates using 2006 and 2015 ACS and PRCS data in the IPUMS.
Notes: Puerto Ricans and Hispanics are based on self-identification. The total population on the U.S. mainland increased by 7.4 percent between 2006 and 2015. Incoming migrants are Puerto Ricans who moved from the island to the mainland within twelve months of the survey.

or otherwise) migrated from Puerto Rico to the U.S. mainland or another country, which represented 16.5 percent of the island's 2006 population (see Table 1.2). This net outmigration flow over the decade represents the largest population loss the island has experienced on an absolute basis, and the second largest loss on a relative basis, since becoming a U.S. territory.[4]

While 2016 data were not available to determine the destination country as this book went to press, the U.S. mainland would have received the vast majority of these migrants. Indeed, when focusing on the 2006–2015 period, Table 1.2 shows that the mainland received three-quarters (74.4%) of the migrants (433,955 out of 582,175), equivalent to 12.5 percent of the island's 2006 population. When focusing exclusively on individuals who identified themselves as Puerto Ricans, the net outmigration between the island and U.S. mainland was smaller, at 277,988 (64.1% of these migrants, and 7.4% of the island's 2006 Puerto Rican population), but was nevertheless substantial.[5]

Table 1.2   Net Outmigration from Puerto Rico: 2006–2016 Overview Plus 2006–2015 Detailed Estimates by Puerto Rican Ethnicity

Characteristic	Estimates
Panel A: Changes between 2006 and 2016	
Population in Puerto Rico in 2006	3,926,744
Population in Puerto Rico in 2016	3,411,307
Total change in population	-515,437
Natural increase (live births-deaths) in Puerto Rico	131,495
Net outmigration from Puerto Rico: 2006–2016	*646,932*
(Percentage of Puerto Rico's 2006 population)	*(16.5%)*
Panel B: Changes between 2006 and 2015, by Puerto Rican and non-PR ethnicity	
Population in Puerto Rico in 2006	3,926,744
Population in Puerto Rico in 2015	3,473,181
Total change in population	-453,563
Natural increase (live births-deaths) in Puerto Rico	128,612
Net outmigration from Puerto Rico: 2006–2015	*582,175*
(Percentage of Puerto Rico's 2006 population)	*(14.8%)*
Net outmigration to U.S. mainland	*433,955*
(Percentage of net outmigrants)	*(74.5%)*
Net outmigration of Puerto Ricans to mainland	277,988
(Percentage of net outmigrants to mainland)	(64.1%)
Net outmigration of non-Puerto Ricans to mainland	155,967
(Percentage of net outmigrants to mainland)	(35.9%)
Net outmigration to other countries	*148,220*
(Percentage of net outmigrants)	*(25.5%)*

Source: Authors' estimates using data on the population and natural increase estimates from the U.S. Census Bureau (http://www.census.gov/popest/estimates.html) and from data on recent migrants in the 2006–2015 ACS in the IPUMS.

Notes: Puerto Ricans versus non-Puerto Ricans (non-PR) are based on self-identification. Data (2016) were not available to provide detailed estimates by ethnicity and outmigration to the U.S. mainland versus other countries as the book went to press.

Given the island's already low fertility rate and the higher propensity of younger versus older individuals to migrate, the recent outmigration has left behind a rapidly aging population that is experiencing negative population growth. As Table 1.1 shows, between 2006 and 2015, the Puerto Rican population on the island declined by 11.1 percent, which was the first time the island experienced a population loss, on record.[6] In contrast, fueled by the massive net migration from the island and relatively high mainland fertility rates, the Puerto Rican population living stateside increased by 34.8 percent between 2006 and 2015 (from 3.99 million to 5.37 million), which was nearly five times greater than the 7.4 percent growth rate in the mainland population overall.

For a better understanding of the Puerto Rican diaspora, Panel A in Figure 1.1 shows the percentage of all Puerto Ricans (regardless of birthplace) who resided in Puerto Rico between 2006 and 2015. In 2006, nearly half (48.4%) of all Puerto Ricans lived on the island; nine years into Puerto Rico's crisis, the share of Puerto Ricans residing on the island had fallen by ten percentage points (to 38.2%). These numbers suggest that the prediction made by Edwin Meléndez and Vargas-Ramos in 2013—that two-thirds of all Puerto Ricans will reside on the U.S. mainland as early as 2020—is well on track to becoming a reality.

An Overview of Puerto Rican Population Growth by Region

Table 1.1 also shows the states which received at least four percent of Puerto Rican migrants from the island between 2006 and 2015.[7] Despite New York's history of being the traditional gateway area, Florida received a full third of all incoming migrants from the island during this time, and is poised to overtake New York as the state with the largest Puerto Rican population (if it has not done so already). In fact, during the first nine years of La Crisis Boricua, the Puerto Rican population grew by 57.3 percent in Florida, but shrank by 1.6 percent in New York. These population shifts over a relatively short period of time are presented in Panel B of Figure 1.1, which documents how Florida became home to an increasing share of the Puerto Rican population since 2006, while New York lost ground. Net migration from the island as well as from other states and relatively high fertility rates are explanatory factors for the population increase of Puerto Ricans in Florida.

In four of the five traditional receiving areas shown in Table 1.1 (Pennsylvania being the exception), the Puerto Rican population growth rates were close to (in the case of Massachusetts) or below the mainland's average growth in this population. In contrast, over the nine-year period, the number of Puerto Ricans in Texas more than doubled. It follows that La Crisis Boricua affected states and regions well beyond those with traditional Puerto Rican

Chapter 1

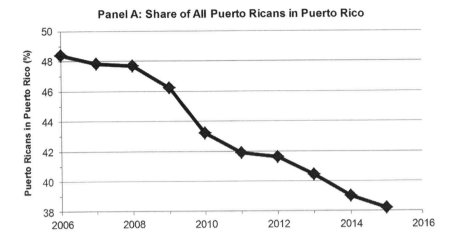

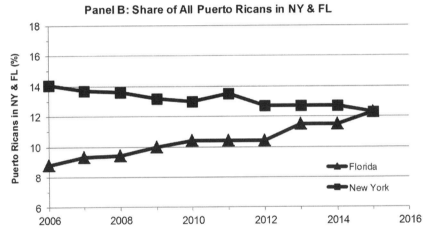

Figure 1.1   Percentage of All Puerto Ricans Residing in Puerto Rico, New York, and Florida: 2006–2015. *Source*: Authors' estimates using ACS and PRCS data in the IPUMS. *Notes*: The sample only includes individuals who identify themselves as Puerto Rican. The percentages of all Puerto Ricans in 2006 who lived in Puerto Rico (48.4%), New York (14.1%), and Florida (8.8%) statistically differed (at the 1% level) from the corresponding percentages in 2015 (38.2%, 12.3%, and 12.3%, respectively).

communities, including areas in which few Puerto Ricans resided at the turn of the millennium.

Despite their growing presence on the mainland, and the interest in recent years in Hispanic-related socioeconomic issues by social scientists, policymakers, the media, and the public at-large, Puerto Ricans are often overlooked in comprehensive and rigorous (yet publicly accessible) studies examining demographic and social mobility outcomes on both the mainland and island.[8] As a consequence of La Crisis Boricua, it has become imperative that we have a better understanding of the demographic, socioeconomic, and political realities and implications for this large and rapidly growing group of U.S. citizens who have experienced social, economic, and political marginalization for nearly 525 years (first under Spain, and then 120 years as a U.S. territory). Moreover, as this book went to press, the literature offered few comprehensive analytical analyses and insights into the socioeconomic and demographic outcomes of La Crisis Boricua for island and mainland Puerto Ricans even though it had been surging for over a decade. We believe this book is an important and major step in addressing these research voids.

IDENTIFYING AND ADDRESSING ISSUES AND CHALLENGES

Chapter 2 provides an overview of Puerto Rico's demographic, social, and economic development over time, starting with the conquest by Spain 525 years ago, especially after Puerto Rico became part of the United States as a result of the Spanish American War. We also pay close attention to Puerto Rico's population and economic development policies, strategies, and initiatives, along with their impacts on the island's growth and development and migration trends between the island and the mainland.

In chapter 3, we make the case that the massive migration flows of Puerto Ricans from the island to the mainland were primarily the result of significant economic and policy changes in Puerto Rico that led to the "perfect storm" of events in 2006. These changes included a fiscal crisis that resulted in the imposition of a sales tax and a significant reduction in public sector jobs (compounding the already weak labor market); the elimination of income tax breaks for corporations operating on the island, which resulted in a significant decline in manufacturing jobs; and rising energy prices on the island. Combined with already high levels of unemployment and poverty, these factors contributed to the recent unprecedented net migration flows to the mainland.

We also analyze the socioeconomic and demographic characteristics of Puerto Ricans migrants after conceptually discussing how such characteristics affect decisions to migrate in chapter 4. Unlike headlines in the popular press published during Puerto Rico's crisis, we do not find that the recent migrants were overwhelmingly drawn from a highly educated population. (That said, the outmigration of physicians, nurses, and other healthcare professionals has been a real problem for the island, contributing to its humanitarian crisis.) We conclude the chapter with a conceptual and empirical discussion of migrants who returned to the island despite the ongoing crisis.

Along with analyzing differences across the major destination states with respect to the reported reasons for leaving the island during La Crisis Boricua, chapter 5 explores the increased interstate migration and continued geographic dispersion of Puerto Ricans on the mainland. Our results show that while Puerto Ricans living stateside are relatively geographically concentrated (particularly those with lower levels of schooling), they became more dispersed after 2006. The increased incidence of geographic dispersion was not only driven by migrants from the island; it was especially pronounced among Puerto Ricans born in the continental United States

In chapter 6, we further document important demographic and socioeconomic differences between Puerto Ricans residing in traditional receiving states relative to those moving to other destinations, such as Florida and Texas. Previous literature has documented a process of selective migration among Puerto Ricans with high levels of education and other human capital who relocate to new destinations. Consistent with this literature, we find that Puerto Ricans in these new areas (especially in Texas) have higher labor force participation rates and income relative to those remaining in the so-called traditional states. At the same time, when further adjusting for skill levels, Puerto Ricans fared worse in Texas with respect to labor market earnings (although this was not the case for the likelihood of being impoverished).

Given the important and critical role of Puerto Rican women in the socioeconomic well-being of their families, chapter 7 focuses on gender-related outcomes. Island-born women have more education on average than their male counterparts; however, compared to women remaining on the island, less educated women appear to have been disproportionately represented among the outmigration flow to the mainland, more so than men. Some of these differences appear to relate to gender differences in the reported reasons for moving. We also highlight the critically dire economic circumstances among Puerto Ricans in the traditional receiving states, especially among women, who migrated during La Crisis Boricua.

We consider in chapter 8 some of the potential socioeconomic and political impacts of Puerto Ricans on the U.S. mainland, particularly since 2006. We assess these impacts by examining changes in the number and characteristics of businesses owned by Puerto Ricans on the mainland overall as well as within the major receiving states. Socioeconomic and demographic characteristics associated with the likelihood of being self-employed are also considered. We further discuss recent changes in voter participation rates and turnout at the national level, and consider potential implications in future elections. Finally, chapter 9 discusses the likely near-term future of Puerto Rico, including under the Puerto Rico Oversight, Management, and Economic Stability Act (PROMESA). It also describes steps being taken (at the time this book went to production) to address La Crisis Boricua, and concludes with a set of policy recommendations.

SUMMARY AND CONCLUDING REMARKS

The economic and humanitarian crisis currently permeating Puerto Rico through the unprecedented national debt, the major exodus of Puerto Ricans to the mainland, and the increasing geographic dispersion of Puerto Ricans on the U.S. mainland mean that migration patterns, employment, and socio-economic outcomes of Puerto Ricans have increasingly important implications nationally and regionally, far outside of the Commonwealth. Our book explores many of the challenges Puerto Ricans are facing, along with the implications, as a result of La Crisis Boricua. We argue in our final chapter that this is a time not only for disaster response, but also for mitigation and preparedness to curtail similar events in the future, providing Puerto Ricans on the island and the mainland the economic opportunities they merit and deserve to achieve the ever-elusive American dream.

NOTES

1. We identify Puerto Ricans and other ethnic groups based on self-identification in surveys. Unless otherwise indicated, our empirical estimates are from our analyses of Public- Use Microdata from the American Community Survey (ACS) and the Puerto Rican Community Survey (PRCS), made available by the Integrated Public Use Microdata Series (IPUMS); details of these datasets can be found in appendix A.

2. Puerto Rico's total population was 3.47 million in 2015, 3.33 million of whom identified as Puerto Rican.

3. Florida, particularly central Florida, began emerging as a major destination area for Puerto Ricans in the 1970s, as migration patterns shifted due to the deindustrialization and relatively high cost of living in the Northeast and Midwest (e.g., Silver and Vélez 2014; Delerme 2013; Silver 2010).

4. As we note in chapter 2, during the period of its Great Migration, Puerto Rico lost 470,000 residents due to net outmigration between 1950 and 1960 alone, which represented 21.3 percent of the island's population in 1950. The net outmigration during Puerto Rico's Great Migration remains one of the largest, proportionally speaking, migratory movements of the twentieth century (Rivera-Batiz and Santiago 1996; Whalen and Vázquez-Hernández 2005).

5. Non-Puerto Ricans were disproportionately represented among these migrants. They represented over one-third (35.9%) of the migrants, but additional estimates from the PRCS indicate non-Puerto Ricans represented 4.3 percent of the island's total population between 2006 and 2015. A detailed analysis of the migration patterns

among non-Puerto Ricans goes beyond the scope of our study, but it serves as topic worthy of future research.

6. Examining the island's total population on an annual basis indicates that it began shrinking between 2009 and 2010. Since then, the island has continued to face a negative population growth rate on an annual basis. (Putting this into context, even during the height of the Great Migration in the 1950s, the island's population continued growing). The population of individuals identified as Puerto Rican on the island started falling a year earlier.

7. The distribution of location settlements of Puerto Rican migrants—both between the island and mainland as well as interstate migrants—will be explored extensively in chapter 5.

8. Noteworthy exceptions include Francisco Rivera-Batiz and Carlos Santiago (1996), Carmen Whalen and Giovani Vázquez-Hernández (2005); Edna Acosta-Belén and Carlos Enrique Santiago (2006); the volume edited by Susan Collins, Barry Bosworth, and Miguel Soto-Class (2006); and other edited volumes on Hispanic/Latino populations (e.g., Rodríguez, Sáenz, and Menjívar 2008). The Pew Research Center Hispanic Trends Project, and under Edwin Meléndez, the Center for Puerto Rican Studies at Hunter College, also have a history of disaggregating by Hispanic subgroups when possible. Both centers have been reporting on various aspects of La Crisis Boricua.

Chapter 2

The Growth and Emergence of the Puerto Rican "Nation"

Economic Development, Mass Migration, and Population Composition

After more than four centuries of Spanish control, the successful invasion of Puerto Rico by the United States resulted in an intertwined and often complicated relationship that laid the groundwork for La Crisis Boricua. To provide insight into the Puerto Rico of today, this chapter first presents a brief historical overview of the island,[1] and then highlights key policies and initiatives related to industrialization, fertility and birth control, and migration that have taken place over the decades. We also provide an overview of changes in socioeconomic and demographic outcomes in Puerto Rico during the twentieth century as a contextual basis for the conditions the island has been undergoing since the start of La Crisis Boricua in 2006—the year that we describe in the next chapter as the "perfect storm."

A BRIEF HISTORICAL OVERVIEW

For over 400 years, Puerto Rico remained a colony of Spain, after Cristopher Columbus first arrived in Puerto Rico in 1493. As a result of the invasion by the Spanish, the exploitation of the local native population ensued (namely, the Tainos—the indigenous population of the island) to harvest gold for Spain, and new diseases were introduced to the island, which led to significant epidemics. An implication of these events, coupled with the flight of many of these indigenous groups to other parts of the Caribbean, the Tainos were all but decimated on the island once called Borikén. To deal with the declining Taino population and shrinking indentured labor force, the Spanish government began introducing African slaves to the island in relatively large numbers.

With the passing of time and closer to the late nineteenth century, Puerto Rico began gaining some level of autonomy from Spain. The 1868

"El Grito de Lares," a local insurrection by island residents against the Spanish government seeking independence for Puerto Rico, marked the beginning of Puerto Rico's independence from Spain. In 1897, the *Carta Autonómica* (Charter of Autonomy) granted quasi-political and economic autonomy to Puerto Rico. This was a major accomplishment for the island after over four centuries of Spanish colonization, but it was extremely short-lived. In 1898, Puerto Rico was ceded to the United States as a bounty or compensation for the expenses of the Spanish-American War under the Treaty of Paris. Puerto Rico's struggle to become a sovereign nation was trumped by these historical developments, and has now been curtailed for well over half a millennium. As indicated by Raul Figueroa-Rodríguez, "Puerto Rico, after all, is a territory that for centuries has been unable to chart its own destiny or make its own choices" (2013:1).

When the United States invaded Puerto Rico in 1898, the population (estimated at over 950,000 one year later) was characterized by extreme poverty, astronomical rates of illiteracy (over 85%), and high fertility and mortality rates. Malnutrition was widespread, infectious diseases were the order of the day, and Puerto Rico's economy was almost exclusively dependent on agriculture. Along with the island and its inhabitants, the United States "inherited" a major health, social, and economic crisis.

Just two years after the invasion, the Foraker Act (1900) allowed for the establishment of a civilian government in Puerto Rico with limited powers under the jurisdiction and control of the United States. In 1917, despite the fact that the Puerto Rican House of Delegates unanimously voted against it,[2] under the Jones-Shafroth Act (more commonly known as the Jones Act), from April 25, 1917 onward, U.S. citizenship was automatically (and retroactively) granted to everyone born in Puerto Rico. However, the newly acquired citizenship came at a significant cost as shortly thereafter, Puerto Ricans were required to serve in the U.S. military and drafted in large numbers to serve in World War I to defend their new "homeland" (Carr 1984; Picó 1988).[3]

It was not until 1948, when the first democratic elections were held on the island, that Puerto Rico elected its first governor, José Luis Alberto Muñoz Marín—better known as Luis Muñoz Marín. With the approval of the Constitution of Puerto Rico in 1952, the island became the Estado Libre Asociado (ELA) or the Commonwealth of Puerto Rico. The literal translation of the ELA is "Associated Free State." However, Puerto Rico is neither a state nor a sovereign and free nation, but remains a territory which, as we discuss in more detail in chapter 9, has been characterized as a colony of the United States.

This fact was highlighted in June 2016, with the establishment of the "Oversight Board"[4] as part of the Puerto Rico Oversight, Management and

Economic Stability Act (PROMESA). The Governor of Puerto Rico only serves as a nonvoting ex-officio member of the Board, and the Puerto Rican government has no power, oversight, or control over the Board's work, decisions, or outcomes. Regardless of the intent or potential inevitability of PROMESA, as we note in chapter 9, social scientists, policymakers, legal analysts (including in an April 2017 issue of the *Harvard Law Review*), community activists, and others have voiced concerns about the significance of PROMESA for Puerto Rico's status as a U.S. territory.

From the "Poorhouse" to the "Shining Star of the Caribbean": Social, Economic, and Demographic Transformations

Despite its new status as a U.S. territory, unemployment, poverty, and malnutrition remained endemic problems that were greatly exacerbated during the Great Depression.[5] With its relatively high poverty rates, Puerto Rico became known as the "poorhouse of the Caribbean" (Carr 1984). As such, and in an attempt to spur the island's economic growth and reduce widespread poverty, economic development strategies were launched under the auspices of the Popular Democratic Party (PPD[6] for its acronym in Spanish), particularly after World War II, with the support of the federal government. The island's first elected governor in 1948, Luis Muñoz Marín, would become known as the Arquitecto (Architect) of the Commonwealth and "father" of modern Puerto Rico after having been involved in the island's politics since the 1930s.

These strategies resulted in significant and unprecedented political, social, and economic development, which transformed the island from a rural-agricultural to an urban-industrial society within a couple of decades. As a consequence of these transformational changes, in a relatively short period of time, Puerto Rico became a regional, if not an international, model for economic development and social prosperity.

Three major strategies led to this designation. First, in 1947, Puerto Rico launched an ambitious economic development strategy titled *Operación Manos a la Obra* (also known as Operation Bootstrap). This initiative aimed at the industrialization of Puerto Rico by providing financial incentives and tax exemptions to attract industry and jobs (primarily in manufacturing) from the U.S. mainland to the island. Second, from the 1950s to the 1970s, Puerto Rico underwent a massive net migration flow to the U.S. mainland encouraged by the government as a means to "export" unemployment. Proportionally speaking, this migration (often referred to as Puerto Rico's "Great Migration") is seen as one of the largest migration flows on a global scale. Third, starting in the 1930s and lasting through the 1970s, Puerto Rican women suffered from a massive sterilization campaign, which resulted in one of the most significant and proportionally largest number of women sterilized at the international level. These government-sponsored initiatives had (and continue to have) significant consequences for population growth on the island and for Puerto Ricans on the mainland. As such, we will address each in more detail later in this chapter.

These three strategies led to significant growth of employment opportunities in labor-intensive, manufacturing jobs on the island due to the increase in labor demand resulting from Operation Bootstrap and due to a decrease in labor supply resulting from the net outmigration and declining population growth. Many Puerto Ricans experienced significant upward economic mobility on the island within a few decades, such that Puerto Rico was described as the "Shining Star of the Caribbean." Still, this economic progress was short-lived. In the absence of a new comprehensive economic development plan for the island and the cessation of major economic incentives for corporations (including the phasing out of tax breaks, which we describe in more detail in chapter 3), manufacturing jobs began to migrate to low-income countries. To compensate, the Commonwealth government became one of the largest employers on the island; low-paying service jobs continued to grow; the ranks of the unemployed began to swell; and poverty became rampant throughout the island.

In the 1980s, Raymond Carr characterized the economy of Puerto Rico as one with "mass unemployment; one out of every three Puerto Ricans was without a steady job and their plight would be made more painful in the coming years by cuts in federal welfare payments" (1984: 1). Francisco Rivera-Batiz and Carlos Santiago reported that, in the 1980s and 1990s, Puerto Rico experienced a "sustained decline of a series of socioeconomic indicators that reached alarming levels" (1996: 3).

Despite a modest recovery in the 1990s and early 2000s with the U.S. economic expansion underway, the previously established economic and political initiatives and processes set the stage for La Crisis Boricua that started in 2006—the year we consider to be the "perfect storm" (discussed in more detail in the following chapter). Puerto Rico's now more-than-decade-long economic crisis and its ensuing humanitarian crisis fit with Raymond Carr's observation made more than three decades ago: "Recession falls with particular severity on an island that has the poorest regional economy of the United States" (1984: 2).

OPERACIÓN MANOS A LA OBRA (OPERATION BOOTSTRAP): FROM AN AGRARIAN TO AN INDUSTRIAL ECONOMY

As mentioned in the previous section, with support from the federal government, the PPD officially launched *Operación Manos a la Obra* (or Operation Bootstrap) in 1947. This was an economic revitalization campaign aimed at promoting (export-based) industrialization to stimulate economic growth, create employment opportunities, increase income levels, and diminish widespread poverty by transforming the island into a desirable location for the investment of external (U.S.-based) capital through the development and implementation of tax exempt policies, combined with an abundance of cheap labor. This new economic development initiative was modeled on some of the premises of President Franklin D. Roosevelt's New Deal. Further, as part of this process, the government generated an agrarian reform program primarily focusing on the sugarcane industry in Puerto Rico.

The strategy initially seemed to work. According to Rivera-Batiz and Santiago (1996), there were about ninety-six manufacturing plants in Puerto Rico in 1950, but 910 in 1963. Moreover, Puerto Rico experienced significant economic growth during the 1950s and 1960s, as measured by the gross national product (GNP). Carr (1984) reports that, from 1947 to 1959, Puerto Rico's GNP doubled; by 1956, for the first time ever, "the proportion of the gross national product (GNP) derived from manufacturing overtook that produced by agriculture" (1984: 231); and "in 1958 Puerto Rico's per capita income was the highest in Latin America" (1984: 75).

Thus, Operation Bootstrap was a major impetus to move Puerto Rico's economy from one dependent on sugar cane and other agricultural products, to one based primarily on manufacturing. Operation Bootstrap transformed Puerto Rico from a rural-agrarian to an urban-industrial society in a relatively short period of time—basically, in a couple of decades.[7] However, by the 1970s the effects of what had been characterized as an "economic miracle" and a "spectacular success" (Carr 1984) of Operation Bootstrap quickly diminished. While Operation Bootstrap led to significant growth of labor-intensive manufacturing jobs, it was not sufficient to compensate for the significant decline in agricultural jobs,[8] such that unemployment remained high and subsequently led to unprecedented large-scale outmigration to the mainland, as discussed in the next section. Poverty rates, after falling in the 1940s and 1950s (corresponding to the massive exodus from the island), also escalated by 1970.

Even in the period of the most rapid economic development in Puerto Rico, unemployment rates on the island varied from about 11 percent to 16 percent, from 1950 to 1965 (Junta de Planificación de Puerto Rico 1984; Center for Puerto Rican Studies 1978). Moreover, Operation Bootstrap's lifespan and its short-lived economic impact coincided with a reduction in the number of individuals in the labor force, as well as high and increasing unemployment and poverty rates. As reported by Rivera-Batiz and Santiago, "The picture of Puerto Rico as a showcase did not survive the 1970s. By mid-decade, the island had entered a period of stagnation that would last for more than ten years. Economic growth resumed in the mid-1980s, only to be stopped on its tracks by the recession of the early 1990s" (1998: 63).

Table 2.1 Net Outmigration from Puerto Rico to the U.S. Mainland: 1900–2015

Decade	Net Number of Outmigrants	Outmigrants Relative to Puerto Rico's Population at Start of Decade (%)
1900–1910	2,000	0.2
1910–1920	11,000	1.0
1920–1930	42,000	3.2
1930–1940	18,000	1.2
1940–1950	151,000	8.1
1950–1960	470,000	21.3
1960–1970	214,000	9.1
1970–1980	65,817	2.4
1980–1990	116,571	3.7
1990–2000	96,327	2.7
2000–2010	244,000	6.4
2006–2015	433,955	11.1

Source: Authors' estimates using data from Vázquez-Calzada (1988), Acosta-Belén and Santiago (2006), Matos-Rodríguez (2013), and for the 2006–2015 period, from the ACS and PRCS in the IPUMS.
Notes: These estimates represent net outmigration from Puerto Rico to the U.S. mainland; as we noted in chapter 1, there was also migration between Puerto Rico and other countries. The most recent data available when this book went to press to determine net outmigration specifically to the mainland were for 2015. These estimates include both Puerto Ricans and non-Puerto Ricans.

Furthermore, the large-scale migration from Puerto Rico to the mainland during the 1950s and 1960s, as shown in Table 2.1 (and discussed in more detail later in this chapter) has been credited with reducing unemployment on the island due to the decline in labor supply more so than Operation Bootstrap's impact on job creation (Rivera-Batiz and Santiago 1996). The massive female sterilization campaign (discussed next) was also critical to Puerto Rico's economic development "success" during this time period.

LA OPERACIÓN: THE PERILS AND OUTCOMES OF POPULATION CONTROL

Even before Operation Bootstrap, in the 1930s, the Puerto Rican government initiated a less traditional economic development strategy—female sterilization—that had dire and significant impacts on women's reproductive health, and resulted in significant immediate and long-term demographic consequences in terms of fertility rates and population growth on the island. In 1937, Law 136 was approved on the island leading to the legalization of sterilization essentially designed to curtail fertility based on eugenics principles.[9] Shortly thereafter, the campaign of *La Operación* (The Operation) was developed to regulate and significantly reduce fertility rates among Puerto Rican women.

The goal of this government-sponsored population control strategy was essentially a government social policy to promote sterilization as a means to facilitate economic growth in Puerto Rico.[10] *La Operación* developed and grew under the auspices of the Puerto Rican government, one funded by "state" and federal dollars (e.g., Hartman 1987). With the support and active participation of the medical/healthcare industry, it became the most prevalent form of fertility control in Puerto Rico. Ramirez de Arellano and Seipp (1983) and Hartmann (1987) further indicate that the Catholic Church (the predominant religion in Puerto Rico) turned a "blind eye" on female sterilization in Puerto Rico.[11]

La Operación resulted in one of the highest (if not the highest) rates of female sterilization in the world.[12] Over one-third of all Puerto Rican women in their reproductive ages (15–49) were sterilized (Ramirez de Arellano and Conrad Seipp 1983; Presser 1973; Hartmann 1987; Vázquez-Calzada, 1988),[13] and it permeated every aspect of Puerto Rican society. For example, as highlighted by Charles Warren and his colleagues, "the use of sterilization pervades Puerto Rican society: at young ages, short durations of marriage, low parity, and in all education and religious groups" (1986: 364). A demographic outcome of this sterilization campaign can be seen in Puerto Rico's rapidly aging population and the low-fertility rates of the population on the island later in the century, both of which are described later in this chapter.

THE PUERTO RICAN EXODUS: MIGRATION AS A MECHANISM FOR ECONOMIC DEVELOPMENT

As a consequence of increasing unemployment and poverty despite rapid urbanization and industrialization during Operation Bootstrap, the island began to experience a massive net outflow of Puerto Ricans to the mainland in search of employment opportunities and economic mobility. In the 1950s and 1960s, the island faced the "Great Migration," losing approximately one-third of its 1950 population size, which represents one of the largest, proportionally speaking, migratory movements of the twentieth century (Rivera-Batiz and Santiago 1996; Whalen and Vázquez-Hernández 2005).

This migration was, in effect, stimulated by the local government as part of its multifaceted economic development strategy for the island. Migration was used as a means to export Puerto Rico's unemployed (Rivera-Batiz and Santiago 1996; Carr 1984), and as highlighted by Acosta-Belén and Santiago, "Early on, migration became an official tool or 'safety valve' to deal with Puerto Rico's widespread poverty and unemployment" (2006: 5).[14] Alexis Santos-Lozada and Alberto Velázquez-Estrada similarly report that the Puerto Rican government "incentivized the poor population to the United States as a means to escape their economic conditions with promises of better jobs and social welfare on the island" (2015: 3).

To provide insight into the scale of the Puerto Rican diaspora, Table 2.1 shows the net migration from the island to the mainland between 1900 and 2015. Net migration in the first forty years of the twentieth century was relatively modest. However, migration outflows accelerated at a rapid rate during the 1940s, with 151,000 outmigrants compared to only 18,000 in the previous decade. This outflow peaked in the 1950s, with a net number of out-migrants totaling almost half a million (470,000) individuals, which tripled the corresponding number in the 1940s; the outmigrants in the 1950s alone represented over one-fifth (21.3%) of the island's total population at the start of the decade. This remains the highest relative outflow of migrants since Puerto Rico became a territory.

Since that period, net migration flows fell substantially until recent years. On a relative basis, the net outmigration from Puerto Rico to the U.S. mainland between 2006 and 2015 reached a level (433,955 or 11.1% of the island's 2006 population) not seen since the 1950s. Recall from Table 1.2 in the previous chapter that an additional 155,967 net migrants left Puerto Rico for other countries. These recent changes have led to local, national, and even international discussions regarding the "new" massive and "historical" migration from Puerto Rico to the mainland among academics and policy-makers, and in the popular press.

Mirroring many of these changes, particularly earlier in the century, the Puerto Rican population *on the mainland* has been increasing from 1910 to the present day. As we note later in this chapter, this population was esti-mated at just over 1,150 in 1910, but above a million in 1960, about 2 million in 1980, 3.4 million in 2000, 4.7 million in 2010, and 5.4 million in 2015. The "Great Migration" of the 1950s and the migration during La Crisis Boricua have resulted from the same social and economic issues that have permeated Puerto Rican society for decades.

SOCIOECONOMIC AND POPULATION PROCESSES AND INDICATORS: PUERTO RICO'S DEMOGRAPHIC TRANSITION

We now provide an overview of other socioeconomic and demographic changes in Puerto Rico over the past century, as a means to contextualize findings discussed in later chapters. The social and economic changes dis-cussed in the previous sections of this chapter, including the industrialization process, population control (e.g., sterilization and other birth control meth-ods), and net emigration to the mainland, have had significant impacts on the demographic profile of the Puerto Rico of today.

In many regards, Puerto Rico's socioeconomic characteristics are more similar to low-income than high-income countries, but its demographic char-acteristics resemble those of high-income countries. That is, Puerto Rico's death, fertility, and population growth rates are more aligned with countries such as the United States, Japan, France, Spain, United Kingdom, Germany, and others. Figure 2.1 shows the natural population increase (fertility-mortality, henceforth "natural increase") for the U.S. mainland, Japan, and Puerto Rico between 1960 and 2014. We can see that while Puerto Rico was characterized by high natural increase in the 1960s, it declined rapidly over the next several decades, which is not surprising in light of our previous discussion of *La Operación*. This significant decline has resulted in the island's natural increase levels that currently fall in between the United States and Japan.

However, many of the economic indicators for Puerto Rico, including GNP, poverty rates, labor force participation, and unemployment rates, among others, show Puerto Rico at a significant economic disadvantage relative to these countries. The first column in Table 2.2 shows the poverty rates in Puerto Rico from 1950 to 2015. Consider the perennial extreme poverty in Puerto Rico, ranging from a "low" of 45.0 percent in 2010 (ironically, in the midst of La Crisis Boricua) to almost 60 percent (in 1970 and 1980) during this time period. While the poverty rate fell from its peak of 59.8 poverty in 1980 to 46.1 percent in 2015, it still remained high and more than triple the

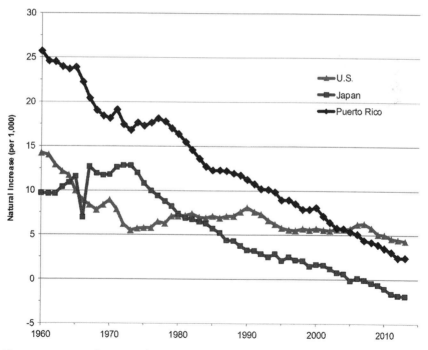

Figure 2.1   Natural Increase for Puerto Rico, the United States and Japan: 1960–2013.
Source: Authors' estimates using World Bank data made available through TheGlobal Economy.com (2016).

Table 2.2　Poverty, Unemployment, and Labor Force Participation Rates in Puerto Rico: 1950–2015

Year	Poverty Rates (%)	Unemployment Rates (%)	Labor Force Participation (LFP) Rates (%)
1950	46.2	14.8	57.9
1960	45.8	11.8	48.9
1970	59.6	10.8	48.0
1980	59.8	17.0	43.3
1990	55.3	14.2	45.4
2000	53.7	10.1	46.1
2010	45.0	16.4	45.3
2015	46.1	12.0	41.9[a]

Source: For 2010 and 2015, authors' estimates using PRCS data in the IPUMS; other years are from Bosworth and Collins (2006, table 2.6).
Notes: The estimates do not account for whether individuals identify themselves as Puerto Rican.
[a] LFP rate is for 2014.

national average of 13.5 percent. It should be noted that Puerto Rico's poverty rate in 2015 was more than double the highest state stateside poverty rate of 22.0 percent in Mississippi.

These poverty rates are closely related to income levels and unemployment rates in Puerto Rico. For example, as shown in the middle column of Table 2.2, the official unemployment rates in Puerto Rico have been in the double digits. In 2015, this rate was 12.0 percent compared to 5.3 percent on the mainland. While it fell between 2010 and 2015 (during La Crisis Boricua), the decline is related to the decrease in the labor force participation (LFP) rate (shown in the final column of Table 2.2). More will be discussed on recent changes in unemployment and LFP rates during the island's crisis in the following chapter, including adjusting the unemployment rate to account for workers who dropped out of the labor force.

The LFP rates in Puerto Rico have been exceedingly low, and generally falling over time, ranging from a high of 57.9 percent in 1950 to a low of only 41.9 percent in 2015. The Federal Reserve Bank of New York noted in a 2012 report that the island's LFP rates have been among the lowest in the world. While we discuss labor force patterns extensively later in the book, suffice it to say that even in the periods of the most rapid industrialization in Puerto Rico, its LFP rate fell nine full percentage points between 1950 and 1960 (to 48.9%), and lost another 0.9 percent point by 1970. It has remained below 50 percent since 1950.

Demographic transition theory indicates that countries move from very high to very low fertility and mortality rates primarily as a result of economic development (recall Figure 2.1, especially in the context of Puerto Rico). In the case of Puerto Rico, although economic development was an important factor in its demographic transition, other factors, such as those discussed already, including the massive female sterilization and an unprecedented exodus to the U.S. mainland, also contributed to these demographic changes.

While it generally takes developed countries several generations to complete their demographic transition, Puerto Rico (as many other low-income countries) accomplished this process in a few decades. Also, once countries reach low levels of fertility and population growth, there is essentially no turning back. In the case of many developed countries, their natural population increases have turned negative, such as the case with Japan shown earlier in Figure 2.1. Some of these countries still experience population growth as a result of positive net in-migration. However, in addition to its net outmigration, as we will see in the following sections, Puerto Rico has been experiencing below replacement fertility levels; it seems unlikely that these trends will reverse themselves in the near future.

The first column in Table 2.3 shows the change in the population in Puerto Rico over time. When the U.S. military invaded Puerto Rico in 1898, the

Table 2.3 Puerto Rico's Population and the Mainland's Puerto Rican Population: 1899/1900–2015

| | Population in Puerto Rico | | Puerto Rican Population on Mainland | |
Year	Total Population	Population Growth since Previous Period (%)	Total Population	Population Growth since Previous Period (%)
1899 (Island) or 1900 (Mainland)	953,243	–	1,150	–
1910	1,118,012	17.3	9,973	767.2
1920	1,299,809	16.3	22,077	121.4
1930	1,543,913	18.8	80,191	263.2
1940	1,869,255	21.1	96,753	20.7
1950	2,210,703	18.3	353,431	265.3
1960	2,349,544	6.3	1,018,836	188.3
1970	2,712,033	15.4	1,438,800	41.2
1980	3,196,520	17.9	2,035,020	41.4
1990	3,522,037	10.2	2,632,326	29.4
2000	3,808,610	8.1	3,400,527	29.2
2010	3,725,789	−2.2	4,682,531	37.7
2015	3,474,182	−6.8	5,371,100	14.7

Source: Authors' estimates using data from http://welcome.topuertorico.org/reference/pophistory.shtml; Rivera-Batíz and Santiago (1996); and for the 2015 mainland population, the 2015 ACS data in the IPUMS.
Notes: Puerto Rico's population in 1860 was 583,308. The 1899 census was conducted by the War Ministry of the United States. The first U.S. Decennial Census in Puerto Rico took place in 1910 and has been occurring every 10 years as is the case in the U.S. mainland. The population estimates for Puerto Rico represent the total number of residents on the island, and do not account for whether individuals identify themselves as Puerto Rican.

island's population was about to reach 1 million inhabitants. As can be seen, from 1899 to 1950, the population grew at an accelerated rate, reaching over 2.2 million individuals in 1950. The population continued growing at a rapid pace through 2000, reaching over 3 million individuals on the island in 1980. However, the island's population never reached 4 million because, as highlighted in the previous section, Puerto Rico experienced a net decline in its population between 2009 and 2010, which has continued falling. These population changes reflect the net outmigration spurred by Puerto Rico's economic crisis starting in 2006 as well as the low-fertility rates on the island.

For comparative purposes, the last column in Table 2.3 shows the growth of the Puerto Rican population on the U.S. mainland. As indicated earlier in this chapter, this population was estimated to be just over 1,150 in 1910, but increased dramatically, particularly during Puerto Rico's Great Migration in the 1940s and 1950s; during these decades, the Puerto Rican population living stateside increased by 265.3 percent and 188.3 percent, respectively. The mainland Puerto Rican population—at 5.37 million in 2015—currently outnumbers the island's population by a margin of almost two-to-one, the ratio of which increased at an accelerated rate as a result of La Crisis Boricua (at least through 2015) and the relatively high-fertility rates among mainland-born Puerto Ricans.

Fertility-Related Measures

Two important and most frequently used measures for fertility include the crude birth rate (CBR), which is expressed as the number of live births per 1,000 population, and the total fertility rate (TFR), which provides a measure of the average number of children that a woman would have, at the completion of her reproductive cycle, if she were to conform to age-specific fertility rates for previous cohorts of women. Some generally refer to the TFR as the average number of children per woman.[15]

The first two columns in Table 2.4 present the fertility trends for Puerto Rico from 1900 to 2015. This table shows significant declines in fertility among Puerto Rican women on the island. For example, in 1910, the CBR was 33.6; this is a high fertility rate, comparable to fertility rates for many African countries in 2015. In 1900, the TFR in Puerto Rico was also quite high at about 5.2 children per women. Both the CBR and TFR remained at these levels in Puerto Rico through at least 1960, resulting in significant population growth rates. It was not until 1970 and subsequent years when significant declines occurred for both CBR and TFR on the island.

Although increasing educational levels and economic development had an important impact on these rates, as discussed earlier in this chapter, population control (through massive sterilization and other birth control methods)

Table 2.4 Selected Vitality Statistics and Average Age in Puerto Rico: 1900–2015

Year	Crude Birth Rate (CBR)	Total Fertility Rate (TFR)	Crude Death Rate (CDR) (%)	Infant Mortality Rate	Life Expectancy (Years)	Average Age (Years)	Population Aged 65 & Over (%)
1900	–	5.2	–	–	33.3	–	–
1910	33.6	4.7	23.8	–	38.2	–	–
1920	38.4	5.1	22.8	–	38.5	–	–
1930	35.2	4.8	20.4	–	40.6	–	–
1940	38.5	5.2	18.3	–	46.0	–	–
1950	38.8	5.0	9.9	63.4[a]	63.5	18.4	3.5
1960	32.4	4.7	6.7	51.4	68.7	18.5	5.2
1970	24.8	3.2	6.7	33.3	71.5	21.6	6.5
1980	22.8	2.6	6.4	19.7	73.7	24.6	7.9
1990	18.5	2.2	7.3	13.8	74.2	28.5	9.7
2000	15.6	2.1	7.5	10.9	76.7	32.3	11.2
2010	11.3	1.7	7.8	7.0	78.8	34.7	14.5
2015	10.9	1.6	8.5	6.3	79.1	36.3	17.0

Source: Population Reference Bureau (2015) and United Nations data from Factfish.com (2016a, 2016b, 2016c).
Note: These figures do not account for whether individuals identify themselves as Puerto Rican.
[a]The infant mortality rate is for 1955.

Table 2.5 Selected Educational Attainment Measures in Puerto Rico: 1940–2015

Year	High School Graduates or Higher (%)	Average Education (Years of Schooling)
1940	3.2	2.7
1950	7.3	3.7
1960	15.0	4.6
1970	27.1	6.9
1980	40.5	8.7
1990	49.6	9.9
2000	61.9	11.0
2010	67.6	11.7
2015	74.9	12.1

Source: Authors' estimates using data from the U.S. Census Bureau, various years, and the PRCS in the IPUMS for 2015.
Notes: These estimates are for adults aged twenty-five and above. They do not account for whether individuals identify themselves as Puerto Rican.

and unprecedented migration to the U.S. mainland also contributed to declining fertility rates on the island.[16] Thus, fertility was being controlled through sterilization and other birth control methods as well as by massive migratory movements to the mainland.

By the year 2000, Table 2.4 indicates that Puerto Rico had achieved replacement level fertility with a TFR of 2.1, and dipped below replacement level fertility by 2010, indicating that even if the net outmigration ceased altogether, Puerto Rico's population would likely decline. Santos-Lozada and Velázquez-Estrada (2015) project that fertility declines will continue to be part of Puerto Rico's demographic reality, possibly reaching their lowest level in 2030.

During this same time period, educational levels underwent significant increases among the island population. Table 2.5 indicates that the percent of high school graduates (or higher) among adults ages 25 and older in 1940 was about 3.2 percent, and the average level of education was 2.7 years of schooling in Puerto Rico. For each decade shown, however, both schooling measures rose over time, such that by 2015, three-quarters (74.9%) of the island population had a high school degree or higher (compared to two-thirds (67.6%) just five years earlier), and the average number of years of schooling was 12.1 years.[17]

Mortality-Related Measures

CDR, expressed as the number of deaths per 1,000 population, is an important and common measure of mortality. Life expectancy at birth represents another such measure, often defined as the average age at death or the average number of years a person is expected to live at birth based on prevailing mortality rates. The infant mortality rate (IMR), which measures the number of deaths among individuals below the age of one year, expressed per 1,000 live births, is often used as a measure or indicator of the health and well-being of a given population at a specified point in time. Of course, there are many factors, including social (e.g., infusion of public health measures, etc.), economic (e.g., higher incomes), and genetic/biological factors, that impact life expectancy and the other indicators of mortality.

These mortality-related metrics are presented in the third through fifth columns of Table 2.4. Again, in the early part of the twentieth century, Puerto Rico was characterized by high mortality rates and a very low life expectancy. In 1910, despite being a U.S. territory, the CDR was approximately twenty-four deaths per 1,000 population and the life expectancy was only thirty-eight years (up five years since 1900). To put this observation in perspective, there are no countries in the world today that have a CDR as Puerto Rico had in 1910. With the exception of Lesotho (which has a CDR of 20), most countries today have CDRs significantly below 15, and they are primarily in the single digits with the exception of countries in Africa (Population Reference Bureau 2015).

However, the CDR quickly declined in Puerto Rico after 1940, reaching just under 10 per 1,000 population in 1950 (which was essentially half of the CDR in 1940). It ranged between 7.3–7.8 in the period of 1990–2010, although it increased by 2015 (likely one of the consequences of the rapidly aging population). Consequently, life expectancy increased on the island at a rapid rate, reaching almost sixty-four years in 1950 (again, a substantial increase from forty-six years in 1940), and 79.1 in 2015. Clearly, there have been significant and positive improvements in life expectancy in Puerto Rico, reaching levels comparable to high-income countries. The 2015 world life expectancy was seventy-one years, with seventy-nine for high-income countries, and sixty-nine for low-income countries (Population Reference Bureau 2015). As is generally the case across the world, life expectancy for Puerto Rican women (83.1) on the island is significantly higher than for their male counterparts (75.9), suggesting that as Puerto Rico's population continues to age, women will play an increased role in driving the demographic and socioeconomic outcomes on the island.

As a consequence of declining mortality levels and increasing life expectancy (and net outmigration), the average age in Puerto Rico has also increased. As can be seen in the penultimate column of Table 2.4, in the 1950s Puerto Rico had a youthful population, with an average age of 18.4 years. With declining mortality levels, the average age reached almost twenty-five (24.6) years in 1980 and 32.3 years in 2000. In 2015, the average age in Puerto Rico had increased to 36.3 compared to 37.7 on the mainland.

This table also shows a significant drop in the IMR over time, which stood at a 63.4 in 1955, but was cut almost in half by 1970 (to 33.3), reaching 10.9 in 2000, and 6.3 in 2015 (compared to 6.1 in the United States overall that year). The precipitous decline in the IMR resulted from significant socioeconomic changes, improvements in the public health infrastructure, and the infusion of public health services provided to the general population on the island.

During this transition in mortality, from very high to low mortality rates and increasing life expectancy, the primary causes of death in Puerto Rico also underwent significant changes. In the early parts of the twentieth century, the primary causes of death in Puerto Rico resulted from infectious diseases, characteristic of low-income and impoverished nations. Currently, the primary causes of death in Puerto Rico resemble those of high-income countries, including chronic and degenerative diseases (Departamento de Salud, 2015; Váquez-Calzada, 1988).

Natural Increase Revisited

As a consequence of the changing demographic patterns (as measured by mortality and fertility), natural increase has changed significantly on the island. We should note that given the high levels (albeit declining) of fertility and relatively low levels of mortality, the natural increase in Puerto Rico was very high, especially from the 1950s through the 1980s. As Figure 2.1 showed earlier in this chapter, in 1960, the rate of natural increase in Puerto Rico was 2.6. However, it declined at an accelerated rate, reaching only 0.2 in 2015. To consider the magnitude of these changes in terms of population growth, we can use what is referred to as the "doubling time" or the number of years it would take the population to double itself at prevailing growth rates. The doubling time for Puerto Rico in 1960 was 26.5 years. That is, it would take almost twenty-seven years for Puerto Rico to double its population size of about 1,018,836 in 1960 at prevailing growth rates. By 2015, the doubling time was a staggering 345 years.

AGE DISTRIBUTIONS AND POPULATION PYRAMIDS

Changing fertility and mortality rates have important implications for the age structure of a population. As fertility and mortality levels decrease and reach low levels, and life expectancy increases, the age structure begins reflecting an elderly population. There are various ways to measure the aging of the population, such as the average age, the percent of the population that is fifteen years of age and below and sixty-five years of age and above, as well as population pyramids, which graphically show the distribution of the population by age and gender.

The last two columns of Table 2.4 show changes through time in the population aged 65 and above in Puerto Rico. In 1950, this segment constituted only 3.5 percent of the population, and Puerto Rico's age structure represented a youthful population. However, the population aged sixty-five and above increased consecutively each decade, reaching 17 percent in 2015. A population in which 12 percent or more of its individuals are aged sixty-five and above is considered an elderly or "old" population. By 2015, Puerto Rico exceeded this threshold, not only as a consequence of declining fertility and increasing life expectancy, but also as a result of the net outmigration of a significant segment of a fairly youthful population. (We will explore the characteristics of the outmigrants in more detail in upcoming chapters.) The Population Division of the United Nations projected in 2002 that the life expectancy in Puerto Rico by 2050 would reach 80.3 years, and that the population aged sixty-five and above on the island would increase to about 22.1 percent. However, even by 2015, these figures had escalated, given the continued increase in life expectancy, declining fertility rates, and massive outmigration. As such, these numbers in 2050 are likely to be somewhat higher than what the United Nations projected.

Population Pyramids for Puerto Rico

We next consider population pyramids for the island, which are graphical representations of a population by age and gender. Comparing population pyramids across time allows us to see how the age and gender composition of a population has changed. The population pyramid for a youthful population has a pyramidal shape, with a wide base representing the younger ages of the population, and a narrow top representing the older population segments. As the population ages, the pyramid changes in shape and starts becoming top-heavy, reflecting more of an irregular pyramid, at times somewhat rectangular, and, in more extreme cases, it seems like an inverted pyramid, reflecting an old or elderly age structure.

Puerto Rico's age structure has gone through a similar transition, representing a change from a youthful to an elderly population. Figures 2.2 and 2.3 graphically depict the changes from a youthful to an aging population, from 1950 to 2000 (the top two panels in Figure 2.3) to 2015 (the bottom panel in Figure 2.3). Even between 2000 and 2015, the shift in Puerto Rico's age distribution toward an elderly population was visible, especially among women.

Further, the top and bottom panels in Figure 2.3 project how the age structure will continue to change (by 2025 and 2050, respectively), reflecting a top-heavy age structure, especially in 2050, in which the pyramid is somewhat inverted. These shifts represent the continued "graying" of Puerto Rico, similar to recent trends in high-income countries throughout the world, such

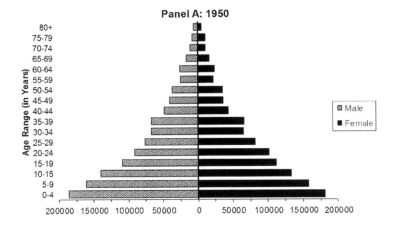

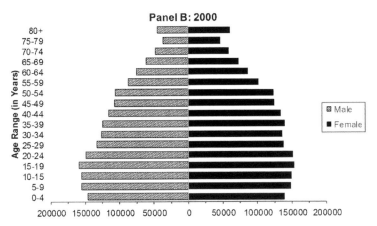

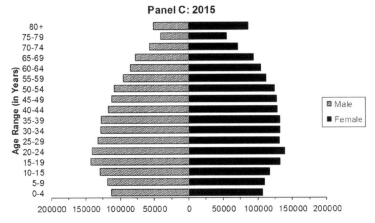

Figure 2.2 Population Pyramids for Puerto Rico: 1950, 2000, and 2015. *Source*: Authors' estimates using United Nations data made available through World Population Pyramid (2017).

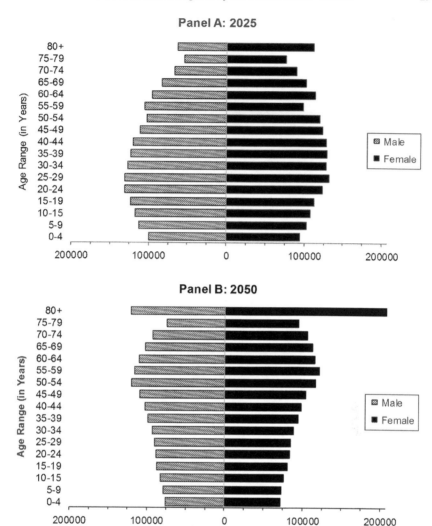

Figure 2.3   Population Pyramids (Projected) for Puerto Rico: 2025 and 2050. *Source:* Authors' estimates using United Nations data made available through World Population Pyramid (2017).

as Japan. It should be emphasized that if it takes several more years for La Crisis Boricua to relent, continued substantial net outmigration from Puerto Rico (which tends to occur among younger populations) will likely result in a more rapidly aging population than what is depicted here. Such rapid changes have important ramifications for the island's already low LFP rates and deteriorating and overstretched healthcare sector (structural issues discuss in the following chapter), particularly for women.

SUMMARY AND CONCLUDING REMARKS

Despite many decades after Muñoz Marín was elected as the island's first governor, the political reality of Puerto Rico is that, in many ways, it appears to operate as a pseudo-colony of the United States (a point we discuss in more detail in chapter 9), and this has permeated the island's national psyche and identity. That said, it cannot be denied that Puerto Rico has gone through an unprecedented economic transformation to become an industrial and urban society. At the same time, appearing to run counter to the increasing educational levels, low LFP rates, high unemployment rates, and chronic poverty have become engrained in the Puerto Rican landscape.

Today, despite being characterized by high levels of unemployment and widespread poverty, Puerto Rico's demographic profile is comparable to high-income, economically "developed" countries. Figueroa-Rodríguez (2013:2–3) indicates that "Puerto Rico is a colony with demographic characteristics of a developed nation, but with an economy of a developing country." Indeed, in 2015, Puerto Rico had low levels of mortality and fertility, a TFR below replacement level, high life expectancy, and an increasingly elderly population.

The *New York Times* Editorial Board wrote a piece titled "Puerto Rico's Last Chance" (June 29, 2016), which highlighted that Puerto Rico was not only confronting a financial crisis, but a humanitarian crisis as well. As we have pointed out (and will continue to do so throughout this book), La Crisis Boricua did not emerge overnight. Indeed, this was the coming together of a "perfect storm" of events that served to magnify and extend the effects and impacts of the mainland's Great Recession, resulting in a massive net migration flow from the island to the mainland not seen since the Great Migration. In the following chapters, we explore the migration patterns and socioeconomic and demographic outcomes and implications for both island and mainland Puerto Ricans during this historic time.

NOTES

1. This brief historical overview of Puerto Rico does not do justice to the very rich history, cultural traditions, political changes, and the extensive social, economic, and demographic transformations that have taken place in this small island about 106 miles long by 37 miles wide (or 3,515 square miles), for 525 years since the arrival of the Spaniards, and almost 120 years after U.S. intervention. For detailed and comprehensive reviews of Puerto Rico's history, see, for example, Fernando Picó (1988) and Francisco Scarano (2008). For a concise timeline of key events starting in 1815 with the Real Cédula de Gracias, which opened Puerto Rico's economy to trade, lowered tariffs, and increased immigration to the island, see Centro (2017).

2. It is important to highlight that the Puerto Rican people were not consulted in the development and implementation of the Treaty of Paris, the Foraker Act of 1900, nor the Jones Act of 1917. These were promulgated to be in the "best interest" of the Puerto Rican people as part of the United States focusing on its "Manifest Destiny" strategies with particular emphasis on expansionism.

3. Throughout the decades, Puerto Ricans' presence and participation in all branches of the military and in every war (including both World Wars) and military conflict have been significant, with great dignity and sacrifice, and the loss of Puerto Rican lives in these conflicts has been described as disproportionately high.

4. We realize that the term "Oversight Board" may be controversial because in the United States, Boards with veto power over elected legislature (which is the case with this Board) are generally not "oversight boards" but "control boards." However, we use the term "Oversight Board" to be consistent with the language used in the legislation.

5. It should be noted that according to José Caraballo and Lara (2016), the impact of La Crisis Boricua on Puerto Rico has been more devastating than the Great Depression.

6. The PPD was founded in 1938 under the leadership of Luis Muñoz Marín. The PPD's banner and its clarion call or slogan was *Pan, Tierra y Libertad* (Bread, Land, and Liberty), which reflected the critical issues of the time that permeated Puerto Rican society.

7. For more details on Operation Bootstrap, for examples, see Dietz (2003); Dietz and Pantojas-Garcia (1993); and Pantojas García (1990).

8. As reported by Carmen Whalen and Victor Vázquez-Hernández, the Puerto Rican government "promoted the industrialization of Puerto Rico, while the island's agricultural economies collapsed." (2005: 27).

9. In 2011, in the fifth Session of the sixteenth Legislature of Puerto Rico, Act No. 125-2011 (H. B. 2085) was approved "to repeal Act No. 136 of May 15, 1937, which authorized the teaching and disclosure of eugenics principles in hospitals, public health units and centers in Puerto Rico."

10. Puerto Rico's high-population growth rate and the focus on "overpopulation" as the root cause of Puerto Rico's economic woes had its inception practically since the U.S. troops landed in Guánica on July 25, 1898. The view was that population control, through fertility-related programs such as sterilization and emigration, would serve as primary "solutions" to the island's social, health, and economic problems (Whalen and Vázquez-Hernández 2005). Moreover, Betsy Hartmann (1987) indicates that the United States began its involvement with sterilization "abroad" in Puerto Rico. According to Hartman, "The Puerto Rican government, with United States government funds, encouraged women to accept sterilization by providing it at minimal or no cost" (1987: 232).

11. Kurt Back, Reuben Hill, and Mayone Stycos indicated in 1960 that "Ironically, it is, in part, the efforts on the part of the strongest moral opponent of birth control, the Roman Catholic Church, that seem to promote the popularity of sterilization."

12. In 1982, Ana María García created a forty-minute documentary titled *La Operación* to chronicle the history and experiences of Puerto Rican women on the island. This documentary shows how Puerto Rican women were sterilized immediately after

giving birth, without being properly informed about the process, and with the belief that the procedure was reversible, when in fact it was not.

13. Also, as documented by Ramirez de Arellano and Seipp (1983), the island and its "captive" population were used by U.S. pharmaceuticals for experimentation with birth control methods, such as "the pill," even before they were available to the general public on the U.S. mainland. Thus, in effect, Puerto Rico was an "ideal" testing ground for these methods. High birth and population growth rates, malnutrition, high unemployment rates, extreme poverty, and a government eager to ensure the success of their economic development plans, facilitated if not incentivized the adoption of population control methods by its population.

14. Acosta-Belén and Santiago (2006:78) indicate that even among "intellectual circles," using migration as a mechanism or "instrument" to foster economic development, and especially industrialization, was also becoming "fashionable."

15. The replacement TFR is set at 2.1 children per woman, which would result in stable (or replacement) population growth (barring net migration). If fertility patterns persist long-term, a TFR above 2.1 would result in population growth, while an ongoing TFR of less than 2.1 would eventually result in negative population growth (not considering migration).

16. Changes in family structures on the island, particularly rising divorce rates, also likely led to reductions in fertility rates. The impact of changing divorce rates on fertility rates goes beyond the scope of our study, but it would be a topic of interest for future studies to examine.

17. The literacy rate for the Puerto Rican population on the island, aged fifteen and above, currently stands at 94 percent.

Chapter 3

2006

The Year of the Perfect Storm and the Onset of La Crisis Boricua

La Crisis Boricua, which started escalating in 2006 and resulted in the second largest massive net outmigration during a decade's time in relative terms (and the largest in absolute numbers) since Puerto Rico became a U.S. territory, contributed to high levels of poverty and unemployment, a shrinking and rapidly aging population, government debt-default, and other dire outcomes. However, it had been brewing for decades. In this chapter, we explore in more detail the "perfect storm" of events that came together in 2006, spurring the crisis and exacerbating the already fragile state of well-being among island residents.

In particular, 2006 witnessed the imposition of the island's first sales tax on an increasingly economically disenfranchised population group, the beginning of a decade's significant loss of public sector jobs, and the complete expiration of corporate income tax breaks, which continued an already significant loss in manufacturing jobs. High and escalating energy prices, a collapsing housing market, the loss of banking assets, and a deteriorating infrastructure (including both education and health care) further contributed to the island's crisis. To contextualize these events, we extend part of the previous chapter's discussion by examining recent labor-market and poverty-related outcomes of Puerto Ricans on both the island and U.S. mainland.

WEAK LABOR MARKETS

Double-digit unemployment rates and dramatically low labor force participation rates have characterized Puerto Rico's labor market for decades.[1] As discussed in chapter 2, one of the traditional "safety valves" has been the potential for outmigration to the mainland, thus reducing the island's labor supply and presumably improving the employment prospects of both

33

the migrants (on the mainland) and those who stay behind. But this escape valve lost some of its luster as a result of the Great Recession that occurred stateside.

Unemployment

Panel A of Figure 3.1 presents the annual unemployment rates of Puerto Rican civilians between 2006 and 2014,[2] and for comparative purposes, panel B presents them for mainland-born Mexican Americans, Mexican

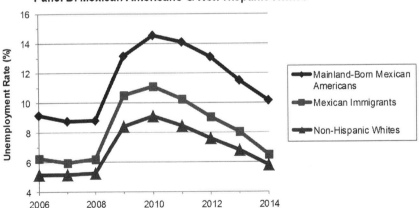

Panel A: Puerto Ricans, by Birthplace & Residence

Panel B: Mexican Americans & Non-Hispanic Whites

Figure 3.1 Unemployment Rates of Puerto Ricans, by Birthplace and Residence, and Other Groups: 2006–2014. *Source*: Authors' estimates using 2006-2014 ACS and PRCS data in the IPUMS. *Notes*: The sample includes civilians aged sixteen and above who were in the labor force. Non-Hispanic whites only include those born on the mainland.

immigrants, and mainland-born non-Hispanic whites. As we have noted elsewhere (Mora, Dávila, and Rodríguez 2017), with few exceptions, unemployment rates of island-born and mainland-born Puerto Ricans working on the island tended to change together during this timeframe. That is, as unemployment rates rose for island-born Puerto Ricans on the island, they generally did so among mainland-born Puerto Ricans, although not necessarily by the same magnitude.

These changes affirm that island-born and mainland-born Puerto Ricans faced similar labor market structural conditions on the island, particularly since 2008, as the unemployment-rate gap between the two groups significantly narrowed. In 2006 and 2007, the unemployment rates of mainland-born Puerto Ricans on the island were relatively high, with the widest gap between island-born and mainland-born workers occurring in 2007 (19.7% vs. 15.3%). However, just one year later, with a steep decline in their unemployment rate, this gap fell to a statistically-insignificant 1.1 percentage-point difference (14.1% vs. 15.2%). As such, by 2014, the two groups had nearly identical unemployment rates on the island for the first time during this timeframe. Panel A thus illustrates that the island's perennially high extent of joblessness is not unique to island-born workers, and it reflects significant and sustained structural problems with the island's labor market.

Since 2008, these differences between island workers and stateside workers have been larger for island-born Puerto Ricans than for mainland-born Puerto Ricans, largely due to the higher unemployment rates of mainland-born versus island-born Puerto Ricans working stateside. These rates also changed similarly between the island and mainland (until 2012), regardless of birthplace. These findings suggest that the intertwined nature of labor markets in Puerto Rico and the U.S. mainland is not unique to island-born Puerto Ricans, as we have noted before (Mora, Dávila, and Rodríguez 2017); many mainland-born Puerto Ricans appear to also consider Puerto Rico within their nexus of labor market opportunities.

Figure 3.1 further shows that the mainland's Great Recession impacted employment prospects in both regions, particularly (and not surprisingly) for stateside workers. Indeed, *both* island-born and mainland-born Puerto Ricans on the island experienced smaller relative and absolute increases in their unemployment rates after 2008 than their mainland counterparts; however, they were already quite high on the island, thus leaving little room for larger increases. The unemployment rates of island-born Puerto Ricans increased by 4.2 percentage points on the island (from this period's "low" of 15.2% to a high of 19.4%) between 2008 and 2010, compared to a 5.2 percentage-point increase on the mainland (from 8.7% to 13.9%). Among mainland-born Puerto Ricans, their unemployment rates rose by 4.5 percentage points on the island versus 6.6 percentage points on the mainland during this time.

The largest components of these changes occurred between 2008 and 2009, in the midst of the mainland's recession. The particularly acute increases among stateside Puerto Ricans likely stems from the fact the island's unemployment rates were already critically high before the mainland's crisis started. Moreover, the scale of the migration from the island may have occurred more rapidly than what mainland labor markets could initially absorb (pushing stateside unemployment up), but it alleviated some of the unemployment effects of the island's excess labor supply.

At the same time, Figure 3.1 shows signs of the subsequent labor market recovery among Puerto Ricans on the mainland after the Great Recession. In Puerto Rico, unemployment rates rose among both island-born and mainland-born workers after 2012, a time when they fell among Puerto Ricans (and the other groups shown in panel B) on the mainland. By 2014, island-born and mainland-born Puerto Ricans had statistically similar unemployment rates on the island (18.8% and 18.3%, respectively), which was not the case on the mainland (9.4% and 12.2%, respectively). These differences marked the largest island-mainland unemployment-rate gap for island-born Puerto Ricans during this entire timeframe, and the largest one for mainland-born Puerto Ricans since 2007.

Labor Force Participation

Despite high unemployment rates in Puerto Rico, both island-born and mainland-born Puerto Ricans had significantly lower labor force participation (LFP) rates on the island than the mainland, as seen in panel A of Figure 3.2. Therefore, island-mainland differences in LFP masked the true effective extent of joblessness on the island, a point on which we elaborate more below. As we discuss elsewhere (Mora, Dávila, and Rodríguez 2017), differences in LFP rates also explain why mainland-born Puerto Ricans have consistently higher unemployment rates than their island-born counterparts on the mainland (a wider gap than between mainland-born Puerto Ricans and Mexican Americans, shown in panel B of Figure 3.2). The relatively high LFP rates among mainland-born Puerto Ricans working stateside might also explain why their unemployment rates escalated the most in both relative and absolute terms during the mainland's Great Recession.

Changes in Puerto Rico's LFP rates in the 2006–2014 period provide further evidence of Puerto Rico's weak and deteriorating labor market during La Crisis Boricua. As panel A in Figure 3.2 indicates, these rates (already low) fell consecutively each year on the island after reaching their highest levels during this timeframe (46.4% in 2009 among island-born Puerto Ricans, and 65.2% in 2010 among mainland-born Puerto Ricans), to their lowest points in 2014 (42.9% and 56.9%, respectively).

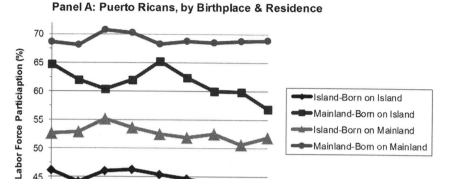

Panel A: Puerto Ricans, by Birthplace & Residence

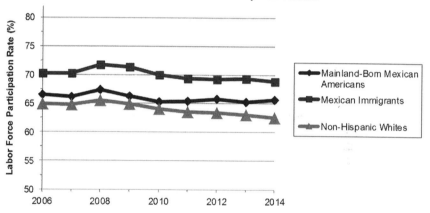

Panel B: Mexican Americans & Non-Hispanic Whites

Figure 3.2 LFP Rates of Puerto Ricans, by Birthplace and Residence, and Other Groups: 2006–2014. *Source*: Authors' estimates using 2006-2014 ACS and PRCS data in the IPUMS. *Notes*: The sample includes noninstitutionalized civilians aged sixteen and above. The LFP-adjusted unemployment rates impute unemployment had the 2006 LFP rate remained constant. See appendix B for more details.

We noted in the previous chapter that LFP rates in Puerto Rico are among some of the lowest in the world. Figure 3.2 illustrates that the substantially low LFP rates on the island are independent of island or mainland birthplace, providing additional evidence that the weak labor market conditions in Puerto Rico are not unique to island-born workers. Figure 3.2 also shows how the low LFP rates among island-born Puerto Ricans spill into the mainland labor market, as their LFP rates were considerably lower than those of mainland-born workers, Mexican immigrants, and mainland-born Mexican Americans and non-Hispanic whites during this time (shown in panel B). Their low LFP rates help explain their low unemployment rates *vis-à-vis* mainland-born Puerto Ricans living stateside. It therefore appears that the mainland labor market might not be as robust with respect to employment opportunities for island-born Puerto Ricans as their relatively low unemployment rates first suggest.

The island-mainland LFP-rate differentials among island-born Puerto Ricans remained fairly steady throughout this time period, and they tended to change in a similar fashion, as they did with other mainland groups in panel B of Figure 3.2. This was not the case for mainland-born Puerto Ricans, however, as their LFP rates moved in opposite directions on the island and mainland until 2010 (at which point they peaked for the former group, and reached their lowest level for the latter). After that year, they fell among the former and stabilized among the latter.

Also, the LFP rates on the island continued falling even after the unemployment rates started rising. This means that the uptick in unemployment on the island did not reflect "added worker effects" caused by rising LFP rates.[3] In fact, the unemployment rates in Puerto Rico would have been even higher at that time had the island's LFP rates remained stable throughout La Crisis Boricua. We explore this point further in the next subsection.

Beforehand, it is worth discussing explanations as to why Puerto Rico has had strikingly low LFP rates and high unemployment rates *vis-à-vis* the mainland. The Federal Reserve Bank of New York (2012) and other studies and reports have contended that these stem from the island's high effective minimum wage, unemployment insurance, welfare and transfer payments, regulatory environment, income tax structures (such as the lack of an Earned Income Tax Credit on the island), unreported work in the underground economy, and relatively low labor demand due to a "mismatch" between workers' skills and those sought by employers, among other factors.[4] However, with respect to the underground economy, Maria Enchautegui and Richard Freeman (2006) reported that such activities only explained approximately 3 percentage points of the low LFP rates on the island. Similarly, Gary Burtless and Orlando Sotomayor (2006) found little evidence that the informal sector explained low LFP rates. At the same time, the large welfare transfer payments also arguably stem from the island's weak socioeconomic conditions; if improved, welfare transfer payments should diminish.

The Hidden Unemployed

It is worth highlighting that the island's LFP rates were significantly lower in 2014 than in 2006, which was not the case for stateside Puerto Ricans. To what extent did Puerto Rico's declining LFP rates distort the observed unemployment rates and "hide" the true rates of joblessness? We provide insight into this question by estimating LFP-adjusted unemployment rates for noninstitutionalized civilians aged sixteen and above, had their LFP rates remained constant at their 2006 values. Figure 3.3 presents these estimates along with the traditionally measured unemployment rates.

Among both island-born and mainland-born Puerto Ricans (panels A and B, respectively), the observed and LFP-adjusted unemployment rates widened on the island since 2010. By 2014, we estimate that nearly 84,900 island-born

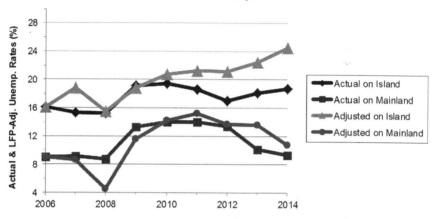

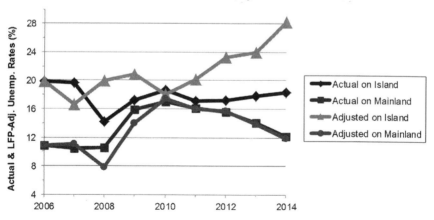

Figure 3.3 **LFP-Adjusted and Actual Unemployment Rates of Puerto Ricans: 2006–2014.** *Source*: Authors' estimates using 2006–2014 ACS and PRCS data in the IPUMS. *Notes*: The sample includes noninstitutionalized civilians aged sixteen and above. The LFP-adjusted unemployment rates impute unemployment had the 2006 LFP rate remained constant. See appendix B for more details.

workers and 10,400 mainland-born workers would have been part of the Puerto Rican labor force had their LFP rates remained the same as in 2006. When adding these "hidden" jobless individuals to the observed 210,100 island-born and 13,700 mainland-born unemployed workers in Puerto Rico, the LFP-adjusted unemployment rates would have been 5.7 percentage points higher (at 24.5%) and 10.0 percentage points higher (at 28.3%), respectively, than the traditionally measured unemployment rates. Moreover, the gap between these LFP-adjusted and measured unemployment rates grew after 2010, which is another indication of the deteriorating labor market conditions in Puerto Rico. Had it not been for the "exporting" of unemployment through the aforementioned labor exodus, Puerto Rico's true extent of joblessness would have been even greater as La Crisis Boricua matured.

Consider that the foregoing was generally not the case for mainland residents. Due to an increase in LFP in 2008 and 2009, some of the observed unemployment can be attributed to added worker effects. In addition, the observed and LFP-adjusted rates among stateside Puerto Ricans were similar in the latter part of this timeframe, particularly among those born on the mainland, owing to their relatively stable LFP rates. Therefore, this analysis indicates that the disparity in joblessness between the island and mainland was even greater than what traditional measures reflect, particularly after the mainland recovered from its Great Recession, while La Crisis Boricua continued to deepen. As policymakers move forward with initiatives to address Puerto Rico's economic, financial, and humanitarian crises, we caution that the human factor is not ignored. Declines in unemployment by themselves should not be interpreted as a positive sign without accounting for the hidden unemployed.

Employment/Population Ratios

In light of La Crisis Boricua, it is not surprising that Puerto Rico experienced declining employment/population ratios on the island after 2006 (with no end in sight as this book went to press), as seen in panel A of Figure 3.4. These ratios, which were already quite low, generally fell each year on the island after reaching their peaks of 39.0 percent in 2008 among island-born Puerto Ricans, and 53.1 percent in 2010 among mainland-born Puerto Ricans. They reached their lows (for this timeframe) in 2014, at 34.9 percent and 46.5 percent, respectively.

While the employment/population ratio among island-born Puerto Ricans living stateside also peaked in 2008 (at 50.3%), it fell to its lowest point of well below 50 percent (44.6%) during this period in 2011, and gradually rose afterwards. With regards to mainland-born Puerto Ricans, their employment/population ratios reached their low in 2010 (the year they peaked for

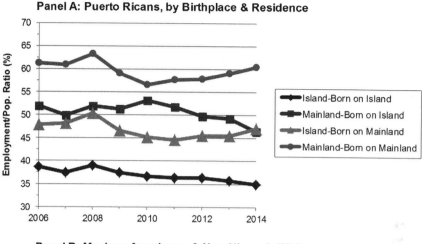

Panel A: Puerto Ricans, by Birthplace & Residence

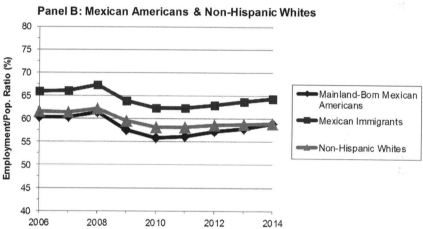

Panel B: Mexican Americans & Non-Hispanic Whites

Figure 3.4 Employment/Population Ratios of Puerto Ricans, by Birthplace and Residence, and Other Groups: 2006–2014. *Source*: Authors' estimates using 2006–2014 ACS and PRCS data in the IPUMS. *Notes*: The sample includes noninstitutionalized civilians aged sixteen and above. Non-Hispanic whites only include those born on the mainland.

their counterparts on the island), but they subsequently increased with the economic recovery on the mainland, returning to over 60 percent by 2014. Such changes mirrored what happened among Mexican immigrants, Mexican Americans, and non-Hispanic whites during this time (shown in panel B), indicating that Puerto Ricans living stateside experienced similar shifts in employment tendencies as other mainland workers.

With just over one-third of island-born Puerto Ricans and not even half of mainland-born Puerto Ricans on the island who were working in 2014, these labor-market patterns raise significant policy challenges to improve the socioeconomic outcomes of island residents. A series of articles in the popular press through the first half of 2017 suggested that unless labor demand is stimulated, the real impact of the fiscal austerity measures proposed by the Financial Oversight and Management Board (discussed later in this chapter) to Puerto Ricans is likely to be dire. Moreover, net migration to the mainland appeared to be serving as a safety valve for some Puerto Ricans to find employment, which had been the case for decades (recall chapter 2), but it was not enough to raise or sustain the employment levels among those who remained on the island as La Crisis Boricua matured. If mainland labor markets become saturated, this crisis may be prolonged with dwindling mainland opportunities serving to stem the flow of net outmigration.

RATES OF IMPOVERISHMENT

As we discussed in the previous chapter, poverty rates in Puerto Rico have been perennially high in absolute and relative terms. However, as seen in panel A of Figure 3.5, despite the deteriorating labor market conditions on the island, the proportion of island-born Puerto Ricans living below the poverty line was consistently high in relative terms, but like the unemployment rates it remained stable between 2006 and 2014, generally hovering between 45 and 46 percent; it reached its high (46.5%) at the end of this period.

These rates were considerably higher than those of island-born Puerto Ricans living on the mainland, which were also high. Among the latter, these rates fell to 27.5 percent in 2014 after peaking the year before (at 29.4%), and remained above those of Mexican immigrants and mainland-born Mexican Americans (shown in Figure 3.5, panel B, for comparison). Of interest, the difference in poverty rates between island-born and mainland-born Puerto Ricans tended to be wider on the island than on the mainland, although this was not the case after 2012, when this poverty-rate gap widened on the mainland.

While the poverty rates of mainland-born island residents also exceeded the national average, they were lower and more erratic than those of their island-born counterparts. After reaching a high of 44.3 percent in 2008 (in the heart of the Great Recession), they generally fell until 2012, when they reached a low in this time period (40.8%). As with island-born Puerto Ricans, they rose thereafter.

Figure 3.5 further illustrates the lingering effects of the mainland's Great Recession on the incidence of impoverishment among island-born Puerto Ricans living stateside. Consider that by 2014, their poverty rates had experienced little recovery, while those of Mexican immigrants had fallen to nearly identical rates as mainland-born Puerto Ricans and Mexican Americans. Some

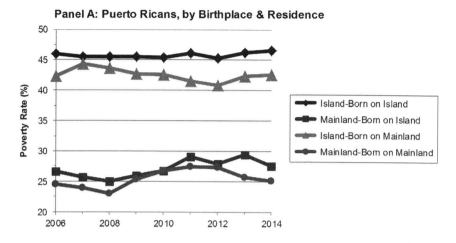

Panel A: Puerto Ricans, by Birthplace & Residence

Legend:
- Island-Born on Island
- Mainland-Born on Island
- Island-Born on Mainland
- Mainland-Born on Mainland

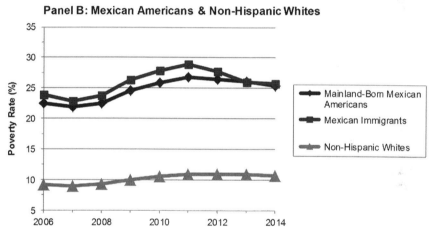

Panel B: Mexican Americans & Non-Hispanic Whites

Legend:
- Mainland-Born Mexican Americans
- Mexican Immigrants
- Non-Hispanic Whites

Figure 3.5 Poverty Rates of Puerto Ricans, by Birthplace and Residence, and Other Groups: 2006–2014. *Source*: Authors' estimates using 2006–2014 ACS and PRCS data in the IPUMS. *Notes*: The sample includes individuals who were not residing in group quarters. Non-Hispanic whites only include those born on the mainland.

of this difference likely relates to the fact that Puerto Ricans who left the island between 2010 and 2013 had significantly higher poverty rates than their counterparts who arrived in 2009—a time when mainland economic conditions were just starting to recover. Moreover, the poverty rates of both island-born and mainland-born Puerto Ricans living in the states substantially exceeded those of non-Hispanic whites. Even when the latter group's poverty rates peaked at 10.9 percent between 2011 and 2013, those of island-born Puerto Ricans were 2.7 times higher on the mainland, and 4.2 times higher on the island.

THE PERFECT STORM AND THE OUTCOMES
OF LA CRISIS BORICUA

While the *relative* rising incidence of unemployment and poverty during the mainland's Great Recession and slow recovery may have deterred some island residents from migrating, significant fiscal policy changes (including the imposition of the island's first sales tax) and losses in public-sector jobs as the perfect storm got underway in 2006 aggravated the already weakened economic conditions on the island, as we discuss elsewhere (Mora, Dávila, and Rodríguez 2017). In addition, many of the policy changes disproportionately affected those who were already facing fragile socioeconomic outcomes.

Imposition of Sales Taxes in Puerto Rico

With respect to the sales tax, in an ironic turn of events, the Governor of the Commonwealth of Puerto Rico, Aníbal Acevedo-Vilá, a member of the Popular Democratic Party (PPD—*Partido Popular Democrático*), signed into law in July 2006 the island's first sales tax: *Impuesto a las Ventas y Uso* (IVU, as it is known for its acronym in Spanish). Prior to 2006, island residents did not pay sales taxes.[5] The Governor argued he had no other option and was forced to do so to "save" Puerto Rico's credit ratings. This political positioning was despite the fact that the fiscal policy threat of federal income taxes and sales taxes had been used in political campaigns, primarily by the PPD, to sway voters away from the New Progressive Party (PNP—*Partido Nuevo Progresista*) and the idea of statehood for Puerto Rico. During his 2004 campaign trail in a highly contested election, then-PPD candidate Acevedo-Vilá upheld his party's political mantra and emphatically rejected the idea or possibility of a sales tax for Puerto Rico. He reiterated that, under no circumstances, would he approve a sales tax for island residents.

Acevedo-Vilá was elected as governor only by a margin of 0.2 percent (3,880 votes), while the PNP controlled the Legislative Assembly, resulting in political gridlock. In April 2006, confronting a significant budget deficit (which adversely impacted Puerto Rico's credit rating) and refusing to approve Acevedo-Vilá's budget, the Legislative Assembly shut down government offices. The political gridlock diminished when the IVU was signed into law. The IVU, which went into effect in November 2006, imposed a "state" tax of 5.5 percent and a municipal tax of 1.5 percent, for a total sales tax of 7.0 percent for island residents. The IVU was increased again, after much political drama, to 11.5 percent in 2015, resulting in Puerto Rico having higher sales taxes than any of the states. This was on top of the already relatively high cost of living in Puerto Rico, given that the majority of goods the island imports have additional transport costs associated with shipping regulations established by the Merchant Marine Act of 1920 (e.g., Marazzi Santiago 2017); also known as the Jones Act of 1920, this Act requires the use of U.S.-owned and U.S.-built ships to transport goods between Puerto Rico and the mainland.

The implementation and subsequent increase of the IVU occurred when Puerto Rico was already confronting weak labor market conditions and high poverty rates, creating further economic hardship for island residents.[6] To help alleviate the IVU's impact, the Puerto Rican government initially enacted a work tax credit that provided a maximum benefit of $450, but as discussed by Maria Enchautegui (2014), the government subsequently eliminated this tax credit due to fiscal constraints. While all island residents have been impacted by the IVU, as we have previously noted (Mora, Dávila, and Rodríguez 2017), the middle-to-low income population has been disproportionately impacted, as sales taxes are regressive income taxes, thus feeding into La Crisis Boricua. Other fiscal policies that subsequently emanated from the perfect storm include "Ley 7" of March 9, 2009, along with its subsequent amendments.[7]

Loss of Public-Sector Jobs

Contributing to Puerto Rico's deteriorating labor market conditions, the number of workers employed in the public sector also declined during this time, as the Commonwealth's government partly dealt with its fiscal crisis by reducing public-sector jobs. According to our estimates (Mora, Dávila, and Rodríguez 2017), the number of public-sector employees at the "state" level in Puerto Rico feli by about 33 percent (from approximately 213,200 to 142,000 workers) between 2006 and 2014, and those employed by local and municipal governments declined by 12 percent (from 67,700 to 59,600 workers). In sum, the total number of sub-federal government jobs on the island shrank by more than 79,000 between 2006 and 2014. Moreover, the public-sector jobs that remained in 2014 tended to be held by workers with higher average levels of education than public employees in 2006 (Mora, Dávila, and Rodríguez 2017), again indicating a disproportionate impact of these changes on more vulnerable segments of the population (i.e., those with lower skill levels).

Expiration of Corporate Income Tax Breaks

Another element of the perfect storm that compounded the loss of public sector jobs was the expiration of Section 936 of the Internal Revenue Code in 2006. Section 936, which went into effect in 1976, exempted U.S. corporations from paying corporate income taxes on profits earned from goods produced in Puerto Rico. In response, U.S. manufacturing companies moved to the island, which continued to shift the industrial structure away from agriculture and toward high-tech manufacturing jobs, especially in the pharmaceutical and electronics' sectors, which had started under Operation Bootstrap (see chapter 2). According to Caraballo Cueto and Lara (2016, p. 5), at the peak of Section 936's utilization (in 1995), manufacturing accounted for 42 percent of Puerto Rico's GNP, created more than 30 percent of its bank deposits, and directly generated 17 percent of its jobs.

However, Section 936 was repealed one year later with the 1996 Small Business Job Protection Act, which established a ten-year window to entirely phase out these corporate income tax breaks by 2006 (technically expiring on December 31, 2005). Many U.S. manufacturing corporations that had moved to the island thus downsized their operations or moved to more attractive locations, such as Ireland, Mexico, or Costa Rica (Caraballo Cueto and Lara 2016). During the phase-out period, tens of thousands of jobs were lost, although the estimates vary. For example, Yaisha Vargas (2005) reported the loss of 30,000 jobs between 1996 and 2005, while the Economic Census estimated the loss of 63,000 jobs between 1997 and 2007.

We estimate that Puerto Rico's manufacturing industry shed an additional 37,400 jobs (approximately 28.5%, from about 131,000 to 93,900) between 2006 and 2014 (Mora, Dávila, and Rodríguez 2017), thus striking an already weak labor market. This loss is in line with the U.S. Census Bureau's (2015) estimates of the loss of 26,900 manufacturing jobs (24.5%) between 2007 and 2012. While not all of these manufacturing-job losses can be directly attributed to the expiration of the corporate income tax breaks, the repeal of Section 936 was nontrivial in this regard. As with the public sector, workers in the manufacturing industry were more educated on average in 2014 than in 2006 (Mora, Dávila, and Rodríguez 2017). As such, less educated workers seem to have been impacted harder than other workers in the manufacturing industry, which may have led to an increase in the migration of less skilled manufacturing workers during this time. The downsizing and relocation of manufacturing firms in response to the repeal of Section 936 would have had the further negative consequence of the corresponding loss in bank deposits, thus reducing access to credit among island residents and businesses when it was needed most.

Economic Contraction, the Public Debt, and Debt Defaults

The contraction of Puerto Rico's economy in all but one of the years between 2006 and 2015 (with 2012 being the exception) under an already weakened budget means that Puerto Rico has not experienced the revenue generation necessary to fund and provide economic relief stemming from La Crisis Boricua.

Even under their optimistic scenario, the economic projections made by the Puerto Rico Planning Board (Junta de Panificación) in 2016 suggested the contraction would continue through at least fiscal year 2017. Estudios Técnicos, Inc. (a Puerto Rican economics consulting firm) projected in 2016 that the contraction would continue for at least four years (until 2020), and it would not be until 2034 that Puerto Rico's economy would be restored to its 2006 level.

With the island's loss in credit ratings on municipal bonds in 2014, the government's unprecedented and ballooning public debt (described in 2015 by the then-governor as a "death spiral"), unfunded pension obligations, and a series of defaults on debt payments since July 2015, the island's government essentially ran out of clear options to use traditional fiscal policy tools to stimulate the economy and employment and reverse the tide of net out-migration. Unable to file for federal protection under Chapter 9 of the U.S. Bankruptcy Code due to Puerto Rico's status as a U.S. territory, as discussed later in this chapter, in June 2016 the U.S. federal government intervened to provide "assistance" to the island's ongoing and deteriorating crisis when President Obama signed into law the Puerto Rico Oversight, Management, and Economic Stability Act (PROMESA).

OTHER EVENTS CONTRIBUTING TO, AND RESULTING FROM, LA CRISIS BORICUA

Other macroeconomic events also fed La Crisis Boricua. As we discuss in this section, the economically fragile island was hit by rising oil prices (which doubled between 2005 and 2012), although they recovered before the crisis ended. Nevertheless, given the island's reliance on oil to generate electricity, energy prices (which were already high) soared during a significant part of our timeframe of study and continue to be higher than most places on the mainland. Moreover, the well-known mainland housing market crisis (spawned by the collapse of housing prices after their 2006 peak) affected both Puerto Rico and the mainland, but Puerto Rico's housing market had yet to recover at the final stages of this book's production. The impact of the housing market on credit access was compounded by the loss in bank deposits during this time, some of which were lost as manufacturing firms scaled down or left the island altogether, as we note earlier.

As such, policies and programs pertaining to collateral, equity, and credit on the island that generally benefit middle-class households stalled, again putting Puerto Rico's future for a near-term recovery at risk after more than a decade of crisis. La Crisis Boricua also witnessed deteriorating conditions in its healthcare industry—conditions made worse by the outmigration of a significant number of physicians, nurses, and other healthcare professionals.

High and Escalating Energy Prices in Puerto Rico

According to the Federal Reserve Bank of New York (2012), electricity prices have been substantially higher in Puerto Rico than essentially anywhere on the mainland because of the disproportionate reliance on imported oil for electricity generation by the Puerto Rico Electric Power Authority (PREPA or Autoridad de Energía Eléctrica [AEE]), a government-owned monopoly. According to a 2015 National Public Radio report, PREPA accounted for $9 billion of the government's debt, more than any other entity. The aforementioned New York Fed report (2012) indicated that oil generated 70 percent of the electricity on the island at the time, compared to only 1 percent on the mainland, leaving Puerto Rico at a major cost disadvantage in producing electricity.[8] Even after restructuring to expand the natural gas firing capabilities, the U.S. Energy Information Administration (EIA) reported in 2016 that petroleum still supplied half of the island's electricity.

As Anne Krueger, Ranjit Teja, and Andrew Wolfe discussed in their 2015 report on Puerto Rico's fiscal crisis, when oil prices doubled between 2005 and 2012, the resulting 3 percent of the GNP increase in Puerto Rico's oil bill represented an equivalent loss of income for the island that could have supported the local economy. The 2016 EIA report further indicated that the increase in oil prices resulted in average electricity prices in Puerto Rico that more than twice exceeded the mainland's average retail prices. Although oil prices subsequently retracted, the sharp increase in electricity prices that hit Puerto Rican residents during critical stages of La Crisis Boricua impacted an already economically vulnerable population, representing another contributing factor to net outmigration.

In addition, the decline in oil prices after 2012 may have only yielded temporary relief from high electricity prices. As a consequence of its inability to make scheduled payments to its creditors, according to a CNN report by Heather Long (2016b), to increase revenue PREPA planned to increase electricity prices by 8 percent in the Summer of 2016, and by up to 26 percent in early 2017. These rate increases, which would have been among the largest in recent U.S. history on a state-wide or territory-wide basis, were put on hold after a legal challenge by nine leading Puerto Rico industry and business associations made jointly with the Puerto Rico Institute for Competitiveness and Sustainable Economy (*Instituto de Competitavidad y Sostenibilidad Económica de Puerto Rico* (ICSE-PR) as it is known in Spanish) (ICSE-PR 2016). Even without this increase, as discussed by Mario Marazzi Santiago (2017), utility prices in the San Juan-Carolina-Caguas metropolitan statistical area (MSA) were 85 percent higher than the U.S. average in 2014, making this MSA the fourth more expensive MSA (behind Hilo, Fairbanks, and Honolulu) out of 325 MSAs across the country with respect to utilities.

Housing Market Crisis, Declining Credit, and the Banking Industry

Both Puerto Rico and the mainland were adversely impacted by the mainland's housing market crisis, but unlike the mainland, Puerto Rico had yet to recover even by 2017. The aforementioned CNN report (Long 2016a) in February 2016 indicated that Puerto Rico ranked second (after New Jersey) in terms of home foreclosures relative to mainland states' levels; even then, its foreclosure rate was also expected to worsen despite exceeding the 2010 national average at the peak of the mainland's housing crisis. The collapse in housing prices left many home owners with unpayable mortgage payments, and given the weak and uncertain economy, the demand for housing remained low, thus keeping property prices down. The massive exodus from the island appears to have exacerbated the loss in real estate value on the island; many homeowners reportedly abandoned their properties when moving to the mainland (Long 2016a), thus increasing the supply of vacant properties.

It follows that with the relatively large stock of vacant homes, the island's construction industry was adversely impacted. Given the importance of housing values as collateral, credit markets in Puerto Rico will presumably remain weak until the housing market begins to recover. Even after such a recovery begins, the widespread foreclosures, abandonment of properties, and the mortgage crisis paint a grim future for many Puerto Ricans with respect to their asset and wealth accumulation.[9]

The loss in commercial bank deposits during La Crisis Boricua, including those related to the shrinking of the manufacturing industry after the end of Section 936, further exacerbated the tightening of the access to credit in Puerto Rico. Krueger, Teja, and Wolfe reported in 2016 that commercial bank assets had fallen by 30 percent since 2005, and that the "fall in the economy and housing was amplified by the associated distress in the banking sector and vice versa" (p. 5). This distress was exemplified by the closure of several major financial institutions, including R-G Premier Bank of Puerto Rico, Eurobank, and Westernbank of Puerto Rico (all in April 2010) and Doral Bank (which at one point had $6.2 billion in assets and $1.8 billion in deposits) in February 2015 (Federal Depository Insurance Corporation 2015).

Deteriorating Healthcare Industry

The events surrounding La Crisis Boricua also negatively impacted Puerto Rico's healthcare industry, which contributed to the island's humanitarian crisis. Coupled with longer life expectancies and below-replacement fertility levels, discussed in chapter 2, the massive net outmigration has led to an increasingly elderly population. These changing demographics, along with a population characterized by Raúl Figueroa-Rodríguez (2013) with long-term chronic illnesses similar to residents of high-income countries (such as cardiovascular diseases, cancer, and diabetes), will presumably create additional challenges for the healthcare system's already-stretched capacity.

Even without this demographic shift, the outmigration of physicians (equivalent to more than one doctor per day as La Crisis Boricua matured), nurses, and other healthcare professionals would have resulted in the significant under-provision of healthcare services on the island.[10] To illustrate, in 2016, the Puerto Rico College of Physicians and Surgeons (Colegio de Médicos-Cirujanos de Puerto Rico) reported that the number of doctors declined from approximately 14,000 to 9,000 between 2006 and 2016; this 36-percent decline more than tripled the overall population decline on the island. The same group reported that the annual outmigration had been increasing in recent years. For example, 500 physicians left Puerto Rico in 2015, up from the 365 who left in 2014.

As reported by Carmen Heredia Rodriguez (2017), the numbers of these outmigrants exceeded the numbers of new medical residents who completed their training in Puerto Rico during those years (265 and 273, respectively), resulting in a net loss of physicians. The loss has been particularly acute in some of the specialized fields; to illustrate, Mary Williams Walsh reported in a 2016 *New York Times* article that there were only 180 surgeons in total serving 3.5 million people on the island (and only six of them were pediatric surgeons).

Many of the reasons healthcare professionals left the island were economic. For example, doctors working on the mainland earned two to three times more than in Puerto Rico (Heredia Rodriguez 2017; Coto 2013). Moreover, while nearly two-thirds of the island's residents are covered by Medicaid or Medicare, the caps on these programs to Puerto Rico have been at levels far below those which states receive, and Medicare payments were reduced in recent years (Allen 2016). Also, payments for doctors and hospitals were a third less than the average payments by Medicaid managed-care organizations on the mainland (Heredia Rodriguez 2017).

Unfortunately, it seems the population's healthcare system will—in all likelihood—continue to deteriorate in the face of declining income and state funding, along with the migration of its doctors and medical students doing their residencies on the mainland. These changes have resulted in what Williams Walsh (2016) described as "the graying of Puerto Rico's doctors" who now individually serve a larger number of patients, and many are, themselves, of retirement age.

PROMESA AND THE FINANCIAL OVERSIGHT AND MANAGEMENT BOARD

In response to Puerto Rico's debt defaults and economic and fiscal crises, on June 29, 2016, President Barack Obama signed into law H.R. 5278—PROMESA (PROMISE in English),[11] after it passed both the U.S. Senate (with a vote of 68 to 30) and the House of Representatives (with a vote of 297 to 127). It should be highlighted that this was not a bailout, as Congress refused a bailout for Puerto Rico, but it established the process for Puerto Rico to restructure its debt while preventing bondholders from suing the Puerto Rican government for payment. Although this measure was led by a Republican Congress, it required strong bipartisan support, and the number of Democrats voting for this bill exceeded the number of Republicans voting for the same.

Earlier that month, the White House had stated that "The only thing that is certain is that without action by Congress, the crisis will get much worse. For those that are fighting for the 3.5 million Americans in Puerto Rico, it would be irresponsible to allow the situation to get even worse when there is no alternative to the current bill" (Zients 2016). Then-President Obama also commented

> It's the only option on the table to save Puerto Rico from spiraling out of control. And that's exactly what would happen if Congress fails to do its job. There's no question this is a trying time for folks in Puerto Rico. They've seen too many jobs lost and too many neighbors leave in search of better opportunity elsewhere. It's clear that it's time for Puerto Rico to chart a new course and make a fresh start. This bill is just a first step. (The White House Office of the Press Secretary 2016)

As part of the legislation, PROMESA created a Financial Oversight and Management Board (known in Puerto Rico as Junta de Supervisión Fiscal) to restructure Puerto Rico's then $72 billion debt. It is important to note that the governor of Puerto Rico (or designee) would serve as an ex-officio member of the Board, but would not have voting rights. As reported by Dávila (2016) in *The Huffington Post*, Section 4 of PROMESA stated, "The provisions of this Act shall prevail over any general or specific provisions of territory law, State law, or regulation that is inconsistent with this Act." Similarly, Patricia Guadalupe (2016) in *NBC News Latino* stated that "The Board would not be accountable to the island government and would have control over Puerto Rico's budget, laws, financial plans, and regulations." That is, PROMESA essentially granted to this Oversight Board[12] unilateral power over Puerto Rico's finances and economic future.

The primary responsibilities of the Oversight Board included the following:

- Approving the governor's fiscal plans;
- Approving Puerto Rico's annual budgets, including the potential to force the island to balance its budget;
- Enforcing the budgets, including the potential to order any reductions in spending;
- Reviewing laws, contracts, rules, and regulations to ensure compliance with the Board-approved fiscal plan; and
- Restructuring Puerto Rico's debt.

Initial Reactions to PROMESA

PROMESA was publicly discussed by U.S. Senators and members of the House of Representatives Puerto Rico's elected officials, the mass media, as well as then President Obama and the 2016 Democratic nominees for U.S. president, Hillary Rodham Clinton and Bernie Sanders. Reactions to PROMESA were (not surprisingly) mixed. In a survey conducted by *El Nuevo Dia* (Puerto Rico's most circulated newspaper) in June 2016, 51 percent of island Puerto Ricans opposed the creation of the Oversight Board, compared to 46 percent who supported it (although the support increased to 69 percent by October 2016).

Some argued that Puerto Rico's government had been unwilling or unable to deal with and resolve Puerto Rico's financial crisis, and that it played a critical role in its generation. Under these circumstances, PROMESA was viewed as not only inevitable and necessary, but represented the only viable mechanism at the time to begin addressing Puerto Rico's crushing debt and avoid a humanitarian crisis.

When PROMESA was signed into law, then-Governor García Padilla stated

> If there is darkness, there is also light. We have to take the good with the bad, and while I may not agree with a control board, this is a way to restructure our debt and move our country forward … I could have stuck to my ideological and political guns and we would have been on a path to misery, or we could do this, and I chose the responsible thing. (Guadalupe 2016b)

President Obama also stated "The task ahead for Puerto Rico is not an easy one, but I am confident Puerto Rico is up to the challenge of stabilizing the fiscal situation, restoring growth, and building a better future for all Puerto Ricans" (Guadalupe 2016b).

However, others argued that a humanitarian crisis already existed and that the law would do little, if anything, to resolve it and address other critical socioeconomic issues directly affecting the island's residents, given its focus on debt restructuring. The media provided extensive coverage regarding such issues and concerns surrounding PROMESA, including the following:

- The absence of provisions to address Puerto Rico's economic development and chronic socioeconomic issues, such as weak labor markets, widespread poverty, and the deteriorating infrastructure;
- Reinforcing Puerto Rico's *de facto* colonial-type status by imposing "totalitarian control" and "sweeping power to a financial oversight board" over Puerto Rico and its finances;
- Threatening Puerto Rico's autonomy and decision-making power, particularly because neither Puerto Ricans nor the Puerto Rican government had any decision-making authority over whom was appointed to the Board, nor would they have power, oversight, or control over the Board's work, decisions, or outcomes;
- The lack of accountability of the Board to the Puerto Rican government or the island's inhabitants;
- The focus on Puerto Rico's fiscal challenges, which might cause the Board to be more inclined to respond to and serve the needs of the bond holders rather than those of Puerto Ricans, thus potentially adversely impacting the provision of public services, such as health care and education;
- The proposed reduction in Puerto Rico's minimum wage from $7.25 to $4.25 for workers aged twenty-six and below; and
- The absence of provisions regarding the Board members' potential conflicts of interest in their deliberations and outcomes.

Early Stages of PROMESA

The initial voting members of the Oversight Board members were appointed by then President Obama on August 31, 2016, based on recommendations made by the House of Representatives and the Senate, with the governor of Puerto Rico or designee serving as a nonvoting ex-officio member of the Board. The seven voting members consisted of four Republicans and three Democrats with backgrounds primarily in financial, banking, and legal industries, such as the Social Security Administration, Puerto Rico's Workers Compensation Board, the Government Development Bank of Puerto Rico, U.S. Bankruptcy Court, Federal Home Loan Bank of New York, and the California Department of Finance. Five Latinos were on the Board, three of whom were Puerto Rican, and one was a woman. When the Board was announced, some expressed concern about the lack of representation from Puerto Rican community members, nongovernmental organizations, local entrepreneurs, social workers, and academics from Puerto Rican universities.

In its first meeting (September 30, 2016 in New York) as an official entity, the Oversight Board elected its Chairman, José Carrión III, a Puerto Rican insurance executive in San Juan, Puerto Rico. Valentín (2016) reported that at its first meeting, the Board placed several public agencies and corporations that were confronting significant financial or fiscal issues under its jurisdiction. These agencies included Puerto Rico's teachers' judicial and employees' retirement systems, the University of Puerto Rico, PREPA, the Puerto Rico Aqueduct and Sewer Authority (recall Note 8), and all other public corporations. Furthermore, the Board requested that then-Governor García Padilla develop an economic or financial plan showing how it would boost the island's revenues while dealing with Puerto Rico's unprecedented debt, which was due on October 14, 2016. The proposed plan and the Oversight Board's response would set the stage to shape future discussions regarding the restructuring of Puerto Rico's debt, as well as the social, economic, and political ramifications for the Caribbean island.

In the following months, the Oversight Board ordered Puerto Rico to cut its public pension system by 10 percent and furlough tens of thousands of government workers, among other fiscal austerity measures, if the government could not find alternatives to increase tax revenue and reduce spending (Associated Press 2017). Its ten-year fiscal plan also called "for everyone on the U.S. territory of 3.4 million people to make sacrifices" (Associated Press 2017), which would be on top of those made during the previous eleven years. In May 2017, the Oversight Board agreed with what then-Governor García Padilla stated nearly two years earlier (in July 2015)—that Puerto Rico's debt was "not payable"; it therefore recommended that Puerto Rico file for the bankruptcy protection that was permitted by Chapter 3 of PROMESA.

SUMMARY AND CONCLUDING REMARKS

In this chapter, we discussed how the year 2006 represented a "perfect storm" of events that marked the beginning of La Crisis Boricua. Yet, the seeds were sown decades before. This crisis brought to the forefront the economic dependence of Puerto Rico and its inhabitants on the U.S. mainland. It was also a manifestation of decades of unsustainable economic policies discussed in the previous chapter, alleged mishandling of public funds, and the inability of government officials to effectively and efficiently ensure Puerto Rico's economic development in the long term.

Fiscal policy changes (including the imposition of the island's first sales tax and its subsequent increase to a level higher than in any state) and the fiscal crisis faced by Puerto Rico since 2006 (which contributed to its unprecedented $74 billion in public debt, $49 billion in pension obligations, its 2015 and 2016 debt defaults, and bankruptcy filing in 2017) exacerbated already weak and deteriorating economic conditions on the island. Even with the passage of PROMESA, significant policy and structural challenges related to the social mobility outcomes of Puerto Ricans remain unresolved after more than a decade of La Crisis Boricua. We will discuss additional proposals and initiatives being designed as this book went to press to address these challenges in chapter 9. These issues have become increasingly critical in light of the island's unfolding humanitarian crisis and the massive net exodus from the island.

NOTES

1. In addition to the historical rates discussed in chapter 2, it should be noted that the U.S. Bureau of Labor Statistics started collecting its monthly unemployment statistics in Puerto Rico in 1976. Over the next forty years, only in five months was the unemployment rate in Puerto Rico in the single digits (July through November 2000); it reached its low (9.7%) in September and October 2000.

2. We end the timeframe in 2014 for many of our analyses presented in the remainder of this book because it was the most recent year of available data when we conducted the vast majority of the empirical work.

3. An "added worker effect" occurs when individuals previously outside of the labor force begin looking for work; because most new (or returning) entrants into the labor market do not immediately find employment, the unemployment rate tends to increase. The effect of "added workers" on unemployment can be detected through simultaneous increases in both unemployment and LFP rates, which was not the case in Puerto Rico.

4. For examples, see Mora, Dávila, and Rodríguez (2017); Meléndez (2016); Center for a New Economy (2016); National Puerto Rican Agenda (2016); Enchautegui (2014, 2003); Federal Reserve Bank of New York (2012); Enchautegui and Freeman (2006); Davis and Rivera-Batiz (2006); Burtless and Sotomayor (2006); Bosworth and Collins (2006); and the U.S. Government Accountability Office (2006: 69–70).

5. This is not to say that the sales tax represented the first consumption tax on the island; Puerto Rico had an excise tax on imports of 6.6 percent, which was eliminated in 2006 with the imposition of the sales tax.

6. Perhaps this is one of the primary reasons why the Puerto Rican government was only able to collect about half of the revenue from the IVU that had been expected. Because tax evasion by local businesses was suspected to increase its revenue through IVU and to increase compliance of local businesses, Puerto Rico established the "IVU Loto." According to Puerto Rico's Department of Treasury (2011:4), the IVU Loto is an "oversight program for the Sales and Use Tax (SUT or IVU, in Spanish). In this program, the consumer assists with the merchant's compliance process, by requesting a purchase receipt. The receipt will have a number that

will allow them to participate in a specific draw." A pilot program of the IVU Loto was initiated in the municipality of Ponce in late 2010 and implemented island-wide in 2011. Another explanation for the lower-than-expected sales tax revenue is that the sales survey used as a benchmark overestimated total sales and hence overestimated potential sales tax revenue (Caraballo 2016).

7. Among other initiatives, Ley 7 ("Special Law for the Declaration of a Fiscal Emergency and the Establishment of an Integrated Plan for Fiscal Stabilization to Save the Credit of Puerto Rico," or "Ley Especial Declarando Estado de Emergencia Fiscal y Estableciendo Plan Integral de Estabilización Fiscal para Salvar el Crédito de Puerto Rico") included a temporary increase in residential and business property taxes; significant limitations on the utilization of previously granted tax credits; and a moratorium on the issuances of new tax credits.

8. The inefficiencies of Puerto Rico's electricity generation were highlighted in the summer of 2016 when the island experienced selected blackouts due to the electric grid's inability to support the number of users. Moreover, the entire island experienced a blackout in September 2016, leading to an estimated $1 billion in immediate economic losses, after a fire broke out at PREPA's power plant in Aguirre (Stanchich 2016). It should be noted that PREPA was not the only government-owned monopoly straddled with inefficiencies. For example, Danica Coto reported in a 2017 *Associate Press* article that the National Resources Defense Council (NRDC) found that Puerto Rico had the worst rate of drinking water violations of any U.S. jurisdiction. Coto noted this group found that nearly all of Puerto Rico was supplied with water from systems that violated the U.S. Safe Drinking Water Act in 2015 (the most recent year of data they had), and there had been almost 34,000 violations between 2005 to 2015.

9. Much has been written about the effects of homeownership on wealth accumulation. For example, Tracy Turner and Heather Luea (2009) estimate that each additional year of homeownership increased the total net wealth of low-to-moderate income households between $6,000–$10,000 in the 1990s, even after controlling for other socioeconomic and demographic characteristics.

10. In the following chapter, we discuss how less educated Puerto Ricans were disproportionately represented in the net migration flow to the mainland. However, this should not be interpreted as a sign that the outmigration of highly skilled professionals, including physicians, did not present significant challenges to island residents.

11. PROMESA was developed by the Committee on Natural Resources, chaired by Rob Bishop; see www.congress.gov/bill/114th-congress/house-bill/4900.

12. We realize the term "Oversight Board" has had some controversy because it has veto power over Puerto Rico's elected government officials, suggesting its function is more of a control board. However, we use "Oversight Board" to be consistent with the language in the PROMESA legislation and popular press.

Chapter 4

On the Recent Puerto Rican Migrants

Who were the Puerto Ricans migrating to the U.S. mainland during La Crisis Boricua? After discussing conceptual and empirical observations regarding migration decisions since the "perfect storm" of events commenced in 2006, in this chapter, we provide a socioeconomic and demographic profile of the recent migrants on the mainland. In particular, we show that, unlike the implications from reports in the popular press, highly educated workers were not disproportionately represented in the recent net migration flow from the island to mainland, although the unobservable skills of these migrants were relatively high. Not surprisingly, but contrary to some public perceptions, work-related issues were heavily cited as reasons behind their exodus to the mainland during La Crisis Boricua. We further discuss the Puerto Rican migrants who were all but ignored by the popular press: those who returned to the island after the perfect storm got underway. Our findings indicate that younger but more educated workers tended to be the ones overrepresented among these return migrants.

CONCEPTUAL ISSUES ON MIGRATION

Conceptually, and following a human capital model framework, migration takes place when the expected present value of the migration decision (both in terms of monetary and nonmonetary compensation) exceeds the present value of the migration costs. Placing a high personal value on living in Puerto Rico raises migration costs because moving entails foregoing the sociocultural amenities associated with island residence. This point is consistent with the overrepresentation of non-Puerto Ricans among migrants who left the island during La Crisis Boricua (recall chapter 1), as most Puerto Ricans likely have a greater attachment to the island than non-Puerto Ricans. To help offset some of these costs, Puerto Rican migrants might be more likely to select mainland areas with large Puerto Rican concentrations, thus having access to a "known" community and culture, including food, language, and so forth.

This conceptualization predicts that migrants are likely to be younger as they would have a longer time horizon to reap the benefits from migrating. It also suggests that people from the more depressed regions on the island would be more likely to migrate. Moreover, given that families tend to have higher migration costs than single individuals, unattached individuals may be more likely to migrate from the island than families. We further expect that migrants who move to areas with less established Puerto Rican communities would have better labor market outcomes, to counter the costs associated with foregoing the proximity to Puerto Rican sociocultural amenities.[1]

Migration Push-Pull Framework

For insight into factors affecting skill-based migration, it is useful to consider a "push-pull" framework. Recall from chapter 2 that at different times, including during the island's Great Migration period, Puerto Rico has used outmigration as a safety valve to respond to a weak labor market, essentially encouraging outmigration as a means to "export" unemployment. In the case of La Crisis Boricua, as we discussed in chapter 3, many of the deteriorating economic and fiscal conditions on the island, such as the imposition of sales taxes, a reduction in public sector employment, a loss in manufacturing jobs, and rising electricity prices, would have disproportionately impacted low- to medium-income (skill) groups. As such, these groups were the ones most likely to migrate during this time, *ceteris paribus*.

However, the U.S. mainland experienced the Great Recession (and a weakened labor market) during part of La Crisis Boricua. As such, it is unlikely that major pull factors were at play overall, at least until labor market conditions recovered on the mainland. We therefore expect that much of the island-to-mainland migration, at least initially, reflected push factors that led to the outmigration of less-skilled individuals. At the same time, the growth in the Puerto Rican population on the mainland, including those in new destination areas, might have reduced migration costs for the later waves of migrants during the economic crisis.

Given these conceptual observations, and given the severity and longevity of La Crisis Boricua, we expect that the net outmigration flow from the island contained a disproportionate share of younger, unattached, and less-skilled migrants. We test these propositions by examining the characteristics of migrants as they were leaving the island as well as those of recent migrants on the mainland. Later in this chapter, we consider conceptual issues related to the incidence of return migration, and then analyze the characteristics of migrants who went back to Puerto Rico in the midst of La Crisis Boricua.

CHARACTERISTICS OF ISLAND-TO-MAINLAND PUERTO RICAN MIGRANTS

Two data sets are used for the purpose of analyzing the demographic and socioeconomic profiles of Puerto Rican migrants to the U.S. mainland: The Puerto Rican Travelers Survey (TS) and the American Community Survey (ACS) data. As discussed in appendix A, the TS was conducted in Spanish and English by Puerto Rican government agencies to measure tourism and economic conditions in Puerto Rico. The TS surveyed passengers who were ages sixteen and above flying into or out of Luis Muñoz Marín International (San Juan metropolitan area) and Rafael Hernandez (Aguadilla) Airports in fiscal years 2011 and 2012.

One major advantage with using the TS is that, among other travelers, it captures Puerto Ricans moving to the U.S. mainland in the most prevalent departure points from the island; it also includes information about the specific *municipio* (equivalent to a county) from where they were migrating and into which state they intended to move. While the public-use version of the ACS includes the state of residence of new migrants from the island, we cannot determine specifically from where they moved. Moreover, the TS asked people why they were moving; the ACS does not contain any information about the reasons for moving.[2]

Potential shortcomings with the TS are that it does not necessarily contain a nationally representative sample of Puerto Rican *residents*, and despite attempts to approximate a representative sample of adult passengers,[3] it is not a random survey of the travelers. The voluntary nature of this survey might lead to self-selection among those willing to complete it along the lines of certain socioeconomic and demographic characteristics. For example, only one person per set of group of travelers completes the survey, which excludes other family members. If the head of the household tends to be the person who completes the survey, characteristics typically associated with household heads would be overrepresented in the TS as opposed to the ACS. Another potential shortcoming of this survey is the absence of ethnicity identifiers (or self-identifiers), thus preventing us from distinguishing between Puerto Ricans and other population groups.

The public-use ACS data, on the other hand, while not providing the specific sending areas of the migrants, include a nationally representative sample of Puerto Ricans who moved to the U.S. mainland within twelve months prior to being surveyed. Unfortunately, we cannot identify individuals who moved to the states but also returned to Puerto Rico within the past year in the ACS, potentially biasing the sample toward relatively successful migrants on the mainland. In terms of selection issues, unlike the TS, the ACS includes the characteristics of all members of a household rather than just the person who completed the survey. The ACS is therefore more representative of Puerto Ricans moving to the mainland than the TS is of those leaving the island.

Because the ACS includes data for a calendar year, and it is not possible in the public-use version to know which month the survey occurred, this leaves a potential time gap in the comparability of the timeframe between the ACS and TS. That is, the 2006–2014 ACS data include individuals who migrated anytime between 2005 and 2013, while the TS only includes outgoing migrants between July 2010 and June 2012.[4] Another difference to note is that while the TS surveys migrants as they were preparing to leave the island, the ACS surveys them ex-post sometime during the next twelve months. That said, both datasets represent important and critical sources of information that can be used to construct demographic and socioeconomic profiles of Puerto Ricans leaving the island during La Crisis Boricua.

For this end, Table 4.1 provides selected characteristics of migrants to the U.S. mainland in the TS (first column) and ACS (second column) who were between the ages of twenty-five and sixty-four. In the ACS, this table further shows these characteristics when partitioning the sample between Puerto Ricans and non-Puerto Ricans (third and fourth columns, respectively). Note that Puerto Ricans represented seven out of ten migrants (71.0%), the vast majority of whom (85.9%) were born on the island. Approximately 7.5 percent of the non-Puerto Rican migrants did not identify themselves as Puerto Rican, despite having been born on the island.

The representation of Puerto Ricans among the migrants, while high, was considerably lower than their representation among the population of island residents in the same age range (95.1% during this timeframe). This finding fits with our conceptual framework as Puerto Ricans are more likely attached to Puerto Rico and therefore face higher migration costs than other individuals. While non-Puerto Rican migrants represent a population outside of the scope of our study, as we noted in chapter 1, this group would be worthy of exploring in more detail in future studies.

Women represented approximately half of the migrants in both the TS and ACS, and the average age among the TS outgoing migrants from Puerto Rico (41.1 years) was just slightly above that of the recent migrants on the mainland (39.7 years). The similarity in these measures demonstrates empirical validity to some of the basic demographic characteristics observed in the TS.

However, one difference is that TS migrants had higher levels of schooling than their counterparts in the ACS. On average, the outgoing migrants had

Table 4.1   Selected Characteristics of Outbound and Recent Migrants, Aged Twenty-Five to Sixty-Four, from Puerto Rico to the Mainland

| Characteristic | Outbound Migrants from Puerto Rico to Mainland (TS: FY2011–FY 2012) | Recent Migrants from Puerto Rico to the Mainland (ACS: 2006–2014) | | |
		All	Puerto Ricans	Non-Puerto Ricans
Puerto Rican	–	71.0%	100.0%	–
Born in Puerto Rico	–	63.2%	85.9%	7.5%
Female	48.0%	49.0%	50.9%	44.1%
Age	41.1 years	39.7 years	39.4 years	40.3 years
Education measures:				
Average education	13.2 years	12.3 years	12.4 years	12.1 years
Not a high school graduate	17.9%	22.3%	21.7%	23.6%
High school graduate	26.8%	28.6%	30.4%	24.0%
Some college, no degree	20.9%	25.7%	24.9%	27.7%
College graduate	34.4%	23.4%	22.9%	24.7%
Family income:				
Less than $20,000	49.0%	39.4%	42.8%	30.7%
$20,000–$39,999	19.7%	24.2%	24.9%	22.4%
At least $100,000	6.2%	8.1%	5.9%	13.5%
Traveling alone	68.0%	–	–	–
Married	–	40.5%	39.7%	42.3%
Number of children at home	–	0.70	0.76	0.56
Unmarried or separated parent with children at home	–	15.0%	16.7%	10.9%
N	2,223	2,302	1,384	678
Estimated population	455,567	314,558	191,858	91,165

Source: Authors' estimates using data from the TS, 2010–11 and 2011–12, and ACS, 2006–2014.
Notes: The samples include individuals between the ages of twenty-five and sixty-four. The outbound migrants in the TS sample include air travelers who reported the primary purpose of their trip was to move to the mainland. The recent migrants in the ACS are individuals who moved from Puerto Rico within the 12 months prior to the survey. The family income distributions exclude individuals who did not answer this question in the TS (approximately 7.0% of this sample); this information is not reported in the ACS for individuals residing in group quarters. The estimate of the percentage of travelers who traveled alone excludes individuals who did not answer this question.

13.2 years of schooling, and over one-third (34.4%) were college graduates. In comparison, the average education among the recent ACS migrants was a year lower (12.3 years), and less than one-quarter (23.4%) had completed college. One possible explanation for these schooling discrepancies is that less educated individuals were more likely to refuse answering the TS. Still, both of these surveys indicate the vast majority of migrants from the island had at least a high school diploma. Comparing recent Puerto Rican and non-Puerto Rican migrants in the ACS indicates both groups moving to the states had similar educational profiles.

Despite the relatively high level of schooling reported in the TS, one-half (49.0%) of the outgoing migrants reported less than $20,000 in family income. When combining these individuals with those whom reported between $20,000 and $40,000, over two-thirds (68.7%) had less than $40,000 in family income.[5] Such low income levels are not surprising in light of the severity of La Crisis Boricua and the high rates of impoverishment discussed in the previous chapter. They also fit with the conceptual framework noted earlier suggesting individuals from more depressed regions or circumstances would be more likely than wealthier individuals to move due to stronger "push" factors from the island.

Indeed, this information is consistent with the primary reason for moving stateside reported by the outgoing migrants in the TS. As seen in Figure 4.1, nearly two-thirds (63.0%) of the outgoing migrants in this age range reported work-related reasons (41.4%) or searching for work (21.6%) as their primary purpose for migrating. Additional reasons included family-related issues (12.5%), retiring (8.1%), and "other" issues (18.7%).[6]

The family income distributions between the TS and ACS suggest only a modest improvement within a year of migration; 39.4 percent of the recent

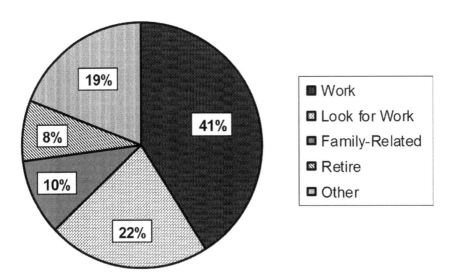

Figure 4.1   Primary Reason for Moving to the Mainland: FY2011–FY2012. *Source:* Authors' estimates using FY2011–FY2012 TS data. *Notes:* The sample does not distinguish between Puerto Ricans and non-Puerto Ricans. Our sample includes air travelers between the ages of 25 and 64 who reported their primary reason for traveling was to move to the mainland.

migrants had less than $20,000 in family income, and nearly two-thirds (63.6%) had less than $40,000. Family income levels were even lower among Puerto Rican migrants than non-Puerto Ricans; one in seven (67.7%) of the former group had family income levels of less than $40,000 compared to half (53.1%) of the latter. The relative lack of progress, particularly among Puerto Ricans, after a year of migration suggests that upward social mobility on the mainland was not immediately apparent.

While marital status is not reported in the TS, we can observe that approximately one-third (32%) were traveling with others to the mainland, with the average number per group being three members. In the 2006–2014 Puerto Rican Community Survey (PRCS), less than half (44.8%) of island residents between the ages of twenty-five and sixty-four were married, and fewer than two-thirds (62.2%) were either married or had their children living with them. The relatively high share of individuals traveling alone in the TS relates to the predictions above that relatively young and unattached individuals are those more likely to migrate. It also suggests that some of the migrants would have been willing to temporarily leave their families behind until they became more settled on the U.S. mainland. The recent migrants in our ACS sample provide some support for this prediction, as 7.8 percent reported being married but did not currently live with their spouse.

SKILL-BASED MIGRATION PATTERNS

As we highlighted in a related study (Mora, Dávila, and Rodríguez 2017), a more detailed analysis of how the skill levels have been shifting among Puerto Rican migrants versus nonmigrants is of particular policy relevance for both the receiving and sending communities. Indeed, an abundance of news articles on Puerto Rico's outmigration during La Crisis Boricua focused on the loss of doctors and other professionals (recall chapter 3), but these studies have not examined the empirical evidence of whether high skilled migrants were disproportionately represented in the outmigration flow.

Extant research investigating island-to-mainland migration patterns have reported mixed results regarding relative skill distributions. For example, Edwin Meléndez and M. Anne Visser (2011) and Ricardo Godoy, Glenn Jenkins, and Karishma Patel (2003) reported through their reviews of the literature that post-World War II Puerto Rican migrants tended to be more educated than nonmigrants. Vilma Ortiz (1986) also reported higher schooling levels among Puerto Rican migrants between 1960 and 1980, but she found these reflected rising education levels on the island and not a shift in the skill composition of migrants favoring the more educated. Using data several decades apart, Orlando Sotomayor (2009) and Eva Sandis (1970) found that Puerto Rican migrants appeared to come from the middle of the skill distribution. Finally, more recent studies have reported that Puerto Rican migrants to the mainland tended to have lower education levels than those remaining on the island.[7]

For our analysis here, we consider changes in both observable skills (primarily measured through education) and unobservable skills (estimated through unexplained earnings differentials). The combination of both types of skill levels provides a more holistic view of underlying characteristics of Puerto Rican migrants. Because the vast majority of the migrants were born on the island, our analysis is restricted to island-born Puerto Ricans.

CHANGES IN OBSERVABLE SKILLS

We report in Table 4.2 the education levels and distributions, age, and other observable characteristics of island-born Puerto Ricans who were between the ages of twenty-five and sixty-four at the beginning (2006), middle (2010), and end (2014) of our timeframe of this analysis. Note that, in 2006, island-born Puerto Ricans residing on the island had similar education levels on average as their counterparts living on the mainland (11.8 years vs. 11.7 years). By 2010, however, a schooling gap of 0.4 years emerged, as average education rose by 0.6 years among island residents compared to 0.3 years among mainland residents. This education gap remained in place by 2014, as both groups experienced an additional 0.3-year increase in average schooling (to 12.7 years among island residents and 12.3 years among mainland residents). The widening of the average schooling gaps between island-born Puerto Ricans on the island versus mainland between 2006 and 2014 was statistically significant.

The increase in the average education levels of island-born Puerto Ricans indicates education investments in Puerto Rico have continued rising in recent years, even during a relatively short period of time. The larger rise in the average schooling levels among island residents compared to those living stateside suggests less educated migrants were the ones more likely to leave, at least in the early stages of Puerto Rico's crisis.

The schooling distributions in Table 4.2 provide support for these conclusions. While a smaller share of island residents than mainland residents had completed at least eight years of schooling, this share fell for both groups, particularly among those living in Puerto Rico (from 16.8% to 10.3% between 2006 and 2014 for this group, and from 13.1% to 9.7% among island-born Puerto Ricans on the mainland). The percentage of college graduates also rose for both groups (by 5.6 percentage points, to 27.7% in 2014 among the former, and by 4.7 percentage points, to 19.1% among the latter).

Table 4.2   Education and Age of Island-Born Puerto Ricans, Ages Twenty-Five to Sixty-Four, by Island versus Mainland Residence: 2006, 2010, and 2014

Characteristic	Island Residents			Mainland Residents		
	2006	2010	2014	2006	2010	2014
Years of	11.82	12.42	12.73	11.72	11.95	12.32
education	(4.19)	(3.76)	(3.67)	(3.55)	(3.46)	(3.44)
Highest level of schooling:						
Up to 8 years	16.8%	12.8%	10.3%	13.1%	11.6%	9.7%
Some high school	10.7%	9.9%	8.7%	18.6%	17.1%	14.8%
High school graduate	27.2%	27.2%	29.2%	30.9%	29.7%	28.7%
Some college	23.2%	25.1%	24.2%	23.0%	25.5%	27.7%
College graduate	22.1%	25.0%	27.7%	14.4%	16.1%	19.1%
Female	52.9%	52.9%	52.8%	53.0%	52.0%	64.9%
Age (in years)	43.74	44.26	44.54	45.35	45.23	44.92
	(11.58)	(11.53)	(11.53)	(11.29)	(11.32)	(11.32)
N (unweighted)	15,475	15,932	13,761	7,034	7,746	7,206
N (weighted)	1,763,768	1,676,001	1,578,882	874,506	961,949	936,332

Source: Authors' estimates using ACS and PRCS data in the IPUMS.
Notes: The parentheses contain the standard deviations for the continuous variables. The sample includes Puerto Ricans (based on self-identification) between the ages of twenty-five and sixty-four.

Still, the changes were greater among stateside Puerto Ricans between 2010 and 2014 than between 2006 and 2010, suggesting education levels were higher in the net migration flow from the island during the latter stages of the economic crisis, perhaps in response to the mainland's recovery from the Great Recession.

Some of these changes may relate to age-distribution differentials between island-born Puerto Ricans on the island versus the U.S. mainland. As seen in Table 4.2, adults between the ages of 25 and 64 were younger on average among the former than in the latter group (43.7 years old vs. 45.5 years, respectively, in 2006). Since younger populations tend to have higher education levels than older ones, this difference could relate to the higher schooling levels observed among the island residents. At the same time, similar to what we reported in chapter 1 for Puerto Rican residents in general, the average age of island-born Puerto Ricans (between the ages of twenty-five and sixty-four) on the island increased between 2006 and 2014, from 43.7 years to 44.5 years. A larger increase occurred between 2006 and 2010 (0.6 years) than between 2010 and 2014 (0.2 years).

These changes reflect a sharp presence of relatively young Puerto Ricans who left the island during this time, as we predicted above, especially in the early stages of the economic crisis. It is therefore not surprising to observe that the average age of island-born Puerto Ricans in the states declined during this time, from 45.4 years in 2006 to 44.9 years by 2014. This decline led to a statistically significant narrowing in the island/mainland age differential among island-born Puerto Rican adults between 2006 and 2014. To the extent that age reflects experience, such findings again point to the view that migrants leaving the island during the economic crisis had relatively lower observable skills.[8]

In sum, Table 4.2 indicates that differences in the education levels and the average age of island-born Puerto Ricans on the island versus the mainland shifted during the La Crisis Boricua. For more insight, Panel A in Figure 4.2 presents the average years of schooling of island-born Puerto Ricans on the island versus their mainland counterparts in each year since 2006. It also shows the average education levels among the stateside recent migrants.

This figure reveals several important findings. First, as had been implied in Table 4.2, with few exceptions, the average education levels of island-born Puerto Ricans increased each year. This was especially the case among those living on the island, which again indicates that education investments in Puerto Rico have been rising. Second, despite the net outflow of physicians, nurses, and other healthcare professions discussed in chapter 3, the more pronounced rise in the average schooling levels of island-born Puerto Ricans who resided on the island versus the mainland supports the foregoing observations that less skilled individuals, on average, were the ones more likely to leave the island during La Crisis Boricua.

Still, this figure illustrates the *annual* skill-based migration propensities were volatile during the economic crisis.[9] In the early years of the economic crisis, the average education among recent migrants in the states initially exceeded that of their counterparts who remained behind. This tendency did not occur throughout the crisis, however, as each wave of island-born Puerto Ricans migrating from the island after 2007 had lower education levels on average than those who migrated in the previous year until 2011. Between 2011 to 2014, the average schooling levels recovered among each new wave of incoming migrants (with 2013 being an exception); as such, by 2014, they had returned to the average education levels of Puerto Ricans on the island.

As La Crisis Boricua deepened, the initial pressures might have disproportionately pushed less educated individuals into migrating, but over time, this crisis also began impacting middle- and higher-skilled individuals (including doctors), especially as the mainland recovered from its Great Recession. This migration dynamic could further reflect a rising willingness to leave the island as Puerto Rican communities on the U.S. mainland continued growing, especially as La Crisis Boricua showed no signs of relenting.

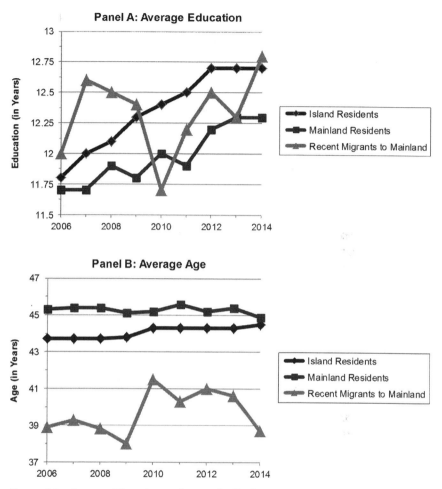

Figure 4.2 **Average Education and Age of Island-Born Puerto Ricans, by Residence: 2006–2014.** *Source*: Authors' estimates using 2006–2014 ACS and PRCS data in the IPUMS. *Notes*: Puerto Ricans are self-identified. Recent migrants are defined as those who moved from the island to mainland within the past twelve months of the survey. The sample includes island-born Puerto Ricans between the ages of twenty-five and sixty-four.

Panel B in Figure 4.2 reveals volatility in the average age among each wave of migrants. Not surprisingly, over the entire time period, recent migrants were younger on average than other Puerto Ricans, which is consistent with human capital predictions. Consider that the relationship between the average age and education of recent migrants shifted between the earlier and later stages of La Crisis Boricua. In particular, between 2006 and 2009, age and education appeared to be complements among recent migrants on the mainland. That is, as the average education of the migrants fell, so too did their average age. To the extent that age reflects experience, this observation reiterates our discussion above that the initial net island-to-mainland migration occurred among adults with below-average observable skills.

Yet after 2009, age and education appeared to serve as substitutes: the average age of recent migrants between the ages of twenty-five and sixty-four rose to its highest level (at 41.5 years) in 2010, but this was the same year their average education reached its trough. Their average age fell each year thereafter (except in 2012), which for the most part coincided with the subsequently rising average schooling levels among migrants. The general increase in the schooling levels observed after 2010 therefore likely relates to a growing presence of the youth leaving the island. Education levels may have been rising, perhaps because of an increase in younger (and less experienced) adults.

OBSERVABLE SKILLS AND THE LIKELIHOOD OF MIGRATION TO THE MAINLAND

An alternative approach to examining skill-based migration, at least in terms of observable skills, involves analyzing how skills related to the likelihood of migrating when accounting for other confounding characteristics involved in such decisions. For example, while the results discussed thus far consistently point to the disproportionate presence of lower skilled migrants from the island in the early part of Puerto Rico's economic crisis, we also note above that one's degree of attachment also matters in terms of migration decisions.

Therefore, we use probit regression analysis with ACS/PRCS data to investigate how education and age related to the likelihood that island-born Puerto Ricans migrated to the U.S. mainland during the crisis when accounting for socioeconomic and demographic traits. Specifically, these include English-language fluency, marital status, the number of children residing at home, whether or not the individual had interest or dividend income (as a proxy for wealth),[10] occupation, and being in a later survey (2011–2014) than in an earlier one (2006–2010). Appendix B provides additional estimation details.

The first column of Table 4.3 presents the empirical results. Education, age, and the lack of English-language fluency were inversely related to the probability of leaving the island during the crisis, with the negative effect of age lessening among older individuals. To illustrate, when computing the marginal effects (not shown), each year of schooling reduced the odds of outmigration by 0.05 percent among island-born Puerto Ricans. While small, this finding points to the disproportionate presence of less educated individuals in the outmigration flow from the island. An additional test (with the details provided in appendix B) indicates that the relationships between the likelihood

Table 4.3 Probit Regression Results for the Likelihood of Island-Born Puerto Ricans Moving between the Island and Mainland: 2006–2014

Characteristic	Migrated from Island to Mainland in Past 12 Months (Base Group: Island Residents)	Migrated from Mainland to Island in Past 12 Months (Base Group: Mainland Residents)
Education	−0.018***	0.029***
	(0.039)	(0.006)
Age	−0.040***	−0.023**
	(0.010)	(0.012)
Age-squared	0.0003***	0.0001
	(0.0001)	(0.0001)
Does not speak English well	−0.409***	0.353***
	(0.029)	(0.039)
Has interest income	0.001	−0.489***
	(0.086)	(0.119)
Female	0.084***	−0.115***
	(0.031)	(0.034)
Number of children at home	−0.033**	−0.062***
	(0.016)	(0.017)
Single	−0.070*	0.081*
	(0.038)	(0.043)
Divorced, widowed, separated	0.062*	0.240***
	(0.035)	(0.040)
Occupation (base = exec., managerial, professional)	Included	Included
Year 2011–2014	0.146***	−0.097***
	(0.027)	(0.034)
Constant	−0.893***	−1.892***
	(0.219)	(0.258)
N	132,658	67,086
χ^2	409.6***	284.1**
Pseudo R^2	0.048	0.041

Source: Authors' estimates using ACS and PRCS data in the IPUMS.
Notes: In the first column, the dependent variable equals one for recent migrants on the mainland, and equals zero for island residents. In the second column, the dependent variable equals one for recent migrants on the island, and equals zero for mainland residents. See appendix B for the empirical details. The parentheses contain robust standard errors. The sample includes island-born Puerto Ricans between the ages of twenty-five and sixty-four.
***, **, * Statistically significant at 1, 5, or 10 percent level.

of migrating to the mainland did not significantly change between the early part of La Crisis Boricua (2006 to 2010) and later stages (2011 to 2014), when accounting for other observable characteristics. It follows that the seeming differences in education and age observed over time in Figure 4.1 were not statistically significant when accounting for other observable characteristics.

Consistent with earlier studies (e.g., Godoy, Jenkins, and Patel 2003; Santiago-Rivera and Santiago 1999), Table 4.3 indicates that individuals lacking English-language fluency were less likely than their English fluent counterparts to move to the mainland. In terms of gender, this analysis shows that Puerto Rican women had greater propensities to migrate than men, other things equal. With respect to family migration decisions, while we had initially expected single individuals to be more likely to move than their married counterparts (because they would be less likely to be attached), our findings indicate the opposite—married Puerto Ricans tended to have a relatively greater likelihood of migration. However, one explanation is that being married does not automatically mean *both* members of the household moved together; recall from above that many of the married recent migrants were not living with their spouses. Consistent with our expectations, having children reduced the likelihood of moving.

We also find that workers with certain occupations were more likely to migrate than others (results not shown). In particular, individuals with white-collar positions were less likely to move than those in the service, blue-collar, and agricultural sectors. This finding is consistent with the disproportionate jobs lost for lower- to medium-skilled positions as noted in the previous chapter. Individuals who did not have an occupation were also more likely to move than workers reporting having one (regardless of the employment status), a finding which provides additional support for the "push" argument behind migration.

CHANGES IN UNOBSERVABLE SKILLS

We now explore changes in unobservable skills and other characteristics among island-born Puerto Ricans during La Crisis Boricua. One common technique to investigate unobservable skills would be to analyze individual earnings while controlling for education and other observable characteristics identified in the literature as being predictors of labor market earnings. However, a potential problem with solely tracking skill-adjusted changes in the earnings of Puerto Ricans working stateside is that such changes reflect both changes in their unobservable skills and other characteristics, such as labor market conditions. More meaningful estimates can be obtained by considering changes in the earnings of island-born Puerto Rican migrants *relative* to a standardized group of workers (e.g., Oaxaca 1973); we use the convention of having mainland-born non-Hispanic whites serve for this purpose.

Consider that earnings differentials between two groups reflect two components: a component that can be explained by differences in observable skills and other characteristics between the groups and an unexplained component (the remainder of the earnings differential). To illustrate, in 2006, island-born Puerto Ricans who worked on the mainland earned 30.3 percent less on average than non-Hispanic whites.

At least part of this earnings gap reflects the fact that the latter group had higher average observable skill levels and other characteristics that generally lead to higher earnings; for example, they had an average of 14.0 years of education that year, compared to 12.5 years among island-born Puerto Ricans who were working. Accounting for differences in such characteristics explains over half (19.8 percentage points) of the total earnings gap between island-born Puerto Ricans and non-Hispanic whites on the mainland (see appendix B for the empirical details).

This leaves an earnings differential of 10.5 percent in 2006 that differences in education and other traits do not explain. This "unexplained" differential reflects differences in the following: (1) unobservable skill levels, such as the quality of education or experience; (2) other unmeasured personal characteristics (e.g., motivation), (3) geographic mobility that affects employment and housing opportunities; (4) the utilization of social networks; (5) hedonic preferences, in which case some individuals forego better economic outcomes because they prefer their current place of residence; (6) the perceived quality of certain attributes by employers, such as education; and last but certainly not least (7) underlying structural factors, including discrimination in labor, housing, and credit markets.

While sizeable, the unexplained earnings differential between island-born Puerto Ricans on the mainland versus non-Hispanic whites was considerably smaller in magnitude than the one accrued by their counterparts on the island (–47.5%). As we discuss elsewhere (Mora, Dávila, and Rodríguez 2017), the sheer magnitude in unexplained earnings differences between island-born Puerto Ricans on the island and in the states points to a substantial "island effect" associated with relatively low earnings in Puerto Rico (e.g., Rivera-Batiz and Santiago 1996), which may reflect the potential underinvestment by corporations in productivity-enhancing activities (e.g., Bosworth and Collins 2006) and underlying structural differences in labor markets between the island and mainland. We offer further support for this when considering the similar large unexplained earnings differential of mainland-born Puerto Ricans (41.7% in 2006) on the island.

To visualize changes in these unexplained earnings differentials since the beginning of Puerto Rico's crisis, panel A in Figure 4.3 presents them annually for island-born Puerto Ricans on the mainland and island as well as those for each wave of recent migrants on the mainland. Throughout the entire period, island-born Puerto Ricans on the mainland and to a much greater extent, on the island, had a persistent unexplained earnings differential *vis-à-vis* non-Hispanic whites. These differentials ranged between –6.1 percent (2011) and -11.9 percent (2013) among those working stateside, and between –41.7 percent (2012) and –51.1 percent (2007) among those working in Puerto Rico.

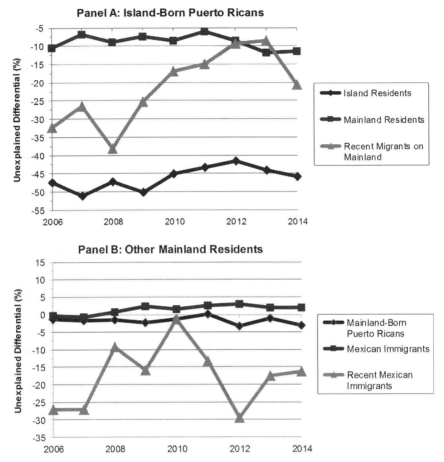

Figure 4.3 Unexplained Earnings Differentials between Puerto Ricans and Non-Hispanic Whites: 2006–2014. *Source*: Authors' estimates using 2006–2014 ACS and PRCS data in the IPUMS. *Notes*: Puerto Ricans are self-identified. Recent migrants are identified as those who moved from the island to mainland within the past 12 months of the survey. The sample includes individuals aged twenty-five to sixty-four who worked within the past 12 months. See appendix B for the estimation of the unexplained earnings differentials.

With the exception of only two years (2011 and 2013), these differentials moved in opposite directions between the mainland and island; as they improved for mainland workers, they deteriorated for island workers and vice versa. This correlation could relate to unobserved skill-based migration patterns between the island and mainland. That is, as workers with higher unobserved characteristics left the island, the average unexplained earnings differential improved on the mainland (as average skill levels increased) and widened on the island.

Empirical support for this supposition can be found with respect to the earnings of recent island-born migrants to the mainland, but mainly for the 2006–2009 period. During these years, their unexplained wage gaps moved together with those of mainland residents (rising except in 2008), and opposite of those of their counterparts who remained on the island. Moreover, Figure 4.3 shows that, between 2009 and 2014, they tended to move together with the unexplained earnings differentials on the island (with 2013 being an exception). A potential explanation for the latter finding is that the net outmigration reduced the relative labor supply on the island, which tended to pull up the wages of those left behind before 2013.

In addition, except in 2008 and 2014, the estimated unexplained earnings differences among incoming migrants to the states increased each year. This finding suggests that, despite the declining observable skill levels among each wave of new island-born migrants early in the crisis, each wave was generally faring better than those who migrated the year before.

We do not observe the same patterns among mainland-born Puerto Ricans or Mexican immigrants on the mainland—groups we include for comparison purposes in panel B in Figure 4.3. When accounting for differences in education and other observable skills, mainland-born Puerto Ricans had considerably smaller unexplained earnings differentials with non-Hispanic whites (hovering between 0 and 3%) than their island-born counterparts. In many of the years, moreover, Mexican immigrants fared slightly better than even mainland-born Puerto Ricans with respect to their unexplained earnings differentials with non-Hispanic whites.

This figure further shows that the unexplained earnings between recent Mexican immigrants and non-Hispanic whites changed differently than those between recent island-born Puerto Rican migrants and non-Hispanic whites. This observation suggests that changes observed in these earnings for island-born Puerto Ricans on the mainland during La Crisis Boricua did not simply mirror those of other migrant groups.

CONCEPTUAL ISSUES FOR TEMPORARY VERSUS PERMANENT MIGRATION

In general, when studying the demographic and socioeconomic profiles of Puerto Ricans migrating from the island to the U.S. mainland, it is important to also consider their migratory intentions. Is the migration permanent or temporary? Do the characteristics of the settlers versus the return migrants differ?

Conceptually, according to Christian Dustmann and Joseph-Simon Gorlach (2015), a migrant decides each time period whether to return to the country of origin or to stay longer. The migrant makes this choice by comparing the value of staying in the host country with the value of returning to his or her home country. When preferences and purchasing power in both areas are identical, and there is no skill accumulation, migration occurs solely because of wage differentials. Under these conditions, when wages are higher in the host country than in the origin country, migrants permanently migrate to the host country. This is the classic case of migration that most research assumes.

But when some of the foregoing assumptions are dropped, temporary migration might occur. Over the wealth-building life span of the migrant, he or she might return to the country of origin if: (1) the migrant receives more pleasure from consumption in the home country; (2) the country of origin has a lower cost of living (allowing the migrant to purchase more goods and services with accumulated wealth); or (3) the migrant acquires human capital in the receiving (host) country that becomes relatively more valuable in the origin country.

The first condition for temporary migration assumes that the migrant moves to the receiving country to accumulate assets to finance consumption in the country of origin, consumption that provides more pleasure in his or her home country than in the host country. One theoretical implication for this type of migration is that temporary migrants accumulate savings in the host country and consume these savings upon returning to the country of origin (this also occurs because of the lower income received in the country of origin). The duration of the migration spell is inversely related to the pleasure of consuming in the country of origin.

The second condition implies that, without earnings differences between the host and origin countries, migration will always be temporary. Keep in mind that the incentive to spend time abroad is assumed to arise solely from a greater purchasing power in the origin country. The third condition will lead to temporary migration if the returns to skills are higher in the origin country than in the host country. Once the migrant accumulates skills in the host country, his or her earnings might become higher in the country of origin.

Note that under this scenario, the migrant has the incentive to borrow while in the host country and not save. Therefore, the consumption profile predicted in the first case differs under this scenario as consumption spending is "smoothed out" between the host and origin countries. This condition will lead to selective return migration as well; migrants with the highest returns to skill in their country of origin will be the ones most likely to return. Finally, this condition captures the case of students who migrate to more rapidly acquire education (both in terms of quantity and quality) in the host country. Once this human capital is acquired, the migrant may return to his/her home country to accrue relatively higher earnings there.

Our data and empirical methodologies cannot adequately measure the migratory intentions of migrants from Puerto Rico to the U.S. mainland, particularly regarding their intentions to *return* to Puerto Rico. Recall from Figure 4.1 earlier in this chapter, that the TS includes information on why the migrants are moving to the mainland. Aside from retiring (which had relatively few responses in the age range we analyze), other reasons for migrating to the U.S. mainland might be construed as being temporary migration decisions.

In particular, the "for work" or "looking for work" reasons only suggest that *at the time of the survey*, the migrants perceived employment opportunities to be more favorable on the mainland than in Puerto Rico. According to the temporary migration framework, we cannot ascertain whether the migration decision, on the basis of employment or job search, is temporary or permanent. Moving for family-related reasons might also be short term, as these reasons might in their own nature be temporary, such as assisting a family member with a pregnancy or temporary illness.

OBSERVABLE CHARACTERISTICS AND THE LIKELIHOOD OF RETURN MIGRATION

We can glean some insights into the observable characteristics of return migrants to Puerto Rico in the 2006–2014 PRCS—in the midst of La Crisis Boricua—by using probit regression analysis to compare them to island-born Puerto Ricans on the mainland in the ACS (who by virtue of their birthplace, had migrated to the mainland).[11] For this purpose, we identify the return migrants as island-born Puerto Ricans on the island who resided on the mainland twelve months before the PRCS. Unfortunately, with these data we cannot determine how long they had resided on the mainland nor can we determine how many times they previously moved between the island and mainland.

The second column in Table 4.3 reports the results from this exercise; the comparison group includes island-born Puerto Ricans living on the mainland. Consistent with temporary migration theory, education significantly increased the likelihood of return migration while age reduced it. That is, educated and older Puerto Ricans tended to be the ones to return to the island during La Crisis Boricua. Recall from the previous chapter that the decline in labor market opportunities on the island hits low-skilled workers the hardest, such that in a relative sense, educated workers would have better opportunities in Puerto Rico than their less educated counterparts. This finding again emphasizes that the *net* migration flow from the island to mainland tended to be characterized by less educated individuals during La Crisis Boricua, but it is less clear in terms of their age distribution.

Other findings shown in Table 4.3 indicate that lacking English-language proficiency increased the odds of returning to the island, which presumably reflects fewer employment opportunities on the mainland versus the island. Women were less likely to move back to Puerto Rico than men, as were married individuals and parents whose children lived with them. The latter findings again relate to higher migration propensities for the relatively unattached. The results further indicate that the likelihood of return migration was lower in the later part of the crisis than earlier, which is not surprising given that the conditions continued to deteriorate over time (moving into a humanitarian crisis), with generally little sign of an economic recovery or relief at the time of the writing of this book.

For the most part, the occupation variables (not shown) did not significantly relate to the likelihood of return migration, with a couple of exceptions. Compared to managers, executives, and other professionals, workers in healthcare and technical positions (and those without occupations) were less likely, while those in agriculture were more likely, to be return migrants. This finding serves as a sobering indicator that the under-coverage in healthcare services on the island mentioned in chapter 3 is unlikely to be alleviated by incoming migrants until La Crisis Boricua dissipates and economic growth and mobility begins to permeate throughout the island once again.

SUMMARY AND CONCLUDING REMARKS

Consistent with the predictions of the human capital model as well as the "push-pull" framework on migration, we provide further evidence that the net migration flow from Puerto Rico to the U.S. mainland between 2006 and 2014 contained a disproportionate share of younger and less-skilled migrants when considering observable skills.[12] Not to lessen concerns over the issue of net outmigration of physicians and other skilled professionals, this finding runs contrary to the impression *created* by some of the media headlines over the past several years (e.g., "Doctors Flee Puerto Rico for U.S. Mainland" (Coto 2013)). At the same time, results for the representation of unobservable skills among recent Puerto Rican migrants in the states were mixed.

We also found that Puerto Ricans heavily cited work-related issues as their main reason for leaving the island during La Crisis Boricua. Not surprisingly, these migrants had relatively low family income levels at the time of their departure from the island, but it is of concern they remained low on the mainland a year after they migrated. If the employment opportunities on the mainland do not emerge as expected, the island's reliance on outmigration as a "safety valve" to alleviate unemployment, as discussed in previous chapters, will be challenged. This will particularly be the case if relatively large numbers of the outmigrants return to the island because their expected mainland employment prospects do not materialize. While our empirical analysis of island-born Puerto Ricans indicates that education enhanced the odds of being a return migrant (as opposed to continuing to live on the mainland) during the 2006–2014 timeframe, it remains to be seen if and when the less skilled migrants (disproportionately represented among recent migrants on the mainland) start to return to Puerto Rico. In light of the unfolding humanitarian crisis and deteriorating infrastructure on the island, however, it is unlikely this will happen anytime in the near future.

NOTES

1. At the same time, as these new communities become more established, other migrants might follow, thus leading to a pattern of "chain migration" and contributing to the rapid growth of the Puerto Rican population in areas in which few had resided just a few years earlier.

2. Reasons for moving are provided in the Current Population Survey, but it has a considerably smaller sample size than the TS, making annual analyses unreliable for Puerto Ricans.

3. In an attempt to approximate a representative sample of passengers aged sixteen and above, the TS dataset includes probability weights for the likelihood an individual was in the sample, based on factors such as the number of passengers on his or her flight, the number of flights, and so forth. We use these weights throughout our analyses using TS data. Still, as indicated in appendix A, the sampling methodology was not necessarily initially designed with the goal of being representative of all travelers. This approach might explain why we detect some differences in the characteristics of migrants between the TS and ACS data, as we describe in this section.

4. We use the entire timeframe of the 2006–2014 ACS in this section to obtain a larger sample size to yield more accurate results. (The 2015 ACS data were not available when we completed this analysis.) That said, when restricting the sample to the 2011–2013 ACS to specifically cover the TS period, the results generally correspond to those discussed here.

5. It should be noted that about 7 percent of our TS sample did not report family income. When including the "nonreports" as a separate category, the percentage of the sample with less than $20,000 in family income falls to 45.5 percent, which is closer to the ACS estimates.

6. These are the only five categories specified in the TS under this question. However, the TS has a question about occupations that includes a category for "student." When considering students versus nonstudents, the former only accounted for 1.1 percentage points of those reporting "other" reason for moving.

7. Examples include Mora, Dávila, and Rodríguez (2017); Birson (2013); Bram, Martínez, and Steindel (2008); Borjas (2008); Enchautegui (2007); Godoy, Jenkins, and Patel (2003); and Ramos (1992).

8. It should be noted that in a related study, we found a similar pattern with respect to the education levels among Puerto Ricans within the same age cohort, such that age differences between the island and mainland are not driving our results in this analysis (Mora, Dávila, and Rodríguez 2017).

9. It should be noted that we observed a similar pattern when focusing on a synthetic cohort of migrants from the island (Mora, Dávila, and Rodríguez 2017).

10. While labor market earnings and home ownership also represent forms of wealth, these measures are "contaminated" for inclusion in this analysis because of issues related to the direction of causation in the migration decision.

11. Of course, we are not the first to consider the socioeconomic and demographic characteristics of migrants returning to Puerto Rico (e.g., see Sotomayor 2009; Duany 2002; Aranda 1996). This issue has only become more critical in light of the massive outmigration during La Crisis Boricua.

12. For examples, see Birson and Meléndez (2013) and Mora, Dávila, and Rodríguez (2017).

Chapter 5

Migration and Changes in the Settlement Patterns of Puerto Ricans

Puerto Ricans have traditionally migrated from the island into the city centers of a small number of urban areas, particularly New York City, but that migration trend began changing decades before La Crisis Boricua. With this in mind, this chapter focuses on where the island-born migrants (particularly stemming from La Crisis Boricua) moved to the mainland and from where they originated in Puerto Rico. Specifically, we consider the major sending areas from Puerto Rico to the mainland to explore how particular regions on the island might have been impacted by this outmigration. We also examine the socioeconomic and demographic characteristics of the major receiving states to "tease out" why certain mainland areas would be more attractive than others. Moreover, we investigate how eduation and other characteristics related to the likelihood of into selected states when Puerto Ricans arrived from the island. Evidence of the continued Puerto Rican diaspora and dispersion during La Crisis Boricua is also discussed.

ADDITIONAL BACKGROUND ON PUERTO RICAN MIGRATION

The traditional Puerto Rican migration from the island into a few city centers primarily in the northeastern mainland, such as New York,[1] has been expanding to other parts of the country particularly since the 1980s.[2] To illustrate, using decennial census data from 1910 to 2000, Angelo Falcón reports in a 2004 study that the share of all Puerto Ricans on the mainland who resided in New York City peaked in 1940 (at 87.8%)—just before the Great Migration got underway—but fell every decade afterwards, reaching its lowest point (during his timeframe of analysis) in 2000 (at 23.2%). This decline has continued, such that by 2014, the share of Puerto Ricans on the mainland residing in New York City had dropped to 17.4 percent.

As we discussed in chapter 1, Florida essentially had the same number of Puerto Ricans as New York as this book went to press, and Florida as well as Pennsylvania received more net incoming migrants from Puerto Rico than New York between 2006 and 2015, resulting in significant (and rapidly growing) Puerto Rican communities. Moreover, beyond shifts in migration patterns from the island, changes in interstate migration patterns have played a significant role in the dispersion of the Puerto Rican diaspora. As highlighted by Acosta-Belén and Santiago (2006:8), "since the 1990s, geographic dispersion has become an important characteristic of Puerto Rican migration." This continued a pattern observed a decade earlier by Rivera-Batz and Santiago (1996).

We analyzed the characteristics of travelers migrating from Puerto Rico to the mainland in chapter 4; the next logical step is to assess from where these migrants emanate. To put this question in perspective, the conceptual migration issues presented in the previous chapter predict that the availability (or lack) of labor market opportunities and, to some extent, hedonics (such as the proximity to other Puerto Ricans, cultural amenities, etc.) in the origin and host areas are at the heart of migration choices. We would expect that Puerto Ricans have the highest destination preference for, and thus gravitate to, areas on the mainland with relatively strong employment outlooks, affordable housing, low cost of living, and nonmonetary amenities resembling those found in Puerto Rico (such as in Puerto Rican enclaves). By the same token, these migrants would be more likely to move out of those areas without these monetary and nonmonetary amenities.

We now consider the conceptual predictions that elaborate on the "where" (from and to which areas) Puerto Ricans migrate (having addressed the "who" in the previous chapter). Our analyses include the reasons behind the migration decisions into certain states as well as the relationship between sending areas from Puerto Rico into specific receiving areas in the states. We also discuss the spatial concept of Puerto Rican dispersion in the states to inform upcoming chapters that discuss how Puerto Ricans have fared in the U.S. labor market and their political and economic impact on U.S. mainland communities.

AN ANALYSIS OF DESTINATION AREAS FROM
PUERTO RICO TO THE U.S. MAINLAND

The major destination areas of migrants from the island during La Crisis Boricua from 2006 through 2014 were, in order of incoming migration flows: Florida, Pennsylvania, New York, Massachusetts, Texas, and New Jersey.[3] We will provide more information on these flows later in this chapter. That these states have become popular migration destinations for island migrants is not surprising. Consider the following. Table 5.1 reports a variety of employment and demographic changes in the Puerto Rican population from 2006 to 2014 using the ACS. From the perspective of employment opportunities, Texas and Pennsylvania provided the strongest growth in both employment and earnings over this period. Employment of Puerto Ricans in Texas grew over 100 percent (matching their population growth) and their wage and salary growth was over 4 percentage points than the national average (14.2% vs. 9.6%) between 2006 and 2014. Pennsylvania reported more modest gains in these two employment dimensions relative to Texas, but both employment growth and wage and salary growth for Puerto Ricans outpaced those in other states.

Table 5.1 also provides potential explanations for the popularity of Florida as a destination for island migrants. While this state's employment and wage and salary growth rates were below those reported for Texas and Pennsylvania, the labor-force statistics of this state outpaced those of most other states. From the perspective of nonmonetary amenities, in addition to close geographic proximity to the island, Florida, unlike Pennsylvania, had an above average share of Hispanics in its population (22.2%) as well as the second highest share of Spanish-language speakers of the states shown (18.7% compared to the national average of 11.9%).

Texas, which had the strongest employment and wage and salary outcomes for Puerto Ricans *and* the highest share of Hispanics and Spanish-language speakers, was the state among those shown in Table 5.1 with the largest Puerto Rican population growth between 2006 and 2014. Still, in terms of migration flows from the island, Texas ranked fifth between 2006 and 2014 (fourth when adding 2015 to the timeframe—see note 3 in this chapter). Perhaps distance from more established Puerto Rican communities, such as those in the northeastern United States, mitigated the popularity of Texas as a destination state for migrants coming from the island (albeit a factor that might be of less interest to Puerto Ricans migrating from other areas of the U.S. mainland).

Indeed, these results suggest that the rank order of destination states for the island migrants to the mainland during La Crisis Boricua (at least up through 2014) were driven by traditional fundamentals, as evidenced by the fact that four out of the top six destination states were in core northeastern parts of the U.S. mainland. Pennsylvania, New York, Massachusetts, and New Jersey remained popular destinations for the island migrants to the mainland, given the traditional settlement patterns and well-established migration networks of Puerto Ricans. In this regard, Pennsylvania provided relatively strong labor-market opportunities for island migrants to the U.S. mainland and afforded this population proximity to traditional Puerto Rican communities. Also, and

Table 5.1 Selected Macroeconomic Characteristics of the Top Receiving States of Puerto Rican Migrants from the Island: 2006–2014

Characteristic	Florida	Pennsylvania	New York	Massachusetts	Texas	New Jersey	All States
Change in PR population (%)	48.2	51.7	1.6	33.7	100.5	22.7	33.5
Change in PR employment (%)	37.3	52.3	4.3	33.3	103.2	34.4	35.4
Change in PR wage and salary earnings (%)	6.1	9.7	6.3	6.4	14.2	11.1	9.6
Change in PR poverty rate (in percentage points)	4.0 pp	1.4 pp	1.4 pp	1.6 pp	0.2 pp	−2.4 pp	2.2 pp
Puerto Rican (%)	4.5	2.9	5.6	3.9	0.5	5.0	1.5
Hispanic (%)	22.2	5.5	17.4	9.4	37.4	17.5	16.2
Spanish speakers (%)	18.7	3.9	13.7	7.3	27.1	14.0	11.8

Source: Authors' estimates using the 2006–2014 ACS in the IPUMS.
Notes: The percent changes are between 2006 and 2014. The percentages of Puerto Ricans, Hispanics, and Spanish speakers and the median housing values in the area are based on a weighted average during the entire time period.

to reiterate, the overwhelming popularity of Florida as a destination state *vis-à-vis* other states likely stemmed from the state's combination of attributes, both monetary and nonmonetary, such as an above-average labor market strength and cultural amenities arguably favored by Puerto Ricans.

Education Differences across the Receiving States

Given that migrants from Puerto Rico have an array of monetary and non-monetary options from which to choose when selecting a destination in the U.S. mainland, how do socioeconomic and demographic factors correlate with decisions to migrate into specific states? To address this question, we first consider the education distributions of the recent Puerto Rican migrants aged twenty-five to sixty-four in the 2006–2014 American Community Survey (ACS) in the six major receiving states. As seen in Figure 5.1, Texas was an outlier with respect to the share of college graduates during this timeframe. Well over half (57.2%) of the incoming migrants in Texas had at least a four-year college degree, which more than twice exceeded the second highest share of college graduates (25.5%, in Florida) among the six states. Less than one of twelve recent migrants in Pennsylvania and Massachusetts (7.1% and 8.2%, respectively), and approximately one in eight in New York (13.1%) had completed college.

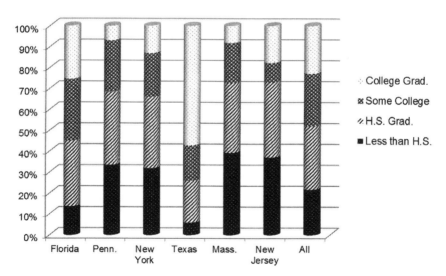

Figure 5.1 Educational Distributions among Recent Migrants from the Island, by Selected States: 2006–2014. *Source*: Authors' estimates using 2006–2014 ACS data in the IPUMS. *Note*: The sample includes Puerto Ricans between the ages of twenty-five and sixty-four who moved from Puerto Rico within the twelve months prior to the survey.

At the other end of the spectrum, Figure 5.1 indicates that nearly four in ten of the new migrants in Massachusetts and New Jersey (39.2% and 37.0%, respectively), and one in three in Pennsylvania and New York (33.4% and 31.8%, respectively) had not completed high school. Only 5.9 percent of those in Texas, and 13.6 percent of those in Florida, had this schooling level. These findings illustrate that Puerto Ricans who moved during La Crisis Boricua settled in different areas according to different levels of educational attainment.[4]

Despite the robust employment opportunities that Pennsylvania seemed to provide to Puerto Ricans, the low schooling levels of recent migrants in the state suggest that the jobs may have required less education on average than those in Texas, and to a lesser extent, in Florida. Moreover, these findings suggest that the selection of one geographic area over another likely goes well beyond potential employment opportunities, which has regional socio-economic implications for the incoming migrants. We provide more insight into these implications in following chapters, when we analyze how Puerto Rican migrants fared across the major receiving states with respect to their labor market earnings and the likelihood of being impoverished.

The Likelihood of Moving to New York versus Other States

We now explore how education, age, and gender affected the likelihood that Puerto Rican migrants went to New York versus another state during La Crisis Boricua. To accomplish this, we conduct a multinomial probit analysis where we analyze how age, education, and gender related to the initial state of residence. Both the TS and ACS datasets are used to conduct this empirical exercise, with the results presented in Table 5.2. Reaffirming the geographic schooling distributions discussed in the previous section, these results indicate that education positively related to the probability that migrants from the island selected Texas and, to a lesser extent, Florida over New York using both datasets. In the TS, when leaving the island, less-educated migrants were significantly more likely to choose Massachusetts over New York.

Based on the ACS, age was negatively related to the decision to move to Pennsylvania and Texas versus New York (i.e., these states attracted younger migrants from the island than New York, which is consistent with the employment-growth differences discussed earlier). Puerto Rican women were also significantly less likely to migrate to Texas than New York in the ACS, but this was the only case where gender played a significant role when accounting for differences in education and age. The results regarding other socioeconomic and demographic characteristics are mixed and for the most part statistically insignificant.

Table 5.2   Multinomial Probit Regression Results for the Likelihood of Migrating from Puerto Rico into Selected States versus New York

Characteristic	Florida	Pennsylvania	Massachusetts	Texas	New Jersey
ACS—2006–2014 (Puerto Ricans only):					
Female	−0.077	0.184	0.058	−0.406**	0.046
	(0.156)	(0.196)	(0.187)	(0.194)	(0.191)
Age	−0.006	−0.022**	0.005	−0.023***	−0.006
	(0.007)	(0.009)	(0.008)	(0.009)	(0.008)
High School	0.558***	−0.073	−0.121	0.592*	−0.074
graduate	(0.211)	(0.249)	(0.008)	(0.304)	(0.232)
Some college	0.899***	−0.057	−0.156	0.825***	−0.541**
	(0.231)	(0.270)	(0.253)	(0.314)	(0.265)
College	1.051***	−0.441	−0.359	1.860***	0.068
	(0.228)	(0.333)	(0.302)	(0.295)	(0.270)
Constant	0.777**	0.888**	−0.232	0.054	0.153
	(0.345)	(0.427)	(0.372)	(0.412)	(0.358)
χ^2: education variables	24.68***	1.93	1.44	47.86***	5.34
χ^2: all variables	29.43888	8.54	2.11	52.86***	5.52

χ^2: education variables (all states) = 116.96***
χ^2 : all variables (all states) = 135.6***

TS—FY2010–FY2011 (All migrants):					
Female	0.046	−0.113	0.112	0.010	0.001
	(0.122)	(0.165)	(0.159)	(0.174)	(0.173)
Age	0.015***	0.004	−0.002	0.009	0.015**
	(0.005)	(0.007)	(0.007)	(0.008)	(0.007)
High School	0.053	−0.406*	−0.644***	0.095	−0.171
graduate	(0.201)	(0.226)	(0.207)	(0.008)	(0.250)
Some college	0.358*	−0.393	−0.901***	0.533*	−0.291
	(0.210)	(0.248)	(0.247)	(0.273)	(0.275)
College	0.589***	−0.190	−0.592***	0.870***	−0.341
	(0.193)	(0.235)	(0.224)	(0.256)	(0.251)
Constant	−0.346	0.022	0.417	−1.257***	−0.792**
	(0.308)	(0.360)	(0.331)	(0.420)	(0.375)
χ^2: education variables	16.22***	4.01	16.13***	16.24***	2.11
χ^2: all variables	21.41***	5.70	17.38***	17.20***	7.62

χ^2: education variables (all states) = 68.81***
χ^2 : all variables (all states) = 81.75***

Source: Authors' estimates using the FY20101–FY2012 TS and the 2006–2014 ACS in the IPUMS.

Notes: The reference state is New York. The parentheses contain robust standard errors. Our ACS sample includes Puerto Rican adults between the ages of twenty-five and sixty-four. Our TS sample, which does not distinguish between Puerto Ricans and non-Puerto Ricans, includes air travelers between the ages of twenty-five and sixty-four who reported their primary reason for traveling was to move to the mainland. We exclude migrants from this analysis who moved into states other than New York, Florida, Pennsylvania, Massachusetts, Texas, and New Jersey.

***, **, * Statistically at the 1, 5, or 10 percent level.

In all, these results show that socioeconomic and demographic characteristics impact the destination-state migration choice among these Puerto Rican groups. Owing to the positive relationship education has with the migration choice to Texas and Florida versus New York, it is important to provide insight into *why*. In particular, education can conceptually be positively associated with migrant information and earnings. To the extent that education provides migrants with greater information and higher potential earnings, it could be that the nontraditional destinations have become more attractive to educated migrants from the island. For example, migration to Texas might be occurring because more educated Puerto Ricans have become increasingly cognizant of employment opportunities in a state expected to provide higher earnings which can, in turn, be used to offset the sociocultural amenities not found relative to the traditional states such as New York. Texas has also been aggressive in recruiting skilled workers (such as teachers and nurses) from the island.[5] Moreover, as more Puerto Ricans make Texas their home, in addition to expanded networks (hence, additional information), these new Puerto Rican communities should begin to offer more cultural amenities, thus likely increasing the attractiveness of the state to future migrants.[6]

As a further explanation, consider differences in the cost of living, including for housing. According to CNN Money (2016), compared to New York, on average, in Dallas housing cost 74 percent less, groceries cost 23 percent less, and utilities cost 24 percent less. Also compared to New York, in Orlando these items cost an average of 67 percent less, 21 percent less, and 26 percent less, respectively. Arguably, the decision to move to new destination metropolitan areas such as Dallas and Orlando would be more attractive to Puerto Ricans leaving the island who consider a broad array of monetary and nonmonetary benefits from these newer destination areas *vis-à-vis* other traditional settlement areas such as New York. This information indicates that the newer destination areas afford Puerto Rican migrants more purchasing power regarding basic expenses and home prices. This was especially the case in Texas, where the average island-born migrant between 2006 and 2014 earned more on average than in New York (although not necessarily so when accounting for differences in skills), as discussed in the following chapter.

SENDING AREAS FROM PUERTO RICO
TO THE U.S. MAINLAND

We next consider the major sending areas from Puerto Rico to the mainland. Appendix A provides details behind the construction of these sending areas using the TS; unfortunately, as noted, we cannot identify the specific sending areas in the public-use version of the ACS. The highest share of outbound migrants during the island's crisis came from the northeastern area (minus the *municipio* of San Juan) of Puerto Rico (30.4%), followed by the northwestern (22.7%), southwestern (15.7%), central (12.1%), San Juan (10.4%), and the southeastern (8.6%) regions.

The rank order of these areas is not surprising, as it tends to be driven by their population sizes. Using the 2006 Puerto Rican Community Survey (PRCS),[7] the northeastern region (excluding San Juan) of the island had the largest population (an estimated 970,600 residents, or 26.0% of the population); another 425,900 (11.4%) resided in San Juan. It makes sense that the largest absolute numbers of migrants to the mainland came from these areas. The southeastern and central areas had the lowest numbers of residents based on these regional breakdowns (388,000 and 568,200, respectively, representing 10.4% and 15.2% of Puerto Rico's population).

That said, relative outmigration patterns likely relate to macroeconomic conditions. On a relative basis, we would expect that the job losses in these latter areas would "push" workers to find employment in the U.S. mainland, given our conceptual framework in the previous section. This may especially be the case when considering that the region with the highest educational levels was San Juan (12.9 years) in 2006, while the central and southeastern areas had the lowest (11.2 years).[8] Such differences are consistent with relative job losses in light of our findings in the previous chapter that less-educated workers in Puerto Rico have been disproportionately affected by La Crisis Boricua. Indeed, using the PRCS, the southwestern region had a loss of employment of 14.5 percent between 2006 and 2011,[9] compared to a 7.4 percent loss in the northeastern region of the island; this loss was 8.8 percent for Puerto Rico as a whole.

To garner more insight into the importance of employment-related reasons reported by respondents in the TS for migrating to the U.S. mainland, we include in Figure 5.2 the reasons for migrating from the respective areas of Puerto Rico. Consistent with the relatively high job losses reported in the southwestern area of Puerto Rico from 2006 to 2011, respondents from this region were more likely to have reported employment-related reasons for migrating to the U.S. mainland. Close to 70 percent of the southwestern respondents indicated that they were moving to the states for employment-related purposes (i.e., to work or look for work). Conversely, just over half (52%) of the respondents from the northeastern area provided these reasons for leaving Puerto Rico, as would be expected given this region lost a relatively low number of jobs over the noted timeframe.

We employ a multivariate analysis to further investigate the relationship between the sending areas and the reasons for moving to a particular state when accounting for other socioeconomic and demographic factors. Specifically, we use multinomial probit regression analysis to consider how age,

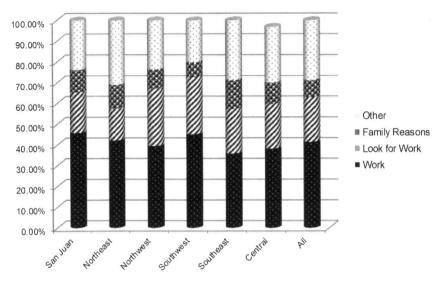

Figure 5.2   Reasons for Moving to the Mainland, by PR Sending Area: FY2011–FY2012. *Source*: Authors' estimates using FY2011–FY2012 TS data. *Notes*: The sample does not distinguish between Puerto Ricans and non-Puerto Ricans. Our sample includes air travelers between the ages of twenty-five and sixty-four who reported their primary reason for traveling was to move to the mainland.

education, gender, traveling alone, and the sending region related to the reasons for leaving Puerto Rico among outbound migrants aged twenty-five to sixty-four. We use the "for work" reason as the reference category. Selected results from this analysis are reported in Table 5.3.

One general result from this analysis is that the sending regions in Puerto Rico by themselves did not consistently relate to the specific reason for leaving the island when accounting for other characteristics. Instead, the specific characteristics of individuals, such as education and age, related to the reason for moving. In particular, education increased the odds of migrating for the reason of finding employment versus other reasons, as did age (unsurprisingly) for the probability of migrating for retirement reasons. Women were also more likely to cite family-related reasons for moving to the U.S. mainland, consistent with the gendered role of family caretaking.

Sending Areas from Puerto Rico and Receiving States in the U.S. Mainland

To our knowledge, few studies have empirically explored the migration patterns between specific sending areas in Puerto Rico and the receiving states on the mainland using large datasets, largely due to the lack of public-use

Table 5.3 Selected Multinomial Probit Regression Results for the Likelihood of Moving from Puerto Rico for Work versus Other Reasons

Characteristic	To Look for Work	To Retire	To Attend to Family	Other Reasons
Female	0.352***	0.342**	1.275***	0.783***
	(0.125)	(0.158)	(0.162)	(0.129)
Age	0.001	0.121***	0.067***	0.031***
	(0.006)	(0.011)	(0.007)	(0.006)
High School graduate	-0.317*	-0.033	-0.398*	-0.575***
	(0.192)	(0.241)	(0.233)	(0.207)
Some college	-0.547***	0.043	-0.409	-0.400*
	(0.190)	(0.251)	(0.252)	(0.212)
College	-1.310***	-0.300	-0.808***	-0.762***
	(0.187)	(0.235)	(0.236)	(0.205)
Traveling alone	-0.061	-0.435***	0.503***	0.043
	(0.130)	(0.158)	(0.166)	(0.128)
PR sending areas	Included	Included	Included	Included
Constant	-0.026	-6.569***	-4.452***	-1.747***
	(0.293)	(0.620)	(0.360)	(0.342)
χ^2: education variables	67.53***	3.17	12.32***	15.07
χ^2: all variables	83.76***	181.45***	211.56***	81.06***
χ^2: education variables (across all reasons) = 77.70***				
χ^2: all variables (across all reasons) = 443.47***				

Source: Authors' estimates using data from the FY2010–FY2011 TS.

Notes: The reference category is moving "for work." The parentheses contain robust standard errors. The TS sample does not distinguish between Puerto Ricans and non-Puerto Ricans. Our sample includes air travelers between the ages of twenty-five and sixty-four who reported their primary reason for traveling was to move to the mainland. The results for the sending areas in Puerto Rico are not statistically significant at conventional levels.

***, **, * Statistically significant at the 1, 5, or 10 percent level.

data availability. However, it is now possible with the TS dataset to analyze these geographic patterns in terms of outmigration flows from the island. We estimate using the TS that migration from Puerto Rico to the U.S. mainland between 2010 and 2012 stemmed largely from the northern areas of Puerto Rico, with over 60 percent of migrants coming from the northwestern, San Juan, and northeastern areas. We alluded earlier in this chapter to the relatively large populations of these areas, and to the role that their above-average education of residents had in sending migrants to seek employment to the mainland during La Crisis Boricua.

At the same time, migrants from the sending areas did not randomly migrate into the receiving areas. As seen in Figure 5.3, the migration choice to specific states on the mainland differed according to the geographic sending area in Puerto Rico. Consider Texas as the destination state. Nearly two-thirds (62.6%) of travelers moving to Texas came from San Juan and other northeastern areas—areas with above average education. Contrast this finding for travelers moving to Pennsylvania, New Jersey, and Massachusetts, where 25–30 percent came from these population centers. Less than 5 percent of migrants going to Texas were from the central region, and there were none from the southeast (areas with relatively low schooling levels). Yet, Pennsylvania and Massachusetts drew approximately 30 percent of migrants from these regions.

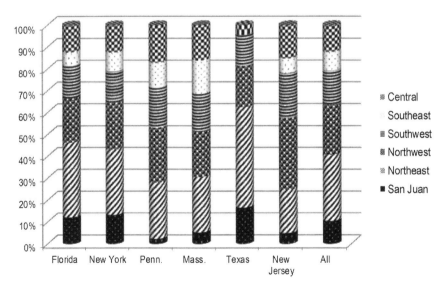

Figure 5.3 Distribution of PR Sending Regions to Selected States: FY2011–FY2012. *Source*: Authors' estimates using FY2011–FY2012 TS data. *Notes*: The sample does not distinguish between Puerto Ricans and non-Puerto Ricans. Our sample includes air travelers between the ages of twenty-five and sixty-four who reported their primary reason for traveling was to move to the mainland.

With regards to New Jersey, over 55 percent of the migrants originated from the western part of the island. Note, too, that Figure 5.3 shows both Florida and New York had similar migratory patterns from regions in Puerto Rico as those found in the overall results; this finding makes sense given that migrants are overrepresented among those moving to these states from the island.

Reasons for Moving into Specific States

These regional variations in the distinct migration patterns between Puerto Rico and the mainland reflect differences in the distributions of the reasons for moving. To our knowledge, we are the first to empirically uncover and report such patterns. As Figure 5.4 indicates, nearly half (47.3%) of Texas-bound migrants, and four out of ten migrants bound for New York (42.4%) and Florida (40.1%) reported moving because of work. Another one-fifth moved into Texas and Florida, and one-third into New York, to search for jobs. In contrast, fewer than one-third of the migrants to Massachusetts (28.9%) and Pennsylvania (31.7%) left the island for work. Instead, the migrants into these latter two states disproportionately cited family-related reasons (14.1% and 14.7%, respectively), compared to those moving to the three former states (4.1%, 10.3%, and 6.7%).

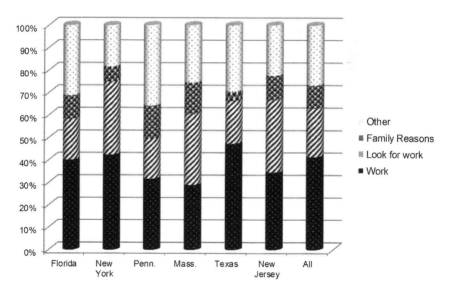

Figure 5.4 Reasons for Moving to the Mainland, by Selected Receiving States: FY2011–FY2012. *Source*: Authors' estimates using FY2011–FY2012 TS data. *Notes*: The sample does not distinguish between Puerto Ricans and non-Puerto Ricans. Our sample includes air travelers between the ages of twenty-five and sixty-four who reported that their primary reason for traveling was to move to the mainland.

The most salient differences in the reasons for moving into particular states likely translated into geographic differences in employment, labor force status, and other social mobility outcomes among the new Puerto Rican migrants. In the following chapter, we empirically examine (and find) variations in these outcomes across the major receiving states since the start of La Crisis Boricua. These differences suggest that social scientists, social workers, and policymakers should consider tailoring specific resources (such as employment assistance vs. child care) according to the receiving area rather than following a "one size fits all" approach to best facilitate the successful integration of new Puerto Rican migrants into their communities.

NET MIGRATION AND THE GEOGRAPHIC DISPERSION OF PUERTO RICANS ON THE MAINLAND

Our discussion thus far has focused on the sending areas from Puerto Rico during La Crisis Boricua, which impacted (and will continue to impact) Puerto Rican communities both on the island and the U.S. mainland. At the same time, as we discussed in the previous chapter, a nontrivial number of Puerto Ricans also moved from the mainland to the island, despite the crisis. Indeed, we estimate that 214,695 Puerto Ricans between the ages of twenty-five and sixty-four moved from the states to the island between 2006 and 2014, which was just under half of the 445,535 Puerto Ricans in this age range who left the island.[10] In fact, the nearly 215,000 Puerto Rican adults who moved to the island made Puerto Rico the second largest destination area after Florida. Puerto Rico's total population decline, then, would have been considerably more severe without the replenishing of migrants from the mainland.

Note that incoming migration kept the size of the Puerto Rican population from shrinking in New York between 2006 and 2014. Indeed, New York represented the third largest receiving area of Puerto Rican adult migrants, into which almost 146,000 migrants moved (40,430 from the island and 105,287 from other states). While this was less than the 247,758 who moved out to other states (211,855) or Puerto Rico (35,903), it was large enough to offset the loss and maintain a positive population growth during this time;[11] the state's total Puerto Rican population grew by almost 17,000 residents.

To better visualize the magnitudes of incoming versus outgoing migration across regions, consider Figure 5.5, which presents the top destination areas of Puerto Ricans between 2006 and 2014, including Puerto Rico. This figure clearly indicates the relatively large net migration from Puerto Rico. Yet, it further shows that interstate migration comprised a larger component of the net migration flow than island-to-mainland migration. This finding agrees with recent studies, including those by D'Vera Cohn, Eileen Patten, and Mark

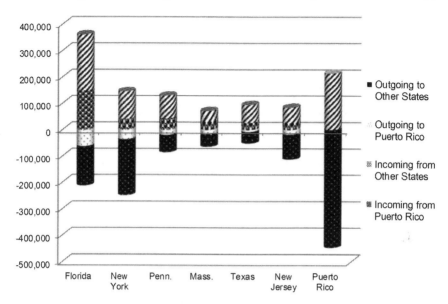

Figure 5.5   Island-Mainland and Interstate Migration of Puerto Ricans: 2006–2014.
Source: Authors' estimates using 2006–2014 ACS and PRCS data in the IPUMS. *Notes:*
The sample includes Puerto Ricans between the ages of twenty-five and sixty-four who
moved between the island and mainland or between states within twelve months prior
to the survey.

Hugo López (2014) and Juan Carlos García-Ellín (2013), highlighting the
increased geographic dispersion of Puerto Ricans on the mainland. However,
part of the interstate migration also likely reflects continued migration from
the island; upon moving to the mainland, migrants may subsequently learn
of additional employment opportunities in other areas, such that some may
soon move onward after using their initial destination point as a temporary
settlement area.

As noted before, Florida was the top receiving area of all the states and
Puerto Rico. Indeed, in addition to the 148,560 migrants from the island
between the ages of twenty-five and sixty-four, we estimate that another
211,873 Puerto Ricans in this age range moved to Florida from other states
between 2006 and 2014. As such, Florida received a total of 360,433 incoming Puerto Rican adult migrants, which was by far, the largest number
received by any state or by Puerto Rico. Even when accounting for the
211,698 Puerto Rican adults who moved out of Florida (62,564 of whom
went to Puerto Rico) during the same time period, on net, the Puerto Rican
population in Florida increased by 148,735. This net increase was also the
largest in magnitude among all the states and Puerto Rico.

Figure 5.5 further indicates that five of these states experienced net population increases due to net in-migration between 2006 and 2014: Florida (again,

with a net increase of 148,735 migrants between the ages of twenty-five and sixty-four), Pennsylvania (44,730), followed closely by Texas (44,481), and Massachusetts (8,020). Proportionately speaking, of these states, Texas had the smallest amount of outflow to Puerto Rico or other states during this time. As with both Puerto Rico and New York, New Jersey (which had the sixth largest number of incoming Puerto Rican migrants between 2006 and 2014) experienced negative net migration.

GEOGRAPHIC DISTRIBUTION OF PUERTO RICANS LIVING STATESIDE

How did the Puerto Rican population size and their geographic distribution across states change during this time period? Figure 5.6 displays the size of the Puerto Rican population (regardless of birthplace or age) in each state in 2006 (panel A) and 2015 (panel B), in rank order of the states with largest number of Puerto Rican residents. In 2006, only New York had at least a million Puerto Rican residents (1,090,564). Among the states with at least 100,000 Puerto Rican residents that year, other than Illinois (which had 162,211) and California (155,276), the location patterns tended to be primarily clustered on the eastern seaboard (Florida, with 678,286; New Jersey, with 398,598; Pennsylvania, with 289,978; Massachusetts, with 228,891;

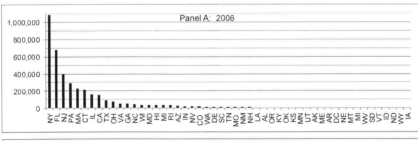

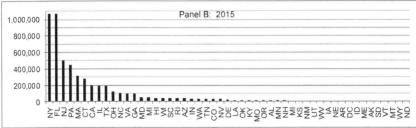

Figure 5.6 Geographic Distribution of Stateside Puerto Ricans: 2006 and 2015.
Source: Authors' estimates using 2006 and 2015 ACS data in the IPUMS.

and Connecticut, with 217,795). A total of twelve states had 50,000 or more Puerto Rican residents that year.

In a decade, however, the Puerto Rican population in Florida had increased to over one million residents (1,066,767) in 2015, and as noted in chapter 1, was essentially the size of the Puerto Rican population in New York (1,073,024) that year, which had fallen slightly. Puerto Ricans are also expected to surpass the Cuban population in Florida in the near future. Moreover, this figure indicates the Puerto Rican population became more dispersed, continuing patterns observed using earlier data, particularly as their presence increased in the east but also in the south, south central, and western states. During this timeframe, Texas, Ohio, and North Carolina joined the list of states with at least 100,000 residents, while Virginia, Georgia, and Maryland joined the list with 50,000 or more Puerto Ricans.

Further insight into changes in these geographic location patterns can be found in Figure 5.7, which shows the net Puerto Rican population change (panel A) and the percentage change (panel B) in each state between 2006 and 2015. Not surprisingly Florida tops the list, with a net increase of 388,451 Puerto Rican residents. Seven states experienced a tripling (or more) of their Puerto Rican population (but they started with very small numbers); Idaho topped the list with a growth rate of 572 percent, followed by Mississippi, West Virginia, Vermont, South Dakota, Wyoming, and South Carolina. Ten

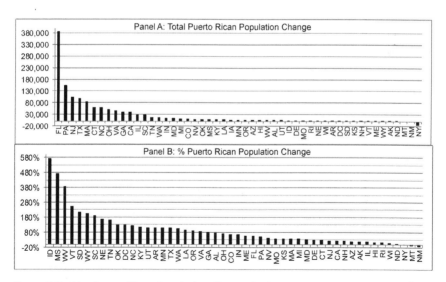

Figure 5.7 Net Puerto Rican Population Change, by State: 2006–2015. *Source*: Authors' estimates using 2006 and 2015 ACS data in the IPUMS. *Note*: Iowa is not reported in panel B, as there were too few Puerto Ricans in the state in 2006 for a reliable estimate of their population growth rate.

states and DC experienced a doubling (or more) of their Puerto Rican population in just ten years.

Again, many of these states admittedly had (and still have) rather small
populations to begin with; for example, despite its acute growth rate, only
5,184 Puerto Ricans resided in Idaho in 2015. However, the Puerto Rican
population in Texas more than doubled, from 90,569 to 189,313 between
2006 and 2015, such that the state had the second largest growth rate (behind
North Carolina) out of all states with at least 20,000 Puerto Rican residents
in 2006.

This figure further indicates that more than half (29) of the states experienced a population growth rate of 50 percent or higher. In only three states
(New Mexico, Montana, and New York) did the Puerto Rican population
decline, and only in another two (Wisconsin and North Dakota) was the
population growth flat. As such, La Crisis Boricua led not only to the massive
outmigration of Puerto Ricans from the island, but the diaspora becoming
increasingly dispersed throughout the mainland, resulting in sizeable Puerto
Rican communities even in areas where few existed a short time before.

MEASURING CHANGES IN THE GEOGRAPHIC
CONCENTRATION OF PUERTO RICANS

In all, many states experienced a relatively large growth in their Puerto Rican
populations, both on an absolute and relative basis, since 2006. Of course,
part of this growth stems from the large exodus from the island since the
beginning of the economic crisis as well as net interstate migration. As discussed earlier in this book, mainland-born Puerto Ricans have relatively high
fertility rates as well.

We have shown that this dispersion of Puerto Ricans was not "across
the board," and that observable characteristics of this population related to
migration into nontraditional areas. An additional metric to analyze changes
in geographic dispersion is through changes in the inverse of the Herfindahl
Index (IHI), measured here at the state level (see appendix B for details). In
this context, the IHI can be interpreted as the equivalent number of states
in which a population resides, which would reflect how many states Puerto
Ricans *seem* to live in. The closer this number is to fifty-one, the more evenly
distributed Puerto Ricans would be across all fifty states plus DC. The closer
it is to one, the more geographically concentrated this population would be.
If it equals one, Puerto Ricans would reside in one state alone.

Table 5.4 presents the IHI for Puerto Ricans in general and also by birthplace and educational attainment in 2006 and 2014.[12] For comparison, we
also present the IHI for Mexican and Cuban immigrants, and mainland-born

Table 5.4   State IHI of Puerto Ricans and Other Groups on the U.S. Mainland: 2006 and 2014

Characteristic	2006	2014
All Puerto Ricans	7.65	9.34
Island-born Puerto Ricans	7.22	7.88
Mainland-born Puerto Ricans	7.59	9.53
Mexican immigrants	4.91	5.16
Cuban immigrants	1.7	1.6
Mainland-born non-Hispanic whites	29.05	29.63
Puerto Ricans Aged 25–64:		
All	7.37	9.08
Less than high school	6.00	7.85
High school graduate, no college	7.27	8.66
Some college	7.85	8.94
College graduate	7.83	9.86

Source: Authors' estimates using 2006 and 2014 ACS data in the IPUMS.
Notes: See appendix B for the construction of these indices. The inverse of the IHI can be interpreted as the equivalent number of states (plus DC) in which each group lived. The maximum value is therefore fifty-one.

non-Hispanic whites. The IHI shows that while Puerto Ricans are more concentrated within states than non-Hispanic whites, they are less so compared to Mexican and Cuban immigrants. The equivalent number of states in which mainland Puerto Ricans resided was 7.7 states in 2006, compared to 29.1 states among non-Hispanic whites, 4.9 among Mexican immigrants, and less than two (1.7) among Cuban immigrants.

Moreover, Puerto Ricans, particularly those born on the mainland, experienced a greater increase in their IHI than the other groups shown by 2014, affirming that their long-term geographic dispersion mentioned earlier continued after La Crisis Boricua began in Puerto Rico. This change also led to a narrowing of their IHI gap with non-Hispanic whites, and a widening with Mexican and Cuban immigrants, as Table 5.4 shows. To illustrate, the equivalent number of mainland states in which Puerto Ricans resided had risen from 7.7 to 9.3 states. When considering birthplace, this equivalency rose by 0.7 states (from 7.2 to 7.9 states) among island-born Puerto Ricans, and by nearly two states (1.9 states, from 7.6 to 9.5) among mainland-born Puerto Ricans. But, for both groups, the increased dispersion was greater than it was for Mexican immigrants (which increased by 0.3 states) and non-Hispanic whites (by 0.5 states); the concentration of Cuban immigrants remained about the same.

These numbers indicate that island-born Puerto Ricans living stateside were more concentrated than their mainland-born counterparts, particularly in 2014, which likely reflects their increased presence in a couple of key net receiving states, such as Florida. Given the particularly strong increase in the geographic mobility of mainland-born Puerto Ricans in a short timeframe (nine years in this analysis), we would initially expect that regional earnings and other socioeconomic differentials converged more for mainland-born Puerto Ricans than for their island-born peers during this time. As previously noted, we will examine changes in their socioeconomic outcomes in the next chapter.

That said, part of the difference between these two groups may relate to differences in their educational attainment. For the most part, Table 5.4 shows a distinct relationship between education and Puerto Rican geographic concentration on the U.S. mainland. In 2014, education was monotonically related to the geographic dispersion of Puerto Ricans (where those with higher levels of schooling were more dispersed than their less-educated counterparts). This was not uniquely the case in 2006 (as Puerto Rican college graduates had a similar degree of geographic concentration as their counterparts with some college but no baccalaureate degree), but the general pattern held otherwise.

This table also shows that the greatest absolute change in the geographic dispersion of Puerto Ricans between 2006 and 2014 occurred among college graduates, who were already more dispersed than those who had not attended college. However, those without a high school diploma experienced the second largest increase in dispersion (and the greatest *relative* increase) during this time, suggesting a bifurcated role of education in the likelihood of migrating and a rising geographic mobility among a vulnerable population. This dispersion is presumably tied to the net outmigration from the island among less-educated workers (recall chapter 4) as well as from traditional mainland settlement areas like New York. As we discuss in the next chapter, Puerto Ricans tend to have greater disparities in educational attainment and other socioeconomic outcomes with non-Hispanic whites in their traditional geographic locations than in the newer communities, possibly due to historical institutional racism (e.g., Vélez 2015; Reyes and Rosofshy 2013). If so, it follows that migration from traditional areas into less traditional Puerto Rican communities may yield more opportunities for upward socioeconomic mobility.

SUMMARY AND CONCLUDING REMARKS

Given that migrants from Puerto Rico have an array of monetary and nonmonetary options to consider when selecting a destination on the U.S. mainland, in this chapter we noted key macroeconomic characteristics in selected major receiving areas. We also compared the characteristics of migrants across the major destination areas, and found that education enhanced the odds that Puerto Ricans selected Florida and especially Texas over New York, which has regional socioeconomic implications for members of this group. Moreover, education in general appeared to play a key role in the growing dispersion of Puerto Ricans on the mainland, although in a bifurcated manner.

We further reported variations in the regional migratory flows between the island and the mainland, along with the reasons for moving. Those migrating to the traditional settlement areas in the midst of La Crisis Boricua tended to disproportionately report moving for family-related purposes compared to those moving to Texas, who tended to report migrating for work. In light of these results, in the following chapter we explore how Puerto Ricans have fared in regional labor markets and with respect to other socioeconomic outcomes in the major receiving areas.

NOTES

1. This is not to infer that, in the past, Puerto Ricans solely migrated to the northeastern United States. Indeed, one of the first significant migratory movements from the island was to Hawaii, near the turn of the twentieth century, when Puerto Ricans were recruited by the Hawaii Sugar Planters Association, as it sought cheap labor for the sugarcane industry (López 2005). Given the acquisition of Puerto Rico by the U.S. government, the island became a fertile ground for this type of recruitment, one that continued throughout the years to many states, and for many industries, from agriculture to manufacturing, to the service industry, and professionals, such as teachers, nurses, and physicians, among others (Whalen and Vázquez-Hernández 2005).

2. For examples, see Cohn, Patten, and López (2014); García-Ellín (2013); Vélez and Burgos (2010); Silver (2010); Marzan (2009); Acosta-Belén and Santiago (2006); Falcón (2004); and Rivera-Batiz and Santiago (1996, 1995).

3. The rank of the states slightly differs from those reported in chapter 1, which included 2015 data. We end our timeframe of analysis at 2014 in parts of this chapter because it was the most recent year of available data when we conducted the majority of the empirical analyses. Texas moved ahead of Massachusetts as the fourth largest receiving area of Puerto Ricans from the island when adding the 2015 data, and the third largest (after Florida and Pennsylvania) when focusing exclusively on adults between the ages of twenty-five and sixty-four.

4. It should be noted that we are not the first to report differences in the socioeconomic characteristics of Puerto Ricans across geographic regions on the mainland (e.g., see Diversitydatakids.org 2016; Vélez and Burgos 2010; Rivera-Batiz and Santiago 1995; Rodríguez 1992; Enchautegui 1992). However, our findings in this chapter (and upcoming chapters) provide more details on how migration patterns might sustain acute differences across geographic areas, suggesting that a "one-size-fits-all" policy consideration and research designs addressing such outcomes among Puerto Ricans may be less effective than those tailored to meet the needs of specific Puerto Rican communities.

5. For example, in 2017 the Dallas Independent School District (ISD) had a section on its website designed to attract teachers for Puerto Rico, stating: "As part of our recruitment efforts to hire effective and dedicated teachers, we will be cultivating relationships with universities and reaching out to certified bilingual educators in Puerto Rico. We are proud to say that Dallas ISD has hired over 100 Puerto Rican teachers … . We will be interviewing for our district on February 9–12, 2017 … in San Juan."

6. This might be why Texas overtook Massachusetts as the fourth largest receiving state from the island when adding the year 2015 to our timeframe of study.

7. These population estimates include both Puerto Ricans and non-Puerto Ricans to be consistent with the TS.

8. These estimates are based on the 2006 PRCS and include both Puerto Ricans and non-Puerto Ricans.

9. Due to changes in the public-use microdata areas (PUMAs) in the PRCS after 2011, we cannot estimate employment losses for the full 2006–2014 period by region with the public-use data; we employ the PUMAs to construct the regions.

10. The reader is reminded that chapter 1 discussed the outmigration flow from Puerto Rico for individuals of all ages. Our focus on this age range pertains to the fact that it includes people at the prime of their working lives.

11. When adding in the 2015 data, however, this was no longer the case; the total Puerto Rican population in New York between the ages of twenty-five and sixty-four declined due to negative net outmigration to both Puerto Rico and other states.

12. We conducted our analysis of the IHI before the 2015 data were available, which is why this section focuses on the 2006–2014 period.

Chapter 6

How Were Puerto Ricans Faring in the New Settlements versus Traditional Areas?

Puerto Ricans became increasingly dispersed during La Crisis Boricua, not only because of their increased migration from the island, but as we discussed in the previous chapter, also through interstate migration on the U.S. mainland. In this chapter, we investigate how Puerto Ricans fared relative to their nonmigrating counterparts with respect to key socioeconomic outcomes, namely labor market earnings and the likelihood of being impoverished, in the newer versus traditional receiving areas during this historic time. Because the large numbers of incoming migrants may have affected these outcomes among other Puerto Ricans in the receiving areas, such as through impacting social networks, we consider recent migrants as well as Puerto Ricans in general on the mainland.

CONCEPTUAL ISSUES FOR MIGRATION INTO NEW VERSUS TRADITIONAL AREAS

According to the "push-pull" framework discussed in chapter 4, deteriorating economic conditions, such as those in Puerto Rico, conceptually push workers into migrating, essentially exporting unemployment out of the sending area. This migration is likely greater into traditional settlement areas (as opposed to nontraditional areas) due to established social and ethnic networks. Attractive labor market and other socioeconomic opportunities can, in turn, pull individuals into migrating, including into nontraditional settlement areas if they provide sufficiently high monetary rewards to offset foregoing the sociocultural amenities associated with more established and long-standing mainland Puerto Rican communities.

In the case of push factors, migrants may fare worse (at least initially) than their counterparts who remain behind, particularly if these forces led to migration into regions with limited avenues for upward socioeconomic mobility. In the case of pull factors, it is expected that the new migrants fare better than their nonmigrating counterparts by virtue of the fact they move to tap into better opportunities. Under both cases, however, it remains unclear how the new migrants compare with Puerto Ricans who migrated in previous time periods (i.e., those with roots in the community), particularly in traditional settlement areas.

Indeed, social scientists have argued that residential segregation affects the quality of institutional resources and capital necessary for upward socioeconomic mobility. For example, in a series of early influential studies, Douglas Massey and his colleagues discussed how the economic and social structures in segregated areas can perpetuate poverty over time among racial and ethnic groups.[1] More recently, Giovanni Burgos and Fernando Rivera (2012) and William Vélez (2015) discuss how residential segregation might be at the root of some of the limited social mobility among Puerto Ricans on the mainland, as this type of segregation depends on the quality and interconnectedness of micro (e.g., human, social, and cultural capital), meso (e.g., neighborhoods, schools, places of work), and macro (e.g., political, economic) structures.

Historical discrimination leading to this type of residential segregation is more likely found in traditional settlement areas, such as New York City. Previous studies, including those by Clara Rodríguez (1989), María Enchautegui (e.g., 1992, 1993), Havidán Rodríguez (1992), and Francisco Rivera-Batiz and Carlos Santiago (1995) provided empirical support for this view a quarter of a century ago. They found that Puerto Ricans in New York, including those born on the mainland, tended to fare worse with respect to a variety of socioeconomic outcomes than Puerto Ricans in other areas on the mainland. More recent work by Diversitydatakids.org (2016) provides further confirmation; indices based on nineteen neighborhood-level indicators related to education, health/environment, and social and economic opportunities show that Puerto Ricans living in the northeast, especially in traditional settlement areas (including New York, Pennsylvania, and Massachusetts) had the lowest access to such opportunities. Their opportunities were greater in Florida, and particularly in Texas.

The geographic dispersion of Puerto Ricans into new destinations mentioned in the previous chapter could therefore bode well for the future socioeconomic prosperity of the Puerto Rican population living stateside. Of course, this optimistic assessment depends on whether new (and growing) enclaves have expanded the social networks of Puerto Ricans and broadened potential employment opportunities associated with growing numbers of individuals who have the same culture and language.

If networks and labor markets in the key receiving areas have not meaningfully absorbed the historically large numbers of Puerto Rican migrants, the expected economic outcomes would be declines in the employment opportunities and earnings for this group. Moreover, despite resource accessibility, as recently discussed by Vélez (2015), moving into traditional enclaves yields the benefits of reducing the effects of "culture shock," decreasing the likelihood of potential discriminatory encounters with non-Hispanic whites, and providing more accessible information on employment and housing through ethnic networks. Therefore, the social mobility benefits in new (nontraditional) destinations must be tempered with these considerations in mind.

Recall from chapter 5 that Puerto Ricans moving to the traditional settlement areas, such as New York, Massachusetts, and Pennsylvania, during the island's crisis tended to disproportionately report moving for family-related reasons. In contrast, those moving to Texas (and to a lesser extent, Florida) tended to disproportionately report work-related reasons. In light of the potential costs and benefits associated with moving into nontraditional versus traditional areas, we next explore whether differences existed in their socioeconomic outcomes, depending on where they settled.

THE LABOR FORCE STATUS OF PUERTO RICANS IN THE MAJOR RECEIVING STATES

Figure 6.1 shows the labor force status of island-born Puerto Ricans aged twenty-five to sixty-four who moved from the island within a year of the American Community Survey (ACS) into one of the largest receiving states; the states are shown in the rank order of the number of incoming Puerto Ricans from the island between 2006 and 2014, based on the ACS. For comparison, this figure also shows the labor force status of island-born Puerto Ricans who returned to the island during this time in the Puerto Rican Community Survey (PRCS). In general, with the exception of Texas, this figure indicates that island-born Puerto Ricans have relatively low labor force participation rates in the states shown, a finding that is particularly pronounced among recent migrants and those returning to Puerto Rico.

Moreover, on the surface, Figure 6.1 supports what the Travelers Survey (TS) revealed in the previous chapter: Puerto Ricans moving from the island into particular destination areas appear to be doing so for consistently different reasons. Indeed, aligned with the relatively large share of migrants in the TS reporting work-related migration reasons, Figure 6.1 shows that two-thirds (66.5%) of the recent migrants in Texas were employed, and four-fifths (79.3%) were in the labor force. These rates were considerably higher compared to those in other states shown. Even in Florida, which had the

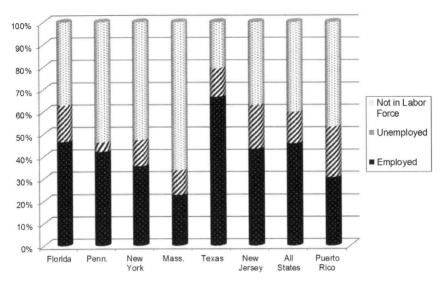

Figure 6.1 Labor Force Status of Island-Born Puerto Rican Recent Migrants, by Residence: 2006–2014. *Source*: Authors' estimates using 2006–2014 ACS and PRCS data in the IPUMS. *Notes*: Only civilians between the ages of twenty-five and sixty-four are included. The percentage of the unemployed represents the percentage of individuals among the population who were unemployed; it does not indicate the unemployment rate. The recent migrants shown residing in the states are those who moved from the island within twelve months prior to the survey. Those residing in Puerto Rico moved from the mainland to island within twelve months prior to the survey.

second highest employment/population ratio of recent island-born migrants from Puerto Rico, fewer than half (46.6%) had jobs. Note also that while the employment/populations ratios among recent migrants in Texas were lower than the national and state averages (both at 72.5%) among civilians in the same age range, their labor force participation (LFP) rates exceeded the national and state averages (77.8% and 77.0%, respectively). Therefore, it appears that "pull" factors were prevalent among island-born migrants who moved to Texas during La Crisis Boricua.

Considering the other extreme, consistent with their relatively low share reporting moving for work, island-born Puerto Ricans who migrated to Massachusetts during Puerto Rico's crisis reported relatively low employment/population ratios and LFP rates; fewer than one in four adults (22.7%) had jobs and only one in three (33.8%) were in the labor force. These labor market outcomes were even lower percentage-wise than the corresponding figures among island-born Puerto Ricans who returned to the island during the crisis (30.6% and 53.3%, respectively). Consistent with the case of "push" factors into traditional receiving areas, recent migrants in New York had the second lowest employment rate (35.5%), followed by the corresponding statistic in Pennsylvania (42.1%).[2] Such information is particularly relevant for social workers and policymakers aiming to facilitate a smooth transition of new migrants into local communities.

The Labor Force Status of All Island-Born Puerto Ricans

Differences in the labor force status of all island-born Puerto Rican adults (shown in Figure 6.2) across geographic dimensions exist, but not surprisingly, they are less extreme than those among the new migrants. Employment/population ratios, and with the exception of Texas, LFP rates, were higher for island-born Puerto Ricans in general than for recent migrants, as would be expected given that the former population more likely mirrors the labor force characteristics of statewide populations. That said, island-born Puerto Ricans in Texas had similar LFP rates (78.3%) as recent migrants in the state, further indicating that employment prospects in Texas served as a major pull factor to attract island residents. Moreover, nearly three-quarters (73.7%) of all island-born Puerto Rican adults were employed in Texas, which was higher than the employment/population ratio among all civilians, regardless of race/ethnicity, birthplace, etc., in the same age range nationwide and statewide.

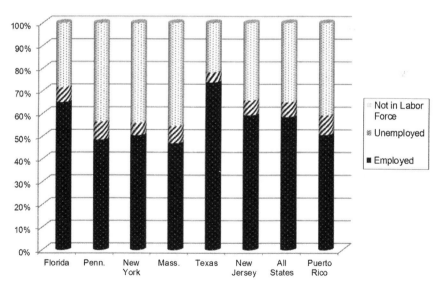

Figure 6.2   Labor Force Status of Island-Born Puerto Ricans, by Residence: 2006–2014. *Source*: Authors' estimates using 2006–2014 ACS and PRCS data in the IPUMS. *Notes*: Only civilians between the ages of twenty-five and sixty-four are included. The percentage of the unemployed represents the percentage of individuals among the population who were unemployed; it does not indicate the unemployment rate.

This figure further reveals that among the states shown, island-born Puerto Ricans in Florida fared the second best with respect to employment opportunities; two-thirds (65.0%) held jobs in the state, and seven out of ten (71.6%) were in the labor force. Such information indicates the relatively robust labor market opportunities for island-born Puerto Ricans that Florida had to offer, likely due at least in part, to the rapidly growing Puerto Rican community and expanding networks.

As with recently arrived migrants, employment prospects were lower in the traditional Puerto Rican communities than the nontraditional areas. Less than half of all island-born Puerto Rican adults in Massachusetts and Pennsylvania, and just half in New York, were employed. These rates were at (in the case of New York) or just below the employment rate among island-born Puerto Ricans in Puerto Rico. Moreover, Puerto Ricans on the island had higher labor force participation rates (59.3%) than in these three states (which hovered between 54 and 56%), suggesting that migrants into these areas had been pushed from the island or had other reasons besides working to leave, including attending to their families. It appears that La Crisis Boricua spurred outmigration into traditional receiving areas, but did not necessarily operate as a "safety valve" in alleviating their lack of labor market opportunities when they arrived to the mainland.

Mainland Employment Opportunities after 2010

One factor yet explored is whether the large number of incoming migrants affected the employment opportunities of island-born Puerto Ricans in these states as La Boricua Crisis unfolded. As noted earlier in this chapter, on the one hand, the influx of large numbers of Puerto Ricans into particular areas may have stimulated employment growth for members of this group owing to expanding social networks and a higher demand for workers who understand the culture and language of the new migrants. On the other hand, if the networks and labor markets in key receiving areas did not expand rapidly enough to absorb the unprecedented numbers of incoming Puerto Rican migrants, employment opportunities may have fallen, particularly in the later stages of La Crisis Boricua after a decade of massive in-migration.

For empirical insight, we compare the employment/population ratios of island-born Puerto Ricans aged twenty-five to sixty-four between 2006 and 2010 versus 2011 and 2014. This exercise indicates that these ratios did not differ between the two time periods in a statistically significant manner for the mainland as a whole or in five of the six major receiving states (the exception being New Jersey). Even in Florida, which received one in every three incoming migrants from the island after Puerto Rico's economic crisis started plus a significant number of Puerto Ricans from other states, the employment/population ratio among island-born Puerto Ricans in this age range remained quite stable (at 65%) between 2006–2010 and 2011–2014 periods. The employment rates among island-born Puerto Ricans in New Jersey significantly fell, from approximately 61 percent in 2006–2010 to 58 percent in 2011–2014.

What Puerto Ricans experienced in five of the six major receiving states was not the same for mainland-born non-Hispanic whites in the same age group (not shown); the latter group's employment/population ratios significantly declined in each of these states plus in the mainland overall (an outcome of the mainland's Great Recession). New Jersey aside, it therefore appears that the relative stability of the employment rates among island-born Puerto Rican adults was not merely a product of underlying labor market conditions. Our findings are consistent with an increase in labor demand for island-born Puerto Ricans that offset the potential labor market crowding associated with growing numbers of incoming migrants. Later in this chapter, we further analyze labor market earnings among island-born Puerto Ricans.

The Labor Force Status of Island-Born Interstate Migrants

We now explore how the labor force status of interstate migrants compared to their counterparts who remained behind. Recall from the previous chapter that the volume of Puerto Rican migration was not solely dependent on island-to-mainland migration; there was considerable migration on the mainland—and from the mainland to island—during this timeframe. For insight into this issue, Figure 6.3 presents the labor force status of island-born Puerto Ricans by the major sending states between 2006 and 2014.

It is not a surprise that in nearly all cases (Massachusetts being the exception), the internal migrants had higher shares of unemployed workers than among those residing in the sending areas, given the transition time it often takes migrants to find employment. At the same time, the LFP rates of the internal migrants exhibited a large degree of variability *vis-à-vis* those in the sending areas. The LFP rates among island-born Puerto Ricans who left Florida, Pennsylvania, Massachusetts, and Texas during this time were lower than those of their counterparts who remained in these states. In contrast, Puerto Ricans who moved from New York and New Jersey had higher LFP rates than those left behind.

These differences likely reflect differences in internal migration selectivity from the sending states. The fact that those leaving New York and New Jersey exhibited greater labor force attachment than those left behind (or moving in) suggests that migration "pull" conditions may have been at play, thus leaving behind potentially socioeconomically vulnerable populations in traditional receiving areas. By virtue of the higher LFP rates among island-born

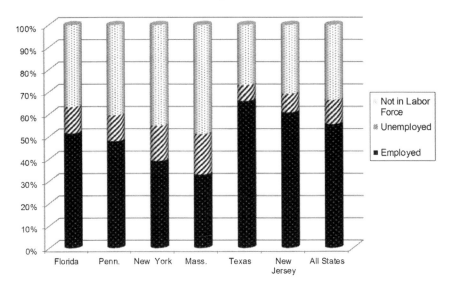

Figure 6.3   Labor Force Status of Island-Born Puerto Rican Interstate Migrants, by Sending State: 2006–2014. *Source*: Authors' estimates using 2006–2014 ACS and PRCS data in the IPUMS. *Notes*: Only civilians between the ages of twenty-five and sixty-four are included. The interstate migrants are those who moved between states or from the mainland to island within the past twelve months. The states shown are where the migrants resided twelve months prior to the survey. The percentage of the unemployed represents the percentage of individuals among the population who were unemployed; it does not indicate the unemployment rate.

residents in the other four states versus those who left suggests that "push" factors led to the outmigration. It therefore appears that as low as the LFP and employment/population ratios were in Pennsylvania and Massachusetts, without interstate migration, Puerto Ricans would probably have had even weaker labor market outcomes in these states.

The Labor Force Status of Mainland-Born Puerto Ricans

With the foregoing changes to the socioeconomic and demographic landscape in key receiving states in mind, it is also important to consider how mainland-born Puerto Ricans have fared. Figure 6.4 presents the labor force status for members of this group between the ages of twenty-five and sixty-four in the largest receiving areas of migrants from the island. As with their island-born counterparts, this figure indicates distinct geographic variations in employment among Puerto Ricans born in the states, although they are less pronounced.

The traditional settlement areas hosted lower employment/population ratios among those born on the mainland, such that selective island-to-mainland

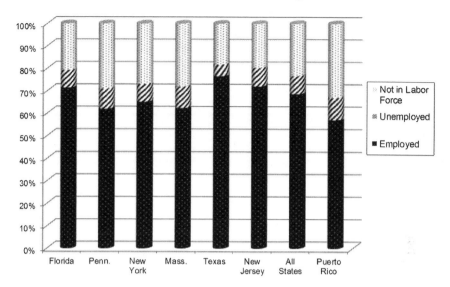

Figure 6.4   Labor Force Status of Mainland-Born Puerto Ricans, by Residence: 2006–2014. *Source*: Authors' estimates using 2006–2014 ACS and PRCS data in the IPUMS. *Notes*: Only civilians between the ages of twenty-five and sixty-four are included. The percentage of the unemployed represents the percentage of individuals among the full population who were unemployed; it does not indicate the unemployment rate.

migration is not the only explanatory factor behind geographic differences in the labor force status of Puerto Ricans. To illustrate, among the states shown, Massachusetts and Pennsylvania had the lowest employment/population ratios (62% in each state) and labor force participation rates (71–72%), followed closely by New York (65% and 73%, respectively). Such findings are consistent with literature mentioned earlier in this chapter on how institutional discrimination in more established Puerto Rican communities limits access to the necessary resources for upward social mobility. In the case of New York, this finding further fits with the selective interstate migration patterns discussed above for island-born Puerto Ricans.

As with their island-born counterparts, employment/population ratios among mainland-born Puerto Ricans were highest in Texas; in fact, Texas represents the only state among the six shown in which employment rates were similar between mainland-born and island-born Puerto Ricans. This finding again reflects relatively robust employment opportunities for Puerto Ricans in Texas. The labor force status of mainland-born Puerto Ricans in New Jersey and Florida was similar and appeared to be more favorable than the national average, which in turn was better than one for mainland-born Puerto Ricans living in Puerto Rico during this time.

Comparing the employment status of mainland-born Puerto Ricans between 2006–2010 and 2011–2014, one difference from their island-born peers is that their employment rates significantly fell overall (from 70% to 68%) and in three of the six states shown: Massachusetts (from 65% to 60%), Florida (from 73% to 70%), and New Jersey (from 74% to 71%). The decline in the employment/population ratio among mainland-born Puerto Ricans in Massachusetts is of particular concern because it was already low, indicating that the mainland's Great Recession (occurring in the midst of La Crisis Boricua) disproportionately impacted already vulnerable populations.

More Details on Labor Force Status and Other Socioeconomic and Demographic Characteristics

Geographic differences in labor force status imply that differences exist with respect to other socioeconomic outcomes, including of course, labor market income and the likelihood of being impoverished. But labor force participation itself depends on other underlying socioeconomic and demographic characteristics, such as education, age, gender, family structure, and English-language fluency. Recall from the previous chapter that education levels varied across Puerto Ricans moving to specific states. Moreover, with respect to gender, a perusal of ACS data indicates that women represented as few as 44 percent of the adult island-born migrants moving from Puerto Rico into Texas (the lowest percentage among the top six receiving states), which was more than 13 percentage points below the representation of women among new migrants in Pennsylvania (57.3%—the highest percentage among these states). Island-born migrants to Texas were also younger, more educated, and more likely to be married than their counterparts moving to other states. It is therefore not surprising to observe relatively high employment/population ratios and LFP rates among Puerto Ricans in Texas.

A more detailed analysis indicates that while such differences explain some of their geographic variations in labor force status, they did not explain all of them. Indeed, when conducting a multivariate probit regression analysis (described in appendix B) of stateside Puerto Rican civilians between the ages of twenty-five and sixty-four, we find that such characteristics related to the likelihood of participating in the labor force in a manner consistent with conventional wisdom and prior literature, regardless of island or mainland birthplace (results not shown to conserve space). For comparison, we also replicated the analysis for mainland-born non-Hispanic whites.

Puerto Ricans who recently migrated from the island or between states were less likely to be in the labor force than their more "settled" counterparts, other things equal. Education, age, and English-language fluency increased the odds of being in the labor force (albeit the effect of age diminished among older adults), while being a woman, being unmarried, or living outside of a metropolitan area reduced these odds. The only initially unexpected finding was that the presence of children at home *increased* the likelihood of labor force participation among both island-born and mainland-born Puerto Ricans, but this was not case for non-Hispanic whites. Nevertheless, this finding appears to have been driven by gender. When replicating the analyses separately for Puerto Rican men and women, having children increased the odds of labor force participation among men, but reduced them among women, which is consistent with traditional gendered roles in the household.

We further investigate how these characteristics related to the likelihood of being employed versus unemployed while accounting for factors affecting labor force participation using a bivariate probit regression analysis (appendix B provides the details). The empirical results are also straightforward. Compared to otherwise similar workers, recent migrants and women were more likely to be unemployed. Education, age (with a diminishing effect), and English proficiency reduced the odds of being unemployed, as did having white collar occupations versus service or agricultural occupations.

When accounting for differences in these characteristics across states, island-born Puerto Ricans in Texas, New Jersey, and to a lesser extent, those in Florida had a significantly higher likelihood of participating in the labor force than their counterparts in New York, Massachusetts, and Pennsylvania. Compared to otherwise similar New York residents, those in the latter two states had significantly lower odds of being in the labor force, which fits with variations in the reasons for migrating as discussed in the previous chapter. Among mainland-born Puerto Ricans, those in Florida, Texas, New Jersey, and other states had statistically similar labor force participation rates on average, which were significantly higher than among their counterparts in New York, Massachusetts, and Pennsylvania—three of the traditional settlement areas.

The differences in the likelihood of being employed versus unemployed among labor force participants suggest the odds of being unemployed were significantly lower among island-born workers in Texas, and significantly higher among those in Massachusetts and Pennsylvania, compared to Florida, New York, New Jersey, and other states on average. Among mainland-born workers, those in Texas fared the best, followed by Florida, with respect to being employed instead of unemployed; those in remaining states had similar unemployment propensities.

These findings do not necessarily reflect interstate differences in labor market conditions in general. Indeed, unlike Puerto Ricans, non-Hispanic whites had significantly *lower* LFP rates in Texas and Florida, and *higher* LFP rates in Massachusetts and Pennsylvania, compared to their otherwise similar counterparts in New York. Among non-Hispanic white labor force participants, while those in Texas also had significantly lower odds of being unemployed than their New York counterparts, so did those in Pennsylvania (although to a lesser extent). Moreover, non-Hispanic whites had lower unemployment odds in New York than those in Florida, Massachusetts, and New Jersey. The recent Puerto Rican employment experiences on the mainland, then, do not seem to simply mirror state-level macro labor market trends.

LABOR MARKET EARNINGS

In addition to differences in the likelihood of being employed, earnings represent an important labor market outcome that often drives other socioeconomic status measures. Therefore, we examine the annual wages and salaries of island-born and mainland-born Puerto Ricans who worked stateside during Puerto Rico's economic crisis. Because of the skewed nature of earnings distributions, as in chapter 4, we use the convention of taking the natural logarithm; the numbers reported in brackets are the 2014-dollar-equivalents. The top panel of Table 6.1 shows that the earnings of Puerto Ricans varied considerably across the main receiving states.

As expected, given their relatively high education levels, island-born Puerto Ricans living in Texas earned considerably more on average per year than their peers in the other states shown. For example, among recent migrants from the island, those in Texas earned nearly $18,171 on average, which despite being relatively low, was more than $1,300 earned by recent migrants in the state with the second highest average earnings (New York, with $16,831), and $4,000 above their peers who moved to Florida (who, with $14,003, had the third highest average earnings among these states). Of the states shown,[3] recent migrants from the island to Pennsylvania earned the least—a mere $9,750, which was about half of the earnings of their counterparts in Texas.

These findings again point to nonrandom settlement patterns of Puerto Rican migrants into specific states. Recall from chapter 4 that migrants from Puerto Rico were considerably more likely to cite work-related reasons when moving to Texas than to other states, whereas those moving to Pennsylvania and Massachusetts disproportionately mentioned family-related reasons. The differences in earnings across these states are generally consistent with the reported differences in the reasons for moving from the island.

New York warrants further attention in light of its relatively low Puerto Rican employment/population ratios and LFP rates and historical significance for stateside Puerto Ricans. It appears that among those who were *employed*, Puerto Rican migrants fared better than those who went elsewhere on the mainland besides Texas. Still, some of this seeming earnings advantage could reflect cost-of-living differences; when compared to the earnings of non-Hispanic whites in the same state (panel B), island-born Puerto Ricans fared slightly better in Florida (where they earned 87.3% less than non-Hispanic whites) than in New York (earning 90.9% less). We will return to the issue of relative earnings later in this chapter.

Table 6.1 Total and Unexplained Earnings Differentials between Stateside Puerto Ricans (PR) and Non-Hispanic Whites: 2006–2014

Characteristic	Florida	Pennsylvania	New York	Mass.	Texas	New Jersey	Entire Mainland
Panel A: Average ln(wages+salaries):							
Island-born PR, recent migrants from island	9.547 [$14,003]	9.185 [$9,750]	9.731 [16,831]	a	9.808 [$18,171]	9.317 [$11,126]	9.525 [$13,698]
Island-born PR	10.153 [$25,668]	9.985 [$21,699]	10.218 [$27,392]	10.025 [$22,584]	10.362 [$31,634]	10.290 [$29,437]	10.185 [$26,503]
Mainland-born PR	10.199 [$26,876]	10.082 [$23,909]	10.378 [$32,145]	10.134 [$25,185]	10.281 [$29,173]	10.444 [$34,338]	10.280 [$29,144]
Mainland-born non-Hispanic Whites	10.420 [$33,523]	10.435 [$34,030]	10.640 [$41,773]	10.679 [$43,434]	10.565 [$38,754]	10.762 [$47,193]	10.479 [$35,561]
Panel B: Total earnings differentials with non-Hispanic whites:							
Island-born PR, recent migrants from island	−87.3%	−125.0%	−90.9%	a	−75.7%	−144.5%	−95.4%
Island-born PR	−26.7%	−45.0%	−42.2%	−65.4%	−20.3%	−47.2%	−29.4%
Mainland-born PR	−22.1%	−35.3%	−26.2%	−54.5%	−28.4%	−31.8%	−19.9%
Panel C: Unexplained earnings differentials with non-Hispanic whites (decomposition estimates):							
Island-born PR, recent migrants from island	−17.0%	−6.8%	−6.9%	a	−34.7%	−47.0%	−22.0%
Island-born PR	−11.9%	−7.4%	−12.1%	−18.5%	−15.7%	−14.2%	−9.2%
Mainland-born PR	−5.7%	−3.0%	−1.1%	−9.1%	−10.1%	−5.2%	−0.3%

Source: Authors' estimates using data from the 2006 to 2014 ACS in the IPUMS.

Notes: The sample includes island- and mainland-born Puerto Rican adult civilians, and mainland-born non-Hispanic white civilians, between the ages of twenty-five and sixty-four. Recent migrants are those who moved from Puerto Rico within the twelve months prior to the survey. The wage and salary income, in 2014 dollars, is adjusted for inflation using the CPI; it is only measured for workers reporting wage and salary income, and excludes self-employment income. The numbers in the brackets refer to the equivalents of the natural logarithm amounts. See appendix B for the empirical methodology and estimation details.

aSample size of workers is too small to produce reliable estimates.

Although not as extreme, similar rank-order differences exist when considering all island-born Puerto Rican adults in these states. Those living in Texas during this timeframe tended to earn $31,634 per year, the highest among the states shown, followed by New Jersey ($29,437), New York ($27,391), and then Florida ($25,668), which fell below the national average ($26,503) earned by this group. Those in Pennsylvania again had the lowest earnings ($21,699).

Turning to panel B in Table 6.1, some of the rank-ordering shifts with respect to the earnings of Puerto Ricans *relative* to non-Hispanic whites in the same state. Island-born Puerto Ricans in Texas still fared better than their counterparts in the other states shown. At the same time, with average earnings 75.7 percent below those of non-Hispanic whites, the distinct socioeconomic disparity among recently arrived island-born Puerto Ricans in Texas should not be disregarded. Recent migrants in Florida and New York fared better than the national average of a 95.4-percent wage disparity, whereas those in Pennsylvania and New Jersey fared considerably worse (with earnings differentials with non-Hispanic whites of 125.0% and 144.5%, respectively).

Among island-born Puerto Ricans in general, these earnings penalties narrow considerably, but are still relatively large in magnitude. The smallest Puerto Rican/non-Hispanic White earnings differential was again accrued by island-born Puerto Ricans in Texas (at 20.3%); it was even smaller than the one for mainland-born Puerto Ricans (at 28.4%) for whom Texas ranked third. Of the major receiving areas, Florida had the second smallest earnings differential (26.7%) among island-born Puerto Ricans (after Texas), and the smallest (22.1%) among mainland-born Puerto Ricans (followed by New York). Island-born Puerto Ricans in New York ranked third in terms of their relative earnings with non-Hispanic whites, although they were closely followed by their counterparts in Pennsylvania and New Jersey. Puerto Ricans in Massachusetts had the largest earnings disparities with non-Hispanic whites in the states shown (a 65.4% disparity among island-born Puerto Ricans, and 54.5 % among mainland-born Puerto Ricans).

In general, these findings again support the empirical observation of relatively robust employment opportunities for Puerto Ricans in new destination versus traditional areas. That said, the existence of significant earnings disparities between Puerto Ricans and other populations even in the new destination areas raises questions about the opportunities for social mobility among Puerto Ricans on the mainland relative to non-Hispanic whites.

UNEXPLAINED PUERTO RICAN/NON-HISPANIC
WHITE EARNINGS DIFFERENTIALS

An important consideration when viewing earnings disparities is the extent to which differences in observable characteristics, such as education, contribute to these disparities. We conducted a similar analysis in chapter 4 at the national level in each year of La Crisis Boricua up until 2014. In this section, we consider how much of the differences in education and other characteristics explain the earnings differentials between Puerto Ricans and non-Hispanics whites across the major receiving states. Due to sample size constraints, however, we cannot report these state-level differentials on an annual basis.

For this purpose, we decomposed earnings differentials into "explained" versus "unexplained" (or skill-adjusted) components, as described in appendix B. The "explained" component reflects how differences in observable characteristics lead to earnings disparities, while the "unexplained" component is the earnings differential that is not accounted for by differences in observable traits between the groups (i.e., the unexplained differential). Recall from chapter 4 that this unexplained differential reflects differences in underlying unmeasurable skills; geographic mobility, including potential locational preferences; the utilization of social networks; and underlying structural factors, such as discrimination in labor, housing, and credit markets.

Panel C in Table 6.1 presents the results for the unexplained earnings differentials between Puerto Ricans and non-Hispanic whites in the key receiving states. Of interest, the rank ordering of the total earnings differentials changes considerably with focusing exclusively on the unexplained earnings gaps across the groups. While island-born Puerto Ricans had the narrowest *total* earnings differential in Texas—both among recently arrived migrants and among island-born Puerto Ricans in general—they had the *second highest unexplained* earnings differential (34.7%) after New Jersey (47.0%) among recent migrants to the mainland, and the second highest (15.7%) after Massachusetts (18.5%) among island-born Puerto Ricans overall. These findings indicate that differences in observable characteristics explained a relatively small part of the Puerto Rican/non-Hispanic white earnings differential in these states in this timeframe.

In contrast, differences in observable characteristics explained all but 7 percent of the total earnings differential between recent island-born Puerto Ricans and non-Hispanic whites in Pennsylvania and New York. The recent migrants in these areas fared better in this regard than those who moved to Florida (who had an unexplained earnings differential of 17.0%) as well as the more settled island-born migrants in these states, other things the same.[4]

These findings thus present a mixed interpretation of how Puerto Rican migrants fared in Texas during La Crisis Boricua. On the one hand, Puerto Ricans moving to the state tended to be highly educated, younger, and employed in white collar occupations. This skill set would have presumably pulled migrants from the island to Texas, and their total earnings were indeed relatively high. On the other hand, despite their higher skill levels, it appears that their *compensation* was considerably below that of comparably-skilled non-Hispanic whites. We will return to this issue in the next subsection.

With respect to the unexplained relative earnings differentials of island-born Puerto Ricans in general, other than in Pennsylvania, these remained in the double-digits in the main receiving states (and were above the national average of 9.2%). Given the growing numbers of Puerto Ricans moving from the island, if local labor markets in the receiving areas cannot absorb them accordingly, as we note above, there are increasingly important implications for their social mobility outcomes, and thus, important implications for the socioeconomic prosperity for the future direction of these states in general.

Another important finding in panel C in Table 6.1 is that when controlling for observable characteristics and traits, at the national level and in New York, mainland-born Puerto Rican workers essentially reached parity with non-Hispanic whites (at least by 2014); this is an outcome not previously observed in the literature. This finding suggests that Puerto Rican workers have made inter-generational socioeconomic progress on the mainland, at least with respect to labor market earnings. Yet, in addition to the point made in note 4 of this chapter, this finding needs to be tempered with the facts that employment rates remain low for this group and the human capital levels of Puerto Ricans lag behind stateside averages. As such, earnings differentials only represent one (albeit critical) facet of the social mobility opportunities Puerto Ricans experience on the mainland.

Education and Occupational Structures

To provide insight into why interstate unexplained relative earnings differences exist among stateside Puerto Ricans, we next consider how their skill levels fit into underlying labor market structures across the major receiving areas. Specifically, in a related study (Dávila, Mora, and Rodríguez 2017), we considered whether the likelihood of being "overeducated" or "undereducated" varied across geographic location. We used the convention employed by Richard Verdugo and Nancy Verdugo (e.g., 1989) to identify overeducated and undereducated workers as those whose schooling levels exceed or fall short of one standard deviation of the average education in their occupations.

Extending this analysis, we find that island-born Puerto Ricans in Texas were significantly more likely to be overeducated, while those in Massachusetts, New York, Pennsylvania, and New Jersey were significantly less likely to be so, than their otherwise similar counterparts in Florida or other states in general. Similarly, the likelihood of being undereducated was significantly lower among island-born Puerto Ricans in Texas, and greater in the other major receiving states, *vis-à-vis* their peers in the rest of the mainland.

These results suggest that despite their higher education and employment levels, Puerto Rican workers moving from the island to Texas during

La Crisis Boricua held jobs for which they were overqualified; this did not appear to occur among those moving into other major receiving states. This finding fits with the relatively high unexplained earnings differential with non-Hispanic whites accrued by island-born Puerto Ricans in Texas, as their skill levels might have been underutilized (hence, undercompensated). It also bodes well for the education-occupation matches in some of the traditional receiving areas; despite their low LFP rates, it appears that among those who found employment, they found jobs well matched to their skills. Precisely why these geographic differences exist with respect to education and occupational structures is an issue worthy of further exploration, particularly as Puerto Rican communities in Texas and other nontraditional receiving areas continue to develop and mature.

Unexplained Relative Earnings after 2010

When further investigating changes in the unexplained earnings differentials throughout the course of La Crisis Boricua that coincided, in part, with the mainland's Great Recession, we find that island-born Puerto Ricans experienced a slight worsening of their earnings penalty *vis-à-vis* otherwise similar non-Hispanic whites from 8.2 percent in the 2006–2010 period to 10.4 percent in the 2011–2014 period (see appendix B). However, when considering the changes within the six major receiving states, it appears that this worsening was largely driven by New York, as the Puerto Rican/non-Hispanic white unexplained earnings differential widened, from 10.5 percent to 14.6 percent, during this time. Island-born Puerto Ricans in the other five major receiving states did not experience statistically significant changes in their unexplained earnings disparities with non-Hispanic whites.

There was a slight deterioration in relative earnings among mainland-born Puerto Ricans on average, who went from a seeming unexplained earnings "premium" (relative to non-Hispanic whites) of 1.0 percent between the 2006–2010 period to a penalty of 1.5 percent in the 2011–2014 period. It might be the case that the Great Recession drove their earnings down relative to otherwise similar non-Hispanic whites because of the particular areas in which they resided (more precisely defined than what we identify here); it might also be the outcome of increased labor market competition with large numbers of incoming migrants into Puerto Rican concentrated areas. Regardless, these changes were quite small.

At the same time, we did not detect statistically significant changes in the unexplained earnings differences between mainland-born Puerto Ricans and non-Hispanic whites in any of the six major receiving areas of island-born Puerto Ricans. This is a topic worthy of future exploration, particularly as skill-based migration and settlement patterns continue to evolve as La Crisis

Boricua moved into its second decade or in response to polices enacted through Puerto Rico Oversight, Management and Economic Stability Act (PROMESA) and other legislative policies and actions.

RATES OF IMPOVERISHMENT

Labor market earnings reveal one important indicator of social mobility, but earnings are only observed among employed workers. Given the relatively low employment/population ratios and high unemployment rates of Puerto Ricans, it is important to consider additional socioeconomic outcomes, including the incidence of poverty. In light of the differences in earnings, labor force status, education (recall the previous chapter), and other observable characteristics, it is not surprising that considerable interstate variation existed among Puerto Ricans with respect to poverty rates between 2006 and 2014.

To illustrate, as panel A in Table 6.2 shows, among civilians aged twenty-five to sixty-four, approximately one out of seven (14.1%) island-born Puerto Ricans recent migrants in Texas were impoverished during this time, compared to one-third who moved from Puerto Rico into Florida (32.8%) and New Jersey (34.1%). Migrants in these states fared better than recent migrants nationally, four out of ten (40.4%) of whom resided below the poverty line. However, nearly two-thirds of the recent migrants moving into New York (59.6%), Pennsylvania (62.2%), and Massachusetts (62.2%) were impoverished between 2006 and 2014, which were considerably higher shares than those among Puerto Ricans on the island (hovering around 45–46%) during this time. This finding provides further evidence that migration "push" factors were at play among those who left the island for these three traditional receiving states.

With lower levels of human capital and labor force attachment rates, it is not surprising that the poverty rates among island-born Puerto Ricans in general in these states were so high, ranging from 31.4 percent in New York to 38.1 percent in Massachusetts. Island-born Puerto Ricans in Texas had the lowest poverty rates (9.9%) between 2006 and 2014 among the states shown, followed by those in Florida (17.3%) and New Jersey (20.6%). Even among mainland-born Puerto Ricans, those in Texas had the lowest poverty rate (12.9%), which (similar to the case of labor market earnings) was the only state during this time among the six shown where island-born Puerto Ricans fared better than their mainland-born counterparts with respect to residing above the poverty line.

As with island-born Puerto Ricans, mainland-born Puerto Ricans in New York, Pennsylvania, and New Jersey had higher poverty rates than among

Table 6.2 Total and Unexplained Poverty-Rate Differentials between Stateside Puerto Ricans (PR) and Non-Hispanic Whites: 2006–2014

Characteristic	Florida	Pennsylvania	New York	Massachusetts	Texas	New Jersey	Entire Mainland
Panel A: Poverty rates:							
Island-born PR, recent migrants	32.8%	62.2%	59.6%	62.2%	14.1%	34.1%	40.4%
Island-born PR	17.3%	36.4%	31.4%	38.1%	9.9%	20.6%	24.4%
Mainland-born PR	15.2%	25.9%	20.6%	28.2%	12.9%	14.1%	18.3%
Mainland-born non-Hispanic whites	9.8%	7.7%	7.4%	6.3%	7.3%	4.6%	8.6%
Panel B: Total poverty-rate differentials (in percentage points) with non-Hispanic whites:							
Island-born PR, recent migrants	23.0	54.5	52.2	55.9	6.8	29.5	31.8
Island-born PR	7.5	28.7	24.0	31.8	2.6	16.0	15.8
Mainland-born PR	5.4	18.2	13.2	21.9	5.6	9.5	9.7
Panel C: Unexplained poverty-rate differentials (in percentage points) with non-Hispanic whites (decomposition estimates):							
Island-born PR, recent migrants	11.3	34.7	19.8	29.4	4.5	17.9	15.5
Island-born PR	4.5	13.6	9.0	15.9	1.9	8.6	7.3
Mainland-born PR	2.5	8.1	4.9	11.0	3.3	5.3	4.0

Source: Authors' estimates using the 2006–2014 ACS in the IPUMS.

Notes: The sample includes island- and mainland-born Puerto Rican adults, and mainland-born non-Hispanic whites, between the ages of twenty-five and sixty-four, who were not residing in group quarters. Recent migrants are those who moved from Puerto Rico within the twelve months prior to the survey. See appendix B for the empirical methodology and estimation details.

mainland-born Puerto Ricans overall (with a national average of 18.3%) between 2006 and 2014. Moreover, these differences do not simply reflect relative rankings of socioeconomic status across states in general. For example, Table 6.2 shows that across these six states, non-Hispanic whites in Massachusetts had the second lowest poverty rate (after New Jersey), while those in Florida had the highest poverty rate. Moreover, when comparing differences in the poverty rates between Puerto Ricans and non-Hispanic whites within the same state (see panel B in Table 6.2), the general rank-ordering stood, with Massachusetts, Pennsylvania, and New York leading in terms of magnitude, regardless of birthplace. Island-born Puerto Ricans had the narrowest poverty-rate differentials with non-Hispanic whites in Texas, followed by those in Florida during this time; these states switched their ranking among mainland-born Puerto Ricans.

Of course, the likelihood of being impoverished tends to be driven by a set of socioeconomic and demographic characteristics, including education, employment, gender, and household structure (e.g., single-headed vs. married households). We already know that many of these characteristics differed across the major receiving states of incoming Puerto Ricans, thus providing context into the geographic variation of their poverty rates (e.g., low education levels in the traditional receiving areas, which also have high rates of impoverishment). When accounting for such differences between Puerto Ricans and non-Hispanic whites between the ages of twenty-five and sixty-four (details are provided in appendix B), we find that while the differentials narrow considerably, the "unexplained" poverty-rate differential remained substantial in most cases (in double-digits, except in Texas), as shown in Table 6.2, panel C.

Among recently arrived island-born migrants during Puerto Rico's economic crisis (at least up until 2014), the relative unexplained poverty rate was highest among those moving to Pennsylvania (34.7 percentage points), followed by Massachusetts (29.4 percentage points), and then with more distance, by New York (19.8 percentage points). At the other end of the spectrum, those in Texas fared the best (4.5 percentage points) in terms of unexplained poverty-rate differentials with non-Hispanic whites, which was the only state among the six shown to be in the single digits. Even in Florida, the state with the second lowest unexplained poverty-rate disparity between recently arrived migrants and non-Hispanic whites, the disparity was well into the double-digits (11.3 percentage points) between 2006 and 2014.

The unexplained relative rates of impoverishment among island-born Puerto Ricans in general were considerably smaller than for the new migrants, but still in the double-digits in Massachusetts and Pennsylvania (15.9 and 13.6 percentage points, respectively), and close thereto in New York (9.0 percentage points). Of the states shown, the unexplained poverty-rate differential with non-Hispanic whites during this timeframe was the smallest in Texas (at 1.9 percentage points [relatively small, but still statistically significant at conventional levels]), seconded by Florida (4.5 percentage points).

The finding for Texas is of particular interest, given the relatively high unexplained earnings penalty of Puerto Ricans in the state discussed in the previous section. It appears that despite a potential skill-occupational mismatch in the state as indicated by our earnings analysis, the misalignment was not enough to disproportionately push island-born Puerto Ricans below the poverty line. In fact, panel C in Table 6.2 shows that only in Texas (of the states shown), island-born Puerto Ricans had a smaller unexplained poverty-rate differential with non-Hispanic whites than their mainland-born counterparts (at 3.3 percentage points) between 2006 and 2014.

Unexplained Relative Poverty-Rate Differentials after 2010

In light of the Great Recession's "push" of millions of Americans into poverty and, as discussed by Elizabeth Kneebone and Natalie Holmes (2016), the number of people on the mainland living below the poverty line as late as 2014 remained at recession-era levels, it is important to highlight that island-born Puerto Ricans in the states—who were already vulnerable socioeconomically—disproportionately felt this push. Their unexplained poverty rates vis-à-vis otherwise similar non-Hispanic whites significantly increased from an average of 7.0 percentage points nationwide between 2006 and 2010 to 7.7 percentage points between 2011 and 2014. At the same time, however, when focusing on specific states, only island-born Puerto Ricans in Pennsylvania experienced a significant deterioration (from 11.8% to 15.4%) in their unexplained poverty rates relative to non-Hispanic whites between these two timeframes; their unexplained relative poverty rates remained stable in the other five major receiving states.

SUMMARY AND CONCLUDING REMARKS

On the U.S. mainland, Puerto Ricans in the newer destinations, including Texas, have had relatively more robust employment opportunities than their counterparts in traditional areas, such as New York and Massachusetts, since 2006. This relates to the fact that Puerto Ricans relocating to Texas tend to be younger, highly educated, and employed in white collar occupations relative to their counterparts residing elsewhere. Given the interstate differences in education and other observable characteristics discussed in the previous chapter, it is not surprising to observe significant earnings and poverty-rate differentials between Puerto Ricans and other U.S. populations, even in these new destination areas.

However, despite faring worse overall in the traditional areas, when accounting for their relatively high levels of education, the earnings of Puerto Ricans in Texas (and to a lesser extent, in Florida) were significantly lower on average than those of otherwise similar non-Hispanic whites between 2006 and 2014. One explanation (with empirical support) was that island-born Puerto Ricans had a greater likelihood of being overeducated in Texas and Florida than in other areas.

The vast differences in the labor force status and other socioeconomic outcomes of Puerto Ricans across specific geographic areas indicate that migrants (including interstate migrants) tend to be consistently selecting their destination areas for different reasons, as discussed in previous chapters. These differences, in turn, may create longer-term disparities in social mobility among Puerto Ricans across geographic areas and socioeconomic and demographic dimensions. Therefore, it behooves social scientists, social workers, and policymakers (including at the local level) to consider not only the numbers, but also the different needs (such as employment assistance vs. childcare), to best facilitate the successful integration of incoming migrants. The consideration of household-specific issues naturally brings forward the issue of gender—an issue we explore in the next chapter.

NOTES

1. Examples include Massey, Gross, and Shibuya (1994); Massey, Gross, and Eggers (1991); Massey and Denton (1993, 1989); Massey and Eggers (1990); and Massey (1990).

2. In terms of rank order, the findings for New York and Pennsylvania appear at odds with the TS; as noted in chapter 5, a higher share of respondents reported work-related reasons for moving to New York than Pennsylvania. Perhaps subsequent outmigration of Puerto Ricans from New York, such as to nearby New Jersey (which had a similar employment rate as in Pennsylvania), would explain this seeming discrepancy.

3. We do not report the earnings of recent island-born Puerto Rican migrants into Massachusetts because the sample size of employed workers is too small to produce reliable estimates.

4. This finding should not be interpreted as a sign that Puerto Ricans in Pennsylvania and New York faced fewer social mobility challenges than those in other states. For example, even though we can "explain" all but 7 percent of the 125 percent total earnings differential in Pennsylvania, we cannot explain why such vast differences in *observable* characteristics exist between Puerto Ricans and non-Hispanic whites. As discussed above, historical discrimination that reduces access to institutional resources may play a role. Future studies should continue to address this issue.

Chapter 7

The Role of Gender on Puerto Rican Social Mobility Outcomes

We reported in chapter 4 that island-born women were more likely than their male counterparts to migrate from Puerto Rico to the U.S. mainland during La Crisis Boricua. We further demonstrated in chapter 5 that the distribution of the reported reasons for moving from the island to mainland, including for family-related reasons, during the crisis varied depending on the intended destination state. Given the traditionally gendered role in family caregiving, in this chapter, we reexamine these outcomes through the prism of gender. Specifically, we investigate gender-related differences in the reasons for leaving Puerto Rico as well as whether gender mattered with regards to other socioeconomic outcomes among Puerto Ricans on the mainland and island.

GENDER, LOCATION, AND REASONS FOR MOVING FROM PUERTO RICO

Earlier in this book, we note that the mainland geographic settlement areas among recent migrants from Puerto Rico were statistically indistinguishable between women and men during Puerto Rico's economic crisis. In the Travelers Survey (TS), women and men leaving the island also reported similar intended destination states. It follows that gender did not appear to be a factor influencing the initial settlement patterns among Puerto Ricans relocating stateside during the island's economic crisis. Of interest, the *sending* regions in Puerto Rico in the TS were also statistically similar between men and women.

However, we further noted in chapter 4 that the distribution of the reasons for leaving the island differed between women and men. Women were more likely to report moving from Puerto Rico for family-related reasons (and less

123

likely to move for work) than their male counterparts. Given that the gender distributions of destination and sending areas were similar for this ethnic group, do these findings imply that the different migration reasons between Puerto Rican men and women were independent of the major destination states in this timeframe?

To answer this question, consider Figure 7.1 (women) and 7.2 (men). First, on average, approximately half (51.6%) of the women aged twenty-five to sixty-four in the TS reported moving to the states either because of work (31.8%) or to look for work (19.8%). In contrast, nearly three-quarters (73.9%) of men reported moving for these two reasons (50.3% and 23.6%, respectively). The relatively low share of women migrating from the island to the mainland for work-related purposes suggests they would have been at an economic disadvantage on the mainland relative to their male counterparts, at least initially, if they had lower rates of labor force attachment without strong family support structures.

However, and related to the question asked here, this relative disadvantage likely varies across the major destination areas in light of the fact that among outbound female migrants in the TS, the reasons for moving varied considerably depending on where they planned to move. Figure 7.1 shows that

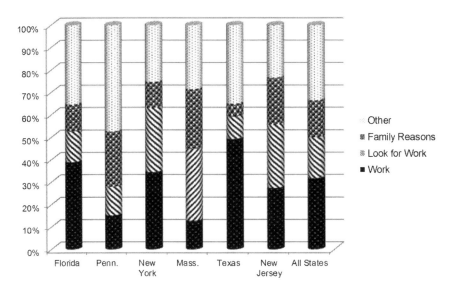

Figure 7.1 Primary Reason for Moving to the Mainland among Women: FY2011–FY2012. *Source*: Authors' estimates using FY2011–FY2012 TS data. *Notes*: The sample does not distinguish between Puerto Ricans and non-Puerto Ricans. Our sample includes female air travelers between the ages of twenty-five and sixty-four who reported their primary reason for traveling was to move to the mainland.

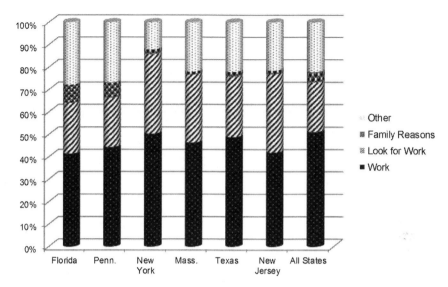

Figure 7.2   Primary Reason for Moving to the Mainland among Men: FY2011–FY2012. *Source*: Authors' estimates using FY2011–FY2012 TS data. *Notes*: The sample does not distinguish between Puerto Ricans and non-Puerto-Ricans. Our sample includes male air travelers between the ages of twenty-five and sixty-four who reported their primary reason for traveling was to move to the mainland.

women moving to Massachusetts and Pennsylvania were considerably less likely to report work-related reasons, and those moving into Texas (and to a lesser extent, into Florida), were significantly more likely to do so, compared to all women migrants during this time. Only 12.8 percent and 15.3 percent of women migrants reported moving to Massachusetts and Pennsylvania because of work, compared to half (49.3%) of women moving to Texas and nearly four out of ten (38.8%) of those moving to Florida.

When further including the share of women moving to search for jobs, these gaps narrow (but remain substantial) in light of the higher shares reporting this reason moving to Massachusetts (a full third) and to a lesser extent, to Pennsylvania (one-eighth), compared to women moving to Texas (one-tenth). Figure 7.1 also indicates that while the share of women moving from Puerto Rico to New York for work-related purposes was similar to the share among women migrants in general, the share of those reporting searching for work was significantly higher than the national average. As such, when combining "work" with "searching for work" as the reasons to move to the U.S. mainland, the highest labor force participation rate (measured in this manner) occurred among female Puerto Ricans moving to New York (63.4%), even higher than among those migrating into Texas (59.2%).

A driving component behind these interstate differences among women migrants related to the incidence of family caretaking. Among the women in the TS migrating from Puerto Rico to the U.S. mainland, approximately one-fourth of those moving to Massachusetts and Pennsylvania (26.7% and 24.7%, respectively), and one-fifth (21.1%) of those moving to New York, reported family-related reasons behind their decisions to migrate. These percentages were considerably higher than the corresponding shares of women moving to Texas (5.6%), and to a lesser extent, to Florida (12.2%) and New York (11.8%).

Among men, Figure 7.2 shows much less variation across states with respect to migration purposes than what is observed for women; in fact, the reasons for moving were not significantly different for men across these geographic regions. Based on these differences, we would expect that among recent migrants from Puerto Rico, women in Massachusetts and Pennsylvania were at a particular socioeconomic disadvantage because of their low labor force attachment, not only compared to their female counterparts migrating to other states, but also compared to their male counterparts in the same state.

DEMOGRAPHIC AND SOCIOECONOMIC CHARACTERISTICS OF PUERTO RICAN WOMEN AND MEN

Beyond the reasons for leaving during Puerto Rico's economic crisis, other demographic and socioeconomic characteristics differed between female and male migrants. Table 7.1 presents selected average demographic and socioeconomic characteristics by gender of the outbound migrants in the TS, and recent migrants from Puerto Rico in the American Community Survey (ACS), who were between the ages of twenty-five and sixty-four. While the specific averages and percentages are not identical between the datasets, both show that women migrants (relative to men): (1) tended to be slightly older (particularly in the TS); (2) had half a year more of schooling; (3) had a smaller share of migrants who did not complete high school; and (4) had a greater share of college graduates.

Moreover, Table 7.1 indicates that in the TS, female migrants were considerably less likely to be traveling alone than men, as just over half (55.9%) of women reported traveling by themselves compared to three-quarters (76.4%) of men. In the ACS, while recent women migrants were less likely than their male counterparts to be married, they were more likely to be unmarried or separated parents; 27.5 percent of recently arrived women from the island were in this category, compared to only 5.5 percent of men. A smaller share of recent female than male migrants on

Table 7.1   Selected Characteristics of Outbound and Recent Migrants from Puerto Rico to the Mainland, by Gender

Characteristic	Outbound Migrants from Puerto Rico to Mainland (TS: FY2011–FY2012)		Recent Puerto Rican Migrants from Puerto Rico to Mainland (ACS: 2006–2014)	
	Women	*Men*	*Women*	*Men*
Born in Puerto Rico	–	–	85.1%	86.7%
Age	42.6 years	39.7 years	39.7 years	39.0 years
Education measures:				
Average education	13.5 years	12.9 years	12.7 years	12.2 years
Not a high school graduate	16.1%	19.6%	18.9%	24.6%
High school graduate	24.2%	29.3%	26.5%	34.5%
Some college, no degree	20.3%	21.4%	29.9%	19.8%
College graduate	39.4%	29.7%	24.7%	21.1%
Natural log. earned income	–	–	9.340	9.668
			~$11,384	~$15,804
Poverty rate	–	–	44.3%	36.1%
Family income:				
Less than $20,000	49.3%	48.6%	45.4%	39.9%
$20,000–$39,999	20.2%	19.2%	23.8%	26.2%
At least $100,000	6.2%	6.3%	5.9%	6.0%
Traveling alone	55.9%	76.4%	–	–
Married	–	–	37.3%	42.3%
Number of children at home	–	–	1.01	0.50
Unmarried or separated with children at home	–	–	27.5%	5.5%
At least person in HH is employed	–	–	76.9%	86.1%
N	1,093	1,130	802	822
Estimated population	218,286	237,283	113,800	109,593

Source: Authors' estimates using data from the FY2011–FY2012 TS, and the 2006–2014 ACS.
Notes: The samples include individuals between the ages of twenty-five and sixty-four. The outbound migrants in the TS sample include air travelers who reported that the primary purpose of their trip was to move to the mainland. The recent migrants in the ACS are individuals who moved from Puerto Rico within the twelve months prior to the survey. The family income distributions exclude individuals who did not answer this question in the TS (approximately 7% of this sample); this information is not reported in the ACS for individuals residing in group quarters. The number of travelers excludes individuals who did not answer this question. The earned income measure is adjusted for inflation and reported in 2014 dollars only for those workers who earned wages or salaries in the paid-employment sector.

the mainland also reported living in households with at least one employed person.

With a disparity in the number of earners in the household, it is not surprising that recent Puerto Rican women migrants on the U.S. mainland had higher poverty rates than their male counterparts (44.3% vs. 36.1%). Still, the poverty rates of both groups were high, and for women, they were even slightly higher than the poverty rates among their female counterparts who remained in Puerto Rico (42.6%). The earned income levels among the incoming migrants to the U.S. mainland were also quite low, equivalent to less than $1,000 per month ($11,384 annually) per year among women, about $4,500 below the $15,804 earned per year by men. Related to these differences, women migrants were slightly more likely than men to have had less than $40,000 in family income. We will return to more detailed analyses of gender-related earnings and poverty-rate differentials later in this chapter, but family and household structures clearly played a role.

These figures point to depressed economic circumstances among Puerto Ricans arriving to the states, especially women, during La Crisis Boricua. Arguably, the demographic and socioeconomic characteristics of these migrant groups impacted (and would continue to impact) their subsequent socioeconomic mobility on the mainland, thus likely sustaining disparities among Puerto Ricans along the lines of gender, and between Puerto Ricans and other populations. Moreover, this recent migrant group might have experienced different adjustment barriers depending on where they settled (e.g., the new vs. traditional settlement areas) and why they moved (e.g., to work vs. to provide family care). Thus, as noted in the previous chapter, to ensure the successful integration of incoming migrants into their new communities, social workers, social scientists, and policymakers should be aware of the particular socioeconomic challenges these groups face.

Table 7.2 presents the characteristics of island-born Puerto Ricans in general (not only for recent migrants) on both the island and U.S. mainland, as well as for mainland-born Puerto Ricans. Among island-born Puerto Ricans, the age gap between men and women was slightly smaller between those living in Puerto Rico versus the mainland (0.5 years on the island vs. 0.7 years on the mainland). The difference in age between men and women in the states was the same as among recent migrants in the ACS, and suggests that men tended to be slightly overrepresented among younger migrants. Some supporting evidence of this can be found when examining the representation of men among incoming Puerto Rican migrants from the island in the ACS; men represented over half (51.2%) of incoming migrants between the ages of twenty-five and thirty-four, and just under half (48.2%) among those between the ages of thirty-five and sixty-four.

Table 7.2 further reveals distinct differences with respect to educational attainment between Puerto Rican men and women, which were particularly pronounced on the island during our timeframe of study. Indeed, island-born women had one more year of schooling on average than their male counterparts in Puerto Rico, compared to 0.4 years more on the mainland. The reason for the larger gender-related difference in schooling on the island versus mainland was the relatively large island-mainland differences in education among women (12.8 years vs. 12.2 years); an island-mainland schooling gap

Table 7.2 Selected Characteristics of Puerto Ricans (PR), by Birthplace, Residence, and Gender: 2006–2014

Characteristic	Island-Born PR on Island		Island-Born PR on Mainland		Mainland-Born PR on Mainland	
	Women	*Men*	*Women*	*Men*	*Women*	*Men*
Age (in years)	44.3	43.8	45.6	44.9	39.6	39.3
Education measures:						
Average education (in years)	12.8	11.8	12.2	11.8	13.0	12.6
Not a high school graduate	19.2%	26.9%	26.2%	30.0%	14.6%	17.4%
High school graduate	25.4%	30.6%	27.1%	32.0%	27.6%	34.8%
Some college, no degree	25.3%	22.9%	28.1%	23.3%	37.3%	32.3%
College graduate	30.1%	19.6%	18.5%	14.7%	20.5%	15.5%
Natural log. earned income	9.726	9.799	10.035	10.319	10.166	10.393
	~$16,747	~$18,016	~$22,811	~$30,303	~$26,004	~$32,630
Poverty rate	42.6%	38.0%	28.5%	19.8%	21.7%	14.5%
Family income:						
Less than $20,000	46.5%	43.0%	32.2%	24.1%	23.5%	17.2%
$20,000–$39,999	26.7%	27.2%	22.9%	23.4%	20.9%	20.1%
At least $100,000	4.1%	4.7%	13.1%	14.1%	18.1%	21.1%
Married	44.7%	46.7%	44.7%	52.0%	41.4%	44.7%
Number of children at home	0.98	0.67	1.08	0.74	1.19	0.73
Unmarried or separated with children at home	25.4%	6.1%	28.5%	6.4%	30.2%	6.5%
At least person in home is employed	89.7%	90.9%	81.4%	86.3%	88.0%	90.7%

Source: Authors' estimates using the 2006–2014 ACS and PRCS.

Notes: The samples include individuals between the ages of twenty-five and sixty-four. The family income distributions and the number of people employed in the household exclude individuals residing in group quarters. The earned income measure is adjusted for inflation and reported in 2014 dollars only for those workers who earned wages or salaries in the paid-employment sector.

did not exist among island-born men. This finding suggests that Puerto Rican women who migrated to the mainland during this time had less education on average than women who stayed in Puerto Rico, but more education than their male counterparts.

Additional support for this supposition can be found in the relatively large island-mainland differences *among women* with respect to: (1) the share of those who did not complete high school (as less than one out of five had this schooling level on the island compared to more than one out of four on the mainland), and (2) the share of those who completed college (nearly one out of three vs. less than one out of five, respectively). The representation of college graduates among women in Puerto Rico also dwarfed the corresponding shares among their male counterparts (less than one out of five on the island). Therefore, we would expect that island-born Puerto Rican females living on the island had an advantage over their male counterparts with respect to securing employment—an advantage that was smaller on the mainland. We will return to the issue of gender-related differences in employment in the next section.

On a related point, despite their significantly higher education levels than men, similar to what we observed for recent migrants, island-born women in general had lower labor market earnings, higher poverty rates, and a slightly higher share with family incomes of less than $20,000 during this time. Even though the schooling levels were closer between island-born men and women on the mainland, the income and poverty-related gaps were further apart. For example, less than $1,300 separated the average earnings of island-born women and men on the island ($16,747 vs. $18,016) compared to about $7,500 on the mainland ($22,811 vs. $30,303). Similarly, the gender-related poverty rate differentials were narrower in Puerto Rico (46.5% vs. 43.0%) than in the U.S. mainland (28.5% vs. 19.8% for island-born men and women, and 21.7% vs. 14.5% for mainland-born women and men). We will further explore issues pertaining to these gender-related disparities in terms of earned income and poverty rates while accounting for differences in education and other observable characteristics later in this chapter.

Table 7.2 also shows that married island-born women were equally represented among female Puerto Ricans regardless if they lived on the island or U.S. mainland, whereas island-born men were more likely to be married if they lived stateside. The average number of children in the household was slightly higher among both island-born women and men living stateside than those in the same gender group on the island. Mainland-born Puerto Rican women had the highest number of children at home of the groups shown, reflecting island-mainland differences in fertility rates discussed earlier in this book.

GENDER AND LABOR FORCE STATUS ON
THE ISLAND AND MAINLAND

The foregoing findings likely explain differences in the labor force status between Puerto Rican women and men. It is not surprising in light of "traditional" gendered roles that women had lower employment rates and labor force participation (LFP) rates than men during our timeframe of study. As Figure 7.3 shows, fewer than half (45.1%) of island-born women aged twenty-five to sixty-four on the island were employed between 2006 and 2014, compared to 56.8 percent of their male counterparts. The gender-related gap was even larger when considering the LFP rates of women (53.9%) versus men (66.5%) on the island.

While not shown in Figure 7.3, when examining the labor force status of recent Puerto Rican migrants between 2006 and 2014, on a proportional basis, fewer women were employed on the mainland versus those who remained in Puerto Rico (36.5% vs. 45.1%), although their LFP rates were much closer together (51.4% vs. 52.9%). In contrast, the employment/population ratios among island-born men were more closely aligned between those who recently left the island (55.5%) and those who stayed (56.8%). It follows that the relatively low employment/population ratios among island-born recent

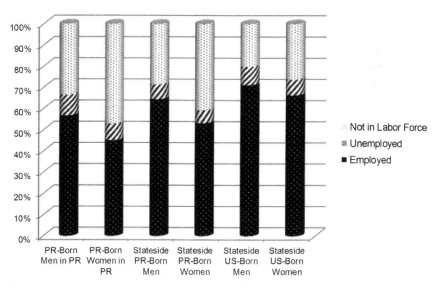

Figure 7.3   Labor Force Status of Puerto Ricans, by Residence and Gender: 2006–2014.
Source: Authors' estimates using 2006–2014 ACS and PRCS data in the IPUMS. *Notes*: Only civilians between the ages of twenty-five and sixty-four are included. The percentage of the unemployed represents the percentage of individuals among the population who were unemployed; it does not indicate the unemployment rate.

female migrants *vis-à-vis* female island residents does not appear to be driven by a large difference in their LFP rates, and instead appears to reflect a dearth of mainland labor market opportunities for incoming women migrants from the island—a dearth that their male counterparts did not seem to experience.

Similar to what we observed in chapter 3, mainland-born Puerto Rican men and women had higher employment-population ratios and LFP rates than their island-born peers in the states. Nonetheless, Figure 7.3 shows that the gender-related differences in labor force status were narrower among mainland-born Puerto Ricans. Such differences tend to translate into differences in other socioeconomic outcomes, which we next explore.

GENDER-RELATED DIFFERENCES IN LABOR
MARKET EARNINGS ON THE MAINLAND

In light of the differences in education levels and other socioeconomic and demographic characteristics between Puerto Rican women and men, we next analyze the extent to which these differences explain gender-related earnings differentials among workers aged twenty-five to sixty-four. In this analysis, similar to our use of mainland-born non-Hispanic whites as the base group of comparison in the previous chapter, we now use mainland-born non-Hispanic white men as the base group of comparison. As part of this analysis, we also consider the earnings of non-Hispanic white women to determine whether the gender-related earning gaps are unique to Puerto Ricans or reflect broader macroeconomic trends on the U.S. mainland. Non-Hispanic white men had the highest average earnings (approximately $44,700) of the groups considered here during the 2006–2014 timeframe.

Panel A in Table 7.3 reports the total earnings differentials between non-Hispanic white men and the other demographic groups on the U.S. mainland overall as well as within the top six receiving states of Puerto Rican migrants. As seen in the final column, on average, island-born Puerto Rican women had the largest earnings differential with non-Hispanic white men of the groups shown (67.3%), followed by mainland-born Puerto Rican women (54.2%), non-Hispanic white women (47.7%), island-born Puerto Rican men (38.9%), and mainland-born Puerto Rican men (31.5%). Note that Puerto Ricans, especially those born on the mainland, had narrower gender-related wage gaps than non-Hispanic whites.[1]

When taking into account differences in observable characteristics between these groups and non-Hispanic white men, island-born Puerto Rican women still had the highest unexplained earnings differential (33.9%), but non-Hispanic white women had the second highest (28.5%), followed by mainland-born Puerto Rican women (21.9%). Puerto Rican men continued to

Table 7.3 Total and Unexplained Earnings Differentials between Stateside Puerto Ricans (PR) and Non-Hispanic White Men, by Gender: 2006–2014

Characteristic	Florida	Pennsylvania	New York	Massachusetts	Texas	New Jersey	Entire Mainland
Panel A: Total earnings differentials with non-Hispanic white men:							
Island-born PR women	-59.6%	-91.0%	-72.7%	-100.9%	-69.7%	-84.5%	-67.3%
Island-born PR men	-32.3%	-49.4%	-53.0%	-75.7%	-29.5%	-63.1%	-38.9%
Mainland-born PR women	-51.1%	-73.3%	-55.0%	-87.0%	-76.2%	-70.7%	-54.2%
Mainland-born PR men	-30.4%	-44.8%	-38.1%	-67.7%	-35.7%	-45.3%	-31.5%
Mainland-born non-Hispanic white women	-38.4%	-48.5%	-42.4%	-45.7%	-55.4%	-54.2%	-47.7%
Panel B: Unexplained earnings differentials with non-Hispanic white men (decomposition estimates):							
Island-born PR women	-35.0%	-32.2%	-35.0%	-41.5%	-46.0%	-37.1%	-33.9%
Island-born PR men	-12.8%	-10.2%	-17.6%	-23.5%	-16.5%	-20.0%	-12.8%
Mainland-born PR women	-25.0%	-26.4%	-20.2%	-25.9%	-36.5%	-27.6%	-21.9%
Mainland-born PR men	-7.5%	-6.7%	-7.5%	-14.5%	-12.1%	-9.3%	-5.0%
Mainland-born non-Hispanic white women	-24.4%	-28.4%	-24.5%	-24.8%	-32.9%	-29.4%	-28.5%

Source: Authors' estimates using the 2006–2014 ACS in the IPUMS.
Notes: The sample includes island- and mainland-born Puerto Rican adult civilians, and mainland-born non-Hispanic white civilians, between the ages of twenty-five and sixty-four. The wage and salary income is adjusted for inflation using the CPI; it is only measured for workers reporting wage and salary income, and excludes self-employment income. The earnings differences are relative to mainland-born non-Hispanic white men. See appendix B for the empirical methodology.

have lower earnings differentials *vis-à-vis* non-Hispanic white men, at 12.8 percent among those born on the island and 5 percent among those born on the mainland. While statistically significant, the relatively small magnitude for men indicates that differences in education and other socioeconomic and demographic characteristics played a major role in explaining the Puerto Rican/non-Hispanic white male earnings gap, at least during the 2006–2014 period.

Gender-Related Earnings Differentials by the Largest Receiving States

A more detailed examination across the major receiving states of Puerto Rican migrants reveals that the gender-related earnings differences varied substantially across states. As panel A in Table 7.3 shows, all Puerto Rican groups, particularly island-born women, in Massachusetts had the lowest relative earnings on average compared to non-Hispanic white men of the states shown. In other states, the rank order shifted across the different groups. To illustrate, whereas island-born women had the second lowest relative earnings in Pennsylvania, their male counterparts fared relatively worse in New Jersey and New York than in Pennsylvania. Of interest, island-born Puerto Rican women encountered the second largest earnings gap with island-born Puerto Rican men in Texas (40.2% = 69.7—29.5), just after Pennsylvania (41.6% = 91.0—49.4). Among mainland-born Puerto Ricans as well as non-Hispanic whites, the gender earnings differentials within the same ethnic group were the largest in Texas.

Turning to panel B, differences in observable characteristics do not explain all of the seeming disadvantages that women workers—both Puerto Rican and non-Hispanic whites—had relative to their male counterparts. For island-born Puerto Ricans, mainland-born Puerto Ricans, and non-Hispanic whites, the largest gender-related own-group earnings differentials existed in Texas during this time, partly because women in Texas had the largest magnitude of the unexplained earnings "penalties" among the states shown, but this was not case for men. This finding indicates that women were driving a large part of the relatively low unexplained earnings of Puerto Ricans in Texas discussed in the previous chapter. Why women in Texas had such an earnings disadvantage, relative to their otherwise similar male counterparts, goes beyond the scope of this book, but we note that it was not an issue unique to Puerto Ricans. However, given that Texas is one of the top receiving states of incoming migrants from the island, this finding has gender-related, and therefore socioeconomic, implications for the future social mobility of Puerto Ricans in that state, including potentially along intergenerational lines.

Island-born women moving to Massachusetts had the second largest unexplained earnings penalty (which is consistent with their relatively large share in the TS who reported moving to the state for family-related reasons), followed by those moving to New Jersey, New York, Florida, and then Pennsylvania. As with their female counterparts, island-born (and mainland-born) men fared the best in Pennsylvania, and second best in Florida (and in New York among mainland-born Puerto Ricans) in this timeframe when accounting for observable socioeconomic and demographic traits.

In all, these results indicate that the relative labor market outcomes of Puerto Rican women versus men differ across geographic regions. A policy implication stemming from these results is that Puerto Rican gender-related labor market differentials can be better addressed by considering local and state job-related dynamics and less by national gender gaps for this ethnic group.

GENDER-RELATED DIFFERENCES IN POVERTY RATES BY THE MAJOR RECEIVING STATES

One issue that arises when solely focusing on labor market earnings is that not everyone works, and the propensity to work consistently varies between men and women. Therefore, we turn our attention to gender-related poverty-rate differentials. Panel A in Table 7.4 shows the poverty rates among Puerto Rican women and men aged twenty-five to sixty-four living on the mainland between 2006 and 2014, partitioned by birthplace and the major receiving states. For comparison, our analysis reports this statistic for mainland-born non-Hispanic white women and men. This analysis shows that the largest gender-related poverty-rate gap within the demographic groups existed among island-born Puerto Ricans on the U.S. mainland: well, over one in four (28.5%) women in this group lived below the poverty line, compared to one in five (19.8%) of men.

While these rates were considerably lower than those of island residents noted earlier in this chapter (42.6% and 38.0% among island-born women and men, respectively), the gender differentials were twice as large stateside versus the island. This finding presumably reflects the lower propensity of women versus men to migrate from Puerto Rico for work-related purposes as discussed earlier in this chapter.

Table 7.4 indicates that these findings masked the differences observed within the major receiving states. Double-digit gender-related poverty-rate gaps occurred among island-born Puerto Ricans in the traditional settlement areas of Massachusetts (43.3% vs. 31.6%), Pennsylvania (41.9% vs. 30.3%), and New York (35.9% vs. 25.6%). The smallest gaps occurred in Texas (12.3% vs. 7.7%—which were lower poverty rates than among their mainland-born peers in the state) and Florida (19.7% vs. 14.8%). Still, even

Chapter 7

Table 7.4 Poverty Rates and Unexplained Differentials between Stateside Puerto Ricans (PR) and Non-Hispanic White Men, by Gender: 2006–2014

Characteristic	Florida	Pennsylvania	New York	Massachusetts	Texas	New Jersey	Entire Mainland
Panel A: Actual Poverty Rates							
Non-Hispanic white men	9.1%	6.6%	6.7%	5.6%	6.2%	4.1%	7.5%
Island-born PR women	19.7%	41.9%	35.9%	43.3%	12.3%	24.4%	28.5%
Island-born PR men	14.8%	30.3%	25.6%	31.6%	7.7%	16.3%	19.8%
Mainland-born PR women	17.5%	31.1%	24.1%	33.0%	16.0%	18.0%	21.7%
Mainland-born PR men	12.9%	20.1%	16.6%	22.7%	9.8%	9.9%	14.5%
Non-Hispanic white women	10.5%	8.7%	8.1%	6.9%	8.4%	5.0%	9.6%
Panel B: Imputed Poverty Rates Based on Observable Characteristics [in brackets—unexplained differential with NHW men, in percentage points]:							
Island-born PR women	15.3%	25.5%	25.8%	23.4%	12.2%	13.5%	20.1%
	[4.4 pp]	[16.4 pp]	[10.1 pp]	[19.8 pp]	[0.1 pp]	[10.9 pp]	[8.4 pp]
Island-born PR men	10.9%	17.9%	19.0%	17.7%	6.4%	9.1%	14.0%
	[3.9 pp]	[12.4 pp]	[6.6 pp]	[14.0 pp]	[1.3 pp]	[7.2 pp]	[5.8 pp]
Mainland-born PR women	14.6%	19.7%	17.3%	16.4%	12.5%	9.9%	16.0%
	[2.8 pp]	[11.3 pp]	[6.8 pp]	[16.6 pp]	[3.5 pp]	[8.1 pp]	[5.6 pp]
Mainland-born PR men	11.3%	14.0%	13.3%	13.2%	7.7%	7.0%	12.0%
	[1.6 pp]	[6.1 pp]	[3.3 pp]	[9.6 pp]	[2.2 pp]	[2.9 pp]	[2.5 pp]
Non-Hispanic white women	11.7%	9.7%	9.4%	7.1%	10.1%	6.2%	10.8%
	[-1.2 pp]	[-1.0 pp]	[-1.3 pp]	[-1.4 pp]	[-1.7 pp]	[-1.2 pp]	[-1.3 pp]

Source: Authors' estimates using the 2006–2014 ACS in the IPUMS.

Notes: The sample includes island- and mainland-born Puerto Rican adult civilians, and mainland-born non-Hispanic white civilians, between the ages of twenty-five and sixty-four. All of the unexplained poverty-rate differentials are statistically significant at conventional levels except for island-born Puerto Rican women in Texas. The unexplained poverty-rate differentials might not equal the differences between the actual and imputed poverty rates because these were estimated based on the empirical methodology described in appendix B that accounts for the nonlinearity of the likelihood of being impoverished. In Puerto Rico, the poverty rates among island-born men and women were 38.0% and 42.6%, respectively; the imputed poverty rates [unexplained differentials] were 20.8% [17.2 pp] and 24.2% [18.3 pp].

among men, these rates were quite high. Consider that the national poverty rate among non-Hispanic white men averaged 7.5 percent between 2006 and 2014, and among the states shown, was as low as 4.1 percent (in New Jersey).

Mainland-born Puerto Ricans also had double-digit differences in poverty rates between women and men in Massachusetts and Pennsylvania, indicating that the incidence of relatively high poverty among women was not a phenomenon unique to island-born Puerto Ricans in the states, even in recent years. This is not a new finding; scholars for decades have recognized that disparities in socioeconomic outcomes of Puerto Ricans on the mainland are not necessarily driven by newly arrived migrants. Instead, as we have discussed throughout this book, they may relate to intergenerational effects and institutional factors limiting upward socioeconomic mobility that tend to be more prevalent in the traditional settlement areas than in new destination states.

Gender and Unexplained Rates of Impoverishment

Education and other socioeconomic and demographic characteristics play a major role in determining gender-related differences in the likelihood of being impoverished. Following the methodology used in chapter 6, we impute the poverty rates for Puerto Ricans and non-Hispanic white women, based on the poverty-rate structure of non-Hispanic white men, which are included in panel B in Table 7.4. For the entire mainland, the imputed poverty rate of island-born Puerto Rican women, given their socioeconomic and demographic characteristics, was 20.1 percent—8.4 percentage points less than their actual poverty rate. Differences in observable characteristics with non-Hispanic white men thus only explained a relatively small portion of their relatively high poverty rates.

Among island-born men, the unexplained poverty-rate differential with non-Hispanic white men was smaller (5.8 percentage points), but not trivial; it was also similar to the one estimated for mainland-born Puerto Rican women (5.6 percentage points). Among non-Hispanic white women, given their characteristics, they fared better than their male counterparts over this time period, as their imputed poverty rates were higher than their actual poverty rates. If their poverty-rate structure had been the same as for men, their poverty rate should have been 1.3 percentage points higher.

Unlike the case for unexplained labor market earnings, Table 7.4 shows that island-born Puerto Ricans, regardless of gender, maintained their rank ordering with respect to unexplained poverty rate differentials with non-Hispanic white men between 2006 and 2014 in the largest receiving states. In particular, both women and men born in Puerto Rico had the highest unexplained differentials in Massachusetts (19.8 and 14.0 percentage points, respectively), followed by Pennsylvania, New Jersey, New York, Florida, and then Texas.

In fact, among island-born Puerto Rican women in Texas, their imputed poverty rate was almost identical to their actual poverty rate in the state, indicating that differences in socioeconomic and demographic characteristics between this group and non-Hispanic white men fully explained the difference in their poverty rates. For island-born Puerto Rican men, the difference was only 1.3 percentage points (albeit a difference that is statistically significant). The finding that observable differences in characteristics explained essentially all of the Puerto Rican poverty-rate differentials with non-Hispanic whites in Texas does not correspond to the findings regarding earnings disparities in that state mentioned earlier in this chapter. Future studies should investigate this issue further, particularly as the Puerto Rican population in Texas continues to grow (as it had been as this book went to press).

Even among mainland-born Puerto Rican women and men, those in Massachusetts and Pennsylvania had the highest unexplained poverty-rate differentials (which for women, were in double digits) with non-Hispanic white men. Why such sharp incidences of *unexplained* impoverishment among mainland-born Puerto Ricans, particularly women, have persisted should be explored by future researchers, particularly in light of the high population growth rate of mainland-born Puerto Ricans and their growing importance in these (and other) states.

SUMMARY AND CONCLUDING REMARKS

Women represented half of all Puerto Rican adults who left the island during La Crisis Boricua, but many migrated for different reasons than their male counterparts. Approximately three-quarters of male migrants, but only half of female migrants, left the island for work-related activities, at least until 2015. Moreover, differences in the reasons for moving were more pronounced among women than men across the major receiving states. For example, among women moving from Puerto Rico to Massachusetts and Pennsylvania, only 12.8 percent and 15.3 percent (respectively) reported doing so for work, compared to half of those moving to Texas. One in four moved to either state because of family-related reasons, which quadrupled the share of those who moved to Texas for this reason.

Given such differences, it is not surprising to observe regional disparities with respect to socioeconomic outcomes along the lines of gender. To illustrate, double-digit differences in the poverty rates existed between island-born Puerto Rican men and women in Massachusetts and Pennsylvania (and

New York as well), but were considerably narrower in Texas and Florida during the 2006 and 2014 timeframe.

As we noted in the previous chapter, social scientists, social workers, and policymakers should recognize that the needs and challenges of Puerto Ricans on the mainland are not "across the board;" they differ according to their settlement areas. Our findings in this chapter illustrate the demographic layer that gender adds to such differences. Effectively facilitating the transition of incoming Puerto Ricans into their new mainland areas of residence has considerable long-term and intergenerational implications for their socioeconomic outcomes (and for overall regional prosperity), especially when considering the traditionally gendered roles of women in the household. If the relatively high rates of impoverishment among island-born women in traditional settlement areas continue, their families will likely face sustained hurdles to socioeconomically advance. Our results in this chapter provide supportive evidence, as even among mainland-born Puerto Ricans, significant gender-related differences exist with respect to socioeconomic outcomes, including double-digit differences in poverty rates between men and women in Massachusetts and Pennsylvania. The longer such differences are sustained, the longer it may take for stateside Puerto Ricans in traditional settlement areas to achieve the American dream.

NOTE

1. The earnings gaps between specific groups can be found by taking the difference of the groups' gaps with non-Hispanic whites. For example, the gender earnings gap among island-born Puerto Ricans on the mainland was 28.2 percent (= 67.3–38.9).

Chapter 8

Shaping the Business and Political Landscape on the Mainland

Throughout this book, we have documented a variety of migratory phenomena and socioeconomic and demographic outcomes among Puerto Ricans on the island and U.S. mainland stemming from La Crisis Boricua. One research void unaddressed thus far is whether the growing Puerto Rican population in the states has translated into economic and political power. Arguably, the growing presence and the regional dispersion of Puerto Ricans across the mainland serve as proxies for the national and regional political impacts of this ethnic group. In this chapter, we consider the influence of Puerto Rican–owned businesses in this regard. We also consider the recent voting tendencies of Puerto Ricans on the mainland, particularly as they related to recent presidential elections.

ASSESSING PUERTO RICAN IMPACT ON THE MAINLAND

While the political impact an ethnic group can have is somewhat elusive to predict, it arguably depends on the size and growth of the population, its location, and its ability to coalesce regionally for a political purpose. We have discussed the growing presence of Puerto Ricans on the mainland since 2006, including in areas which until recently had few Puerto Ricans, due to increased migration from the island as well as across states. We have already noted that mainland-born Puerto Ricans have relatively high fertility rates, resulting in above-average population growth. To what extent have these demographic shifts affected the economic and political power of Puerto Ricans on the mainland?

Of course, the potential increase in their political might and subsequent access to resources among Puerto Ricans living stateside as a result of La

Crisis Boricua will likely take years to determine. However, as noted by Timothy Bates: "Politicians allocate public resources to political strength, which inner cities rarely possess; bankers allocate loan funds seeking secure returns, and their consensus view is that inner-city lending is risky; mobile residents seeking attractive opportunities often depart" (2011: 293). This insight suggests that the political influence of Puerto Ricans might be greater in the newer destination areas (such as Florida and Texas) rather than in the traditional receiving areas (including New York, Pennsylvania, and Massachusetts), particularly when considering the high poverty rates and low earnings in the traditional areas that we discussed in earlier chapters.

This quote also alludes to the stylized notion that political influence often channels through the business power of a population in its community. Alberto Dávila and Marie Mora (2013) discussed how the rapid Hispanic population growth in the first decade of the 2000s stimulated entrepreneurial opportunities for Hispanics. While they analyzed some of the differences across businesses owned by specific Hispanic ethnic groups (including Puerto Ricans), a more detailed investigation of those owned by Puerto Ricans on the mainland is warranted in light of their demographic shift since La Crisis Boricua began.

Another metric of political clout pertains to civic engagement, including voting. Presumably, the growing Puerto Rican population on the mainland should have an impact on certain local and state elections, and if they reach a critical mass in key "swing states," on federal elections as well. Two of these swing states include Florida and Pennsylvania—the two states that received the largest number of incoming migrants from the island during La Crisis Boricua. Both states were pivotal in electing Republican Donald J. Trump as the U.S. president in 2016. However, if their population growth continues, Puerto Ricans may play a role in shifting these states toward a Democratic candidate by 2020, given that preliminary analyses of the 2016 election results by precincts and exit polls show that Puerto Ricans on the mainland overwhelmingly voted for the Democratic candidate, Hillary Clinton. With regard to voter turnout, later in this chapter we discuss the role and turnout Puerto Ricans have had on the mainland in recent presidential elections as a way to gauge their potential future impact on shaping the political landscape.

PUERTO RICAN–OWNED BUSINESSES: EVIDENCE FROM THE SURVEY OF BUSINESS OWNERS

We analyze recent business-ownership patterns of Puerto Ricans on the mainland using data from the 2007 and 2012 Survey of Business Owners (SBO). The 2012 SBO represented the most recent version of this survey at the final stages of the writing of this book, with many of these data just becoming publicly available. Appendix A provides additional details about the SBO. For comparative purposes, we also consider business ownership among Mexican Americans, Cubans, and non-Hispanic whites.

The importance of considering Cuban-owned businesses in this discussion is twofold. First, the entrepreneurial tendencies of Cubans have been well established in the literature, particularly starting with Kenneth Wilson and Alejandro Portes (1980). Second, the vast majority of Cuban-owned businesses are in Florida (four-fifths, according to our estimates from the 2012 SBO), which as we have emphasized throughout this book, has become one of the major settlement areas for Puerto Ricans that rivals New York. As such, factors affecting business formation and success among Puerto Ricans in that state will be reflected in some of the business outcomes observed among Cuban-owned firms.

Table 8.1 contains selected characteristics of these firms, including the total number, their sales in absolute value and per firm, the share and the number of firms with paid employees as well as their payrolls. As this table shows, Puerto Ricans owned 258,221 businesses on the U.S. mainland in 2012, making them the third largest group of Hispanic business owners in the states, after Mexican Americans (who owned 1.6 million firms) and Cubans (who owned 281,982 firms). Given that Puerto Ricans represent the second largest Hispanic group in the United States, these figures suggest an underrepresentation of this group in the mainland business sector, potentially dampening their relative political clout.

At the same time, between 2007 and 2012, the number of businesses owned by Puerto Ricans increased by 65.0 percent, which was the largest increase, percentage-wise, of the four groups shown during the five-year timeframe. Mexican Americans had the second largest increase in business ownership (56.8%), followed by Cubans (12.4%). In contrast, non-Hispanic whites experienced a 5.7 percent decline during this timeframe. Consequently, Puerto Ricans narrowed their firm-ownership gap with these other groups, and in light of their population growth, appeared poised to overtake Cubans as the second largest group of Hispanic entrepreneurs in the United States as this book went to press (if they had not already done so), should recent demographic shifts continue.

This relatively large growth rate in the number of Puerto Rican–owned firms was not a continuation of a trend that started earlier in the decade. When examining the 2002 SBO (results not shown), Puerto Ricans had the third largest growth (at 42.9%), from 109,475 firms to 156,466 firms, among these groups between 2002 and 2007. Cubans had the highest growth rate (at 65.5%) during this time, and Mexican Americans, the second highest (at 47.8%). The recent increase in the number of Puerto Ricans living stateside

Table 8.1   Selected Characteristics of Businesses Owned by Puerto Ricans and Other Groups on the Mainland: 2007 and 2012

Characteristics	2007	2012	Change: 2007–2012
Puerto Ricans:			
# Firms	156,466	258,221	65.0%
Sales (in $1,000)	$16,611,414	$24,397,335	46.9%
Sales per firm	$106,166	$94,482	–11.0%
% Firms w/paid employees	9.2%	6.9%	–2.3 p.p.
# Paid employees	97,076	122,313	26.0%
Payroll (in $1,000)	$3,007,662	$4,388,079	45.7%
Average salary paid	$30,983	$35,876	15.8%
Mexican Americans:			
# Firms	1,035,920	1,624,617	56.8%
Sales (in $1,000)	$154,942,238	$204,712,259	32.1%
Sales per firm	$149,570	$126,006	–15.8%
% Firms w/paid employees	11.5%	8.7%	–2.8 p.p.
# Paid employees	1,028,216	1,272,851	23.8%
Payroll (in $1,000)	$26,015,440	$34,405,855	32.3%
Average salary paid	$25,302	$27,031	6.8%
Cubans:			
# Firms	250,976	281,982	12.4%
Sales (in $1,000)	$58,307,148	$92,600,303	58.8%
Sales per firm	$232,322	$328,391	41.4%
% Firms w/paid employees	12.8%	11.4%	–1.4 p.p.
# Paid employees	248,924	275,875	10.8%
Payroll (in $1,000)	$8,872,834	$11,235,803	26.6%
Average salary paid	$35,645	$40,728	14.3%
Non-Hispanic whites:			
# Firms	20,544,891	19,372,250	–5.7%
Sales (in $1,000)	$9,908,521,325	$10,568,974,566	6.7%
Sales per firm	$482,286	$545,573	13.1%
% Firms w/paid employees	21.5%	21.8%	0.3 p.p.
# Paid employees	50,710,039	48,764,974	–3.8%
Payroll (in $1,000)	$1,772,374,217	$1,872,531,888	5.7%
Average salary paid	$34,951	$38,399	9.9%

Source: Authors' estimates using data from the 2007 and 2012 SBO.
Notes: For firms with multiple owners, ownership is determined by the race/ethnicity of the majority of the owners. These do not include firms equally owned by Hispanics and other groups. The "p.p." is for percentage points.

has therefore resulted in a substantial increase in the number of Puerto Rican–owned businesses.

Similarly, the growth rates in the total number of paid employees, total payroll, and the average salary paid to employees were higher for Puerto

Rican–owned establishments than the other groups shown between 2007 and 2012. The number of paid workers hired by Puerto Ricans rose by 26.0 percent (from 97,076 to 122,313 workers), their payroll (in nominal terms)[1] rose by 45.7 percent (from $3.0 billion to nearly $4.4 billion), and their average nominal salary paid to their employees rose by 15.8 percent (from $30,983 to $35,876). Furthermore, the latter increase outstripped the 10.7 percent inflation rate during this time, which was not the case for firms owned by Mexican Americans and non-Hispanic whites. Puerto Rican establishments also had the second highest growth rate in total sales (46.9%, from $16.6 billion to $24.4 billion), after those owned by Cubans (58.8%, to $92.6 billion).

At the same time, Table 8.1 indicates that other than average salaries, the relatively large growth rates in these metrics were driven by the increase in the *number* of Puerto Rican–owned businesses, not necessarily through improved average business outcomes. Indeed, it appears that this business growth did not, on average, occur in large- or medium-scale firms; arguably, then, the increased Puerto Rican presence in the business sector might not have yielded additional political impact for this group on the mainland.

Consider also that the average sales of Puerto Rican firms were the lowest among the groups in 2007 ($106,166). Their average sales were about 71 percent of those generated by the average Mexican American firm, 46 percent of those generated by the average Cuban-owned firm, and only 22 percent of those in the average non-Hispanic white firm. Five years later, the average sales among Puerto Rican firms had *fallen* by 11.0 percent (to $94,482). Mexican American–owned businesses experienced a larger decline in average sales (of 15.8%, to $126,006), which narrowed the gap in this metric between the two groups to 75 percent. However, Puerto Ricans lost ground in this regard to their Cuban counterparts, whose average sales *increased* well above the inflation rate (by 41.4%, to $328,391), and to a lesser extent, to non-Hispanic whites, whose average sales increased by 6.7 percent. Mexican Americans fared the worst in this comparative analysis in terms of sales per firm.

Furthermore, Table 8.1 shows that Puerto Rican businesses had the lowest share of employer firms among these groups in both years; employer firms represented less than one out of ten (9.2%) of Puerto Rican businesses in 2007, which fell to one of out of fourteen (6.9%) in 2012. The share of employer firms also declined by 2012 among Mexican Americans (to 8.7%), and to a lesser extent, among Cubans (to 11.4%), resulting in a narrower gap with respect to employer firms between Puerto Ricans and Mexican Americans, and a wider one with respect to Cubans.

In addition, the payroll numbers reveal that workers employed by Puerto Rican–owned firms in 2012 earned close to the average salaries paid by businesses owned by non-Hispanic whites and Cubans. Puerto Rican employers paid, on average, $35,876 a year, which was approximately $2,500 less than the average amount paid by non-Hispanic whites ($38,399) and $4,800 less than by Cubans ($40,728); this was higher than the average salaries paid by Mexican Americans ($27,027).

The differences in average employee pay across Hispanic-owned firms could be related to industry composition of these firms: 29 percent of Puerto Rican–owned enterprises were in the education, healthcare, professional, and scientific services industries, compared to 23.5 percent of Cuban-owned firms and 18.6 percent of Mexican American–owned firms. In contrast, nearly one-fifth (19.0%) of firms owned by Mexican Americans were in construction and manufacturing, compared to one-tenth (9.7%) of those owned by Puerto Ricans.

Gender and Business Ownership

When investigating the gender of the business owners (not shown to conserve space), women disproportionately drove the growth in the number of Hispanic-owned businesses during this time span, which continued the phenomenon we previously observed (Dávila and Mora 2013). Moreover, the impact of women on Hispanic business growth was particularly pronounced among Puerto Ricans between 2007 and 2012. The number of businesses owned by Puerto Rican women increased by 116.2 percent (to 136,864 firms in 2012), compared to a 98.4 percent increase in the number owned by Mexican American women (to 694,113), and a 57.8 percent increase in the number owned by Cuban women (to 110,061).

Note that these changes resulted in a larger number of businesses owned by Puerto Rican women than those owned by Cuban women in 2012. This was not the case five years earlier when Puerto Rican women owned 63,297 businesses, compared to 69,745 for Cuban women. Furthermore, these changes meant that women owned more than half (53.0%) of all Puerto Rican firms on the mainland by 2012, up from four out of ten (40.5%) in 2007. This shift did not occur among Mexican Americans or Cubans, as women continued to own less than half of their respective enterprises in 2012. Following the argument earlier that business power translates into political power, it could be argued that Puerto Rican women have gained political clout relative to their male counterparts and to Cuban women.

However, additional research will be necessary to determine whether the sharp growth in the number of businesses owned by Puerto Rican women translated into other impactful outcomes, such as sales, payroll, jobs created, and longevity of the firm. Consider that the three industries (out of twenty categories reported by the SBO) with the largest number of firms owned by Puerto Rican, Mexican American, and Cuban women in both 2007 and 2012 were in services: healthcare and social assistance services, "other services" (a composite category), and administrative and support services. In 2007, respectively, these industries accounted for 24.5 percent, 14.6 percent, and 11.7 percent of the businesses owned by Puerto Rican women; 20.4 percent, 18.5 percent, and 16.4 percent of those owned by Mexican American women; and 18.3 percent, 13.7 percent, and 18.2 percent of those owned by Cuban women. Such service industries tend to be less lucrative than others offering professional/scientific or educational services.

Moreover, the growth rate in "other services" category between 2007 and 2012 was considerably higher for Puerto Rican women entrepreneurs (238.0%) than for their Mexican American and Cuban counterparts (106.4% and 98.5%, respectively). This shift resulted in nearly one-fourth (22.9%) of all businesses owned by female Puerto Ricans belonging to this composite service category in 2012, compared to one-fifth (19.3%) among female Mexican Americans and just over one-sixth (17.3%) among female Cubans. Healthcare services also increased its representation in firms owned by Puerto Rican women (to 25.8%), as did administrative support (to 14.6%) but by smaller margins, particularly the former category.

Previous work indicates that despite high rates of business formation, firms owned by women—particularly Black and Hispanic women—tend to have higher closure rates within the first year of opening than those owned by men (Mora and Dávila 2014). In light of the relatively acute socioeconomic disparities that Puerto Rican women encounter—especially among the new migrants—discussed in the previous chapter, and given the disproportionate increase in the "other service" category among businesses owned by Puerto Rican women, these changes suggest their higher rate of business ownership reflect "push" factors into self-employment (to avoid unemployment) as opposed to "pull" factors,[2] which has implications for their survival rates and other business success measures. A more detailed analysis of push/pull conditions among female Puerto Rican entrepreneurs versus other ethnic and gender groups goes outside of the scope of this study, but they should be explored in future research, particularly if women continue to drive business formation among Puerto Ricans on the mainland.

CHARACTERISTICS OF PUERTO RICAN BUSINESSES IN THE LARGEST RECEIVING STATES

Table 8.2 provides more geographic detail of Puerto Rican firms by presenting SBO data from 2007 and 2012 for the top six receiving states of incoming migrants from the island discussed in earlier chapters: Florida, Pennsylvania, New York, Massachusetts, Texas, and New Jersey (listed in order of magnitude based on migrants from the island between 2006 and 2014). Over two-thirds (68.5%) of all businesses owned Puerto Ricans on the mainland

Table 8.2   Selected Characteristics of Businesses Owned by Puerto Ricans, by State: 2007 and 2012

Characteristics	2007	2012	Change: 2007–2012
Florida:			
# Firms	42,374	71,291	68.2%
Sales (in $1,000)	$3,389,954	$4,812,761	42.0%
Sales per firm	$80,001	$67,509	−15.6%
# Paid employees	15,693	22,911	46.0%
Payroll (in $1,000)	$460,634	$725,449	57.5%
Average salary paid	$29,353	$31,664	7.9%
Pennsylvania:			
# Firms	5,321	13,913	161.5%
Sales (in $1,000)	$347,254	$594,051	71.1%
Sales per firm	$65,261	$42,698	−34.6%
# Paid employees	2,256	3,822	69.4%
Payroll (in $1,000)	$57,215	$113,917	99.1%
Average salary paid	$25,361	$29,806	17.5%
New York:			
# Firms	34,387	55,850	62.4%
Sales (in $1,000)	$3,053,802	$3,192,337	4.5%
Sales per firm	$88,808	$57,159	−35.6%
# Paid employees	15,537	18,675	20.2%
Payroll (in $1,000)	$474,156	$629,717	32.8%
Average salary paid	$30,518	$33,720	10.5%
Massachusetts:			
# Firms	3,232	7,596	135.0%
Sales (in $1,000)	$447,709	$482,117	7.7%
Sales per firm	$138,523	$63,470	−54.2%
# Paid employees	6,532	4,285	−34.4%
Payroll (in $1,000)	$224,158	$145,985	−34.9%
Average salary paid	$34,317	$34,069	−0.7%
Texas:			
# Firms	6,945	8,351	20.2%
Sales (in $1,000)	$1,047,238	$1,386,034	32.4%
Sales per firm	$150,790	$165,972	10.1%
# Paid employees	7,503	9,557	27.4%
Payroll (in $1,000)	$189,831	$286,656	51.0%
Average salary paid	$25,301	$29,994	18.5%
New Jersey:			
# Firms	11,485	19,909	73.3%
Sales (in $1,000)	$1,203,953	$1,451,461	20.6%
Sales per firm	$104,828	$72,905	−30.5%
# Paid employees	7,810	6,404	−18.0%
Payroll (in $1,000)	$201,993	$206,157	2.1%
Average salary paid	$25,863	$32,192	24.5%

Source: Authors' estimates using data from the 2007 and 2012 SBO.
Notes: For firms with multiple owners, ownership is determined by the race/ethnicity of the majority of the owners. These do not include firms equally owned by Hispanics and other groups.

in 2012 were located in these states, which was nearly identical to their over-all population proportion (68.2%).

Florida was home to the largest number of Puerto Rican–owned enterprises in the states, followed by New York, in both 2007 and 2012. This was a new dynamic: in 2002 (not shown), more Puerto Rican businesses existed in New York than in Florida (31,658 vs. 24,480 firms), according to the SBO. By 2012, Florida hosted one-fourth (71,291) of all Puerto Rican–owned firms on the mainland, and New York, one-fifth (55,850). This difference also wid-ened slightly between 2007 and 2012, as the number of firms grew in Florida by 68.2 percent (just above the national average for all stateside Puerto Rican businesses), and by 62.4 percent in New York (just below the national aver-age). These two states, as expected, also had the highest total sales, payroll, and number of paid employees among Puerto Rican–owned firms across all the states and DC. In Florida alone, Puerto Rican businesses generated $4.8 billion in sales, $725.4 million in payroll, and 22,911 jobs in 2012.

Still, Table 8.2 shows that the number of Puerto Rican firms in both Penn-sylvania and Massachusetts, while small, grew by substantially larger margins (161.0% and 135%, respectively) than in other states between 2007 and 2012. Note that by 2012, the number of Puerto Rican firms was the lowest for Mas-sachusetts (with 7,596 businesses in that state) among the states shown, but the relatively large growth in Puerto Rican business formation in Pennsylvania (to 13,913 firms) overtook the number of Puerto Rican firms in Texas (7,596).

At the same time, the expected impact of these businesses in Pennsylvania and Massachusetts is likely to be small. To put these results in perspective, only in Texas were the sales per firm higher (and considerably so) than the national average for Puerto Rican firms in 2012 ($165,972 vs. $94,482). The average sales were lower than the national average in the remaining five states shown that year, with Puerto Rican firms in Pennsylvania ($42,698) having the lowest sales per firm. Moreover, with the exception of Texas, their sales per firm declined in all of these states by a substantially greater rate than the 11.0 percent decline experienced by mainland businesses owned by Puerto Ricans nationwide. This was particularly the case in Massachusetts, where the sales per Puerto Rican firm fell by more than half (54.2%), to $63,470. In Texas, average sales increased by 10.1 percent over the five-year period.

Overall, the SBO results imply that the political clout of the Puerto Rican–owned firms might not be keeping up with their overall population growth within key states. As suggested in Tables 8.1 and 8.2, while Puerto Rican business-ownership patterns increased substantially between 2007 and 2012, they did so among the small, low revenue, firms. For comparative purposes, consider that the average sales per firm among Cubans is $328,370 (nearly 3.5 times the average of $94,482 among Puerto Ricans), and that Cubans owned 281,982 firms compared to 258,221 owned by Puerto Ricans. To the extent that number of firms and their sales value translate into political might, Cuban political influence in recent times has likely been more prominent than for Puerto Rican business owners.

PUERTO RICAN SELF-EMPLOYMENT TENDENCIES

To what extent are the differences in business ownership between Puerto Ricans and other groups driven by differences in entrepreneurial tendencies? One measure to assess these tendencies is through self-employment. Dávila and Mora (2013) reported that Hispanic self-employment, particularly among Mexican immigrants, increased during the first decade of the 2000s, which was not the case among non-Hispanics. Arguably, self-employment activities among Hispanics do not appear to be solely driven by cyclical conditions in the labor market.

While that research studied the self-employment outcomes of specific Hispanic subgroups, the case of Puerto Rican entrepreneurship warrants further attention. In particular, of the five largest Hispanic subgroups on the U.S. mainland, Puerto Ricans have the lowest self-employment rates. To illustrate, according to the American Community Survey (ACS), among civilian workers aged twenty-five to sixty-four in 2014, self-employment rates were 5.4 percent among Puerto Ricans, followed by 8.7 percent among both Mexican Americans and Dominicans, 10.4 percent among Salvadorans, and 13.6 percent among Cubans. These rankings correspond to the groups reported in the SBO, which does not identify Salvadorans or Dominicans.

Figure 8.1 presents the self-employment rates for Puerto Ricans, Mexican Americans, Cubans, and non-Hispanic whites between 2006 and 2014. This figure shows that Puerto Ricans had the lowest self-employment rates on the mainland than any of the other groups throughout the entire timeframe. These self-employment rates started falling after 2008, coinciding with the mainland's Great Recession, reaching a low of 4.8 percent in 2010 and 2011. While there was some subsequent recovery in these rates starting in 2012, they were 0.4 percentage points lower in 2014 than in 2006 (when they were 5.8%).

Recall from our previous discussion that the number of businesses owned by Puerto Ricans grew by a faster pace than they did for Mexican Americans and Cubans. While the SBO does not perfectly align with self-employment trends, the drop in Puerto Rican self-employment rates observed in the ACS suggests that the growth in the number of Puerto Rican businesses was likely driven by their population growth, and not from an intensification of entrepreneurial tendencies within the population.

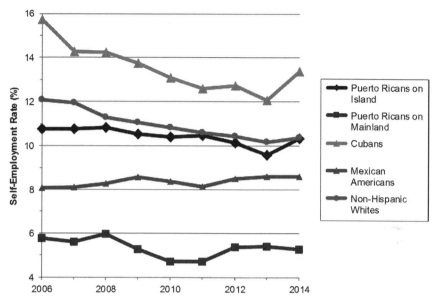

Figure 8.1 **Self-Employment Rates of Puerto Ricans, by Birthplace and Residence, and Other Groups: 2006–2014.** *Source:* Authors' estimates using 2006–2014 ACS and PRCS data in the IPUMS. *Notes:* The sample includes civilians in the labor force between the ages of twenty-five and sixty-four. Mexican Americans, Cubans, and Non-Hispanic whites only include mainland residents; immigrants are included.

An additional feature to highlight in Figure 8.1 is that Puerto Rican self-employment rates (estimated using the Puerto Rican Community Survey [PRCS]) were considerably higher on the island (at 11.1% in 2014). They remained relatively stable for much of the period, with only slight declines until 2011. This finding indicates that throughout La Crisis Boricua (at least through 2014), entrepreneurial tendencies were not uniquely impacted. Between 2011 and 2013, these rates fell a bit more sharply (reaching their low of 10.3% in 2013), but rebounded to 11.1 percent the following year—only 0.2 percentage points below their 2006 self-employment rate (and also the same rate as for non-Hispanic whites on the mainland).

The relatively low self-employment tendencies observed among Puerto Ricans on the mainland are seemingly not driven by cultural factors or practices brought from the island to the mainland, but are indicative of other potential socioeconomic and demographic conditions affecting business formation. Consider that the self-employment rates of island-born and mainland-born Puerto Ricans on the mainland were nearly identical (not shown). With relatively low self-employment rates on the mainland, the impact of Puerto Ricans on the business sector (and thus their political clout) appears to be muted relative to their overall population size.

Figure 8.1 further indicates that Cubans had considerably higher self-employment rates than the groups shown (even higher than those of non-Hispanic whites) between 2006 and 2014. However, their self-employment rates, as well as those of non-Hispanic whites, generally declined over the eight-year period. These declines were slightly steeper than what Puerto Ricans experienced, serving to narrow the self-employment-rate disparities between Puerto Ricans and these two groups. In contrast, with few exceptions, the self-employment rates of Mexican Americans rose during this timeframe, thus widening the self-employment gap between Puerto Ricans and Mexican Americans between 2006 and 2014.

SOCIOECONOMIC AND DEMOGRAPHIC FACTORS AFFECTING PUERTO RICAN SELF-EMPLOYMENT

While numerous studies over the past few decades have examined the relatively intensive nature of Cuban entrepreneurship (including the aforementioned Wilson and Portes' study), few studies have attempted to explain the relatively low incidence of Puerto Rican self-employment on the mainland. This topic warrants more investigation given potential differences in labor market discrimination as well as human, social, and financial capital "intensiveness" among ethnic groups. As the nation's second largest Hispanic subgroup and considering its high population growth rate on the mainland (especially in key states), Puerto Rican entrepreneurial outcomes have become an increasingly important phenomenon to study.

That said, what are the underlying characteristics of self-employed Puerto Ricans on the mainland, and do they differ from those of other populations? To address this question, we estimate how selected socioeconomic and demographic characteristics relate to the probability of being self-employed among Puerto Ricans on the mainland. In this analysis, we separate island-born from mainland-born Puerto Ricans in the event that birthplace affects business formation. We further consider whether the results for Puerto Ricans differ from those of non-Hispanic whites to determine if our findings mirror general national trends or if they are unique to this group.

Table 8.3 presents the selected empirical findings, while appendix B reports the methodological details of this analysis. Suffice it to say that, along with control variables for year of survey and the occupation of individuals, the major factors we consider include the concentration of Puerto Ricans in

Table 8.3   **Selected Probit Regression Results for the Likelihood of Being Self-Employed among Stateside Puerto Ricans and Non-Hispanic Whites**

Characteristic	Island-Born Puerto Ricans	Significant Difference from Non-Hispanic Whites?	Mainland-Born Puerto Ricans	Significant Difference from Non-Hispanic Whites?	Non-Hispanic Whites
Puerto Rican concentration	0.003	No	-0.014***	Yes***	0.007***
	(0.005)		(0.005)		(0.0005)
Local unemployment Rate	0.011	No	0.024**	Yes**	0.002***
	(0.012)		(0.010)		(0.001)
Education	0.028***	No	0.027***	No	0.021***
	(0.008)		(0.007)		(0.0005)
Age	0.058***	No	0.041***	No	0.052***
	(0.015)		(0.013)		(0.001)
Age²	-0.0006***	No	-0.0003**	No	-0.0004***
	(0.0002)		(0.0002)		(0.00001)
LEP	-0.061	Yes*	-0.375***	Yes***	0.058**
	(0.062)		(0.134)		(0.024)
Female	-0.241***	Yes***	-0.233***	Yes***	-0.354***
	(0.039)		(0.032)		(0.002)
Constant	-3.769***	No	-3.355***	No	-3.307***
	(0.363)		(0.296)		(0.022)
Pseudo R²	0.060		0.060		0.058
N	36,603		59,434		6,678,075

Source: Authors' estimates using data from the 2006 to 2014 ACS, available in the IPUMS.
Notes: The dependent variable equals one for the self-employed, and zero for other workers. The parentheses contain robust standard errors. Only employed civilians ages twenty-five–sixty-four are included. Other variables in the probit regression model include marital status, the number of children at home, binary variables for occupation, and binary variables indicating the year of the questionnaire. See appendix B for empirical details.
*** , ** , * Statistically significant at 1, 5, or 10 percent level.

a metropolitan area (as a measure of enclaves), the local unemployment rate (to measure local labor market conditions), education, age, English-language proficiency, gender, and family-structure variables (namely marital status and the number of children at home).

Puerto Rican Concentration

A host of studies finds evidence that ethnically concentrated economies enhance self-employment probabilities, perhaps because of comparative advantages in providing goods and services to fellow-ethnics (given their knowledge of the culture, language, and "tastes"), lower consumer discrimination, greater access to capital via ethnic networks, and the ability to tap into niche labor markets. In such cases, the enclaves would serve to pull Puerto Ricans into self-employment.[3] At the same time, self-employment tendencies might also be higher in enclaves if the greater presence of Puerto Ricans gives rise to bias-type discrimination in the paid-employment sector as predicted by Gary Becker's labor market discrimination theory. The reduced employment opportunities in enclaves would therefore serve to push Puerto Ricans into self-employment. Regardless of pull versus push factors, both scenarios predict relatively high entrepreneurial tendencies among Puerto Ricans in areas with high concentrations of Puerto Ricans.

However, ethnic enclaves might have the opposite effect on Puerto Rican business formation if they provide a wide range of paid-employment and social-networking opportunities for members of the same group, perhaps dampening their need to become self-employed. As we have highlighted throughout this book, in many regards the traditional Puerto Rican settlement areas tend to be associated with relatively low social mobility outcomes, infused by sustained high poverty rates, low employment rates, and low levels of career advancement.

In sum, it appears that for Puerto Ricans, ethnic enclaves have not necessarily been the conduits for upward socioeconomic mobility as they have been for other Hispanic groups. According to our empirical results in Table 8.3, Puerto Rican concentration differently affected the likelihood of being self-employed between island-born and mainland-born Puerto Ricans working stateside between 2006 and 2014. Puerto Rican enclaves had a small and statistically insignificant effect on this likelihood among island-born Puerto Ricans. That is, residing in areas with high concentrations of Puerto Ricans did not appear to provide island-born Puerto Ricans with an advantage or disadvantage in becoming self-employed, *ceteris paribus*. But among mainland-born Puerto Ricans, the relationship between Puerto Rican concentration in a metropolitan area and self-employment probability was *negative*. Puerto Ricans in areas with high concentrations of other Puerto Ricans had lower odds of being self-employed than their counterparts in areas with a limited Puerto Rican presence between 2006 and 2014. This finding does not reflect general business formation tendencies, as metropolitan areas with high concentrations of Puerto Ricans related to *higher* self-employment odds among non-Hispanic whites during this time.

The findings for island-born versus mainland-born Puerto Ricans suggest different enclave dynamics according to birthplace. To the extent that the mainland-born Puerto Ricans have stronger social networks in Puerto Rican enclaves than their island-born counterparts, it is possible that better paid-employment opportunities for the former group mitigated the "push" into self-employment relative to the latter group. Another explanation is that mainland-born Puerto Ricans in traditional enclave areas lacked the access to capital necessary to start businesses, a frequently cited factor in business formation. We cannot disentangle these possibilities given data limitations, but we suspect factors related to the latter possibility are at play, in light of our other findings throughout this book suggesting high concentrations of poverty among Puerto Ricans in traditional settlement areas during La Crisis Boricua.

Enclaves and Self-Employment between 2006–2010 and 2011–2014

We further considered whether the role of enclaves in explaining Puerto Rican self-employment tendencies changed during our timeframe of study. Specifically, we replicated our analysis while splitting our sample between the 2006–2010 and 2011–2014 periods. Among island-born Puerto Ricans, the concentration of Puerto Ricans in the metropolitan areas had no distinguishable impact on the likelihood of being self-employed in either period. Among mainland-born Puerto Ricans, in the earlier time period, Puerto Rican enclaves did not have a statistically significant effect on self-employment tendencies, which parallels the finding for island-born Puerto Ricans. However, between 2011 and 2014, living in areas with larger concentrations of Puerto Ricans significantly reduced the odds of being self-employed among mainland-born Puerto Ricans. This finding implies that self-employment propensities among mainland-born Puerto Ricans intensified *outside* of enclaves relative to those in enclaves over time, and again suggests that the newer destinations fomented additional business formation opportunities than traditional settlement areas.

One implication from the foregoing empirical enclave findings, as it relates to our argument that business power leads to political clout, is that the geographic concentration of Puerto Ricans does not necessarily result in this group's social mobility via political influence. Indeed, it could be argued that Puerto Rican enclaves might be hindering this type of political clout, perhaps due to institutional factors, such as reduced access to capital in the traditional settlement areas, consistent with the point by Bates (2011) cited earlier in this chapter.

Local Unemployment Rates

Macroeconomic conditions in a region are also used in the entrepreneurship literature to explain entry into and exit from self-employment. The most commonly selected macroeconomic variable for this purpose is the unemployment rate despite its ambiguous theoretical link with self-employment (e.g., Mora and Dávila 2014; Thurik et al. 2008; Storey 1991). Consider that an increase in the unemployment rate might push individuals into self-employment without paid-employment prospects. On the other hand, it is conceptually possible that individuals in areas of high unemployment might find self-employment a risky proposition because of a high probability of business failure owing to weak economic conditions.

Table 8.3 reports results that are more consistent with the push explanation for mainland-born Puerto Ricans and to a lesser extent, non-Hispanic whites during the 2006–2014 timeframe: the higher the local unemployment rate, the higher the probability of self-employment for these groups. The particularly strong finding among mainland-born Puerto Ricans regarding being pushed into self-employment (in lieu of unemployment) is also consistent with the findings from the SBO reported earlier in the chapter: businesses owned by Puerto Ricans tended to be smaller than those owned by non-Hispanic whites based on a variety of metrics, particularly in 2012.

At the same time, local unemployment rates did not have a statistically significant effect on the self-employment tendencies among island-born Puerto Ricans on average. As was the case for the enclave effects mentioned earlier, it would appear from these results that socioeconomic and demographic factors differently influenced island-born and mainland-born Puerto Ricans with respect to their self-employment choices. One explanation for the seemingly nonexisting relationship between unemployment rates and the likelihood of being self-employed among island-born Puerto Ricans could pertain to their relatively low rates of labor force participation. Perhaps instead of being pushed into self-employment, members of this group in areas with weak labor markets remained outside of the labor force altogether.

As an additional robustness check, we tested whether the relationship between the local unemployment rate and self-employment tendencies changed for Puerto Ricans between 2006–2010 and 2011–2014. This analysis revealed a stable relationship for both island-born and mainland-born Puerto Ricans: the Great Recession on the mainland did not seem to impact how local labor market conditions affected self-employment choices, at least among Puerto Ricans.

Gender

The literature—both theoretical and empirical—provides insights into gender-related differences in business formation and self-employment. When women face discrimination in the paid-employment sector, some might be pushed into self-employment. According to intersectionality theory, such discrimination might be compounded for women of color. If so, we would expect Puerto Rican women to be disproportionately represented among the self-employed vis-à-vis their non-Hispanic white counterparts. In fact, earlier in this chapter, we reported that the number of businesses owned by Puerto Rican women grew by a substantially greater percentage than those owned by their male counterparts between 2007 and 2012—a time of a weakened mainland labor market. Do other underlying socioeconomic and demographic characteristics explain these tendencies, or did Puerto Rican women have greater self-employment tendencies than their non-Hispanic white counterparts?

Our empirical results, from 2006–2014, for the likelihood of being self-employed support the latter. Table 8.3 shows that while women had lower self-employment tendencies than men on average, the gender-related self-employment gap was weaker among both island-born and mainland-born Puerto Ricans than for non-Hispanic whites. This means that in a relative sense, Puerto Rican women were more likely than their non-Hispanic white counterparts to be self-employed. It could suggest the presence of stronger push factors than pull factors among Puerto Rican female business owners than among non-Hispanic whites, thus dampening their potential impact. At the same time, the literature shows that in many cases women pursue self-employment for household production whereas men tend to pursue self-employment as a vehicle for higher earnings (e.g., Hundley 2000; Boden 1996; Carr 1996), such that self-employment provides women the benefit of a more flexible work environment irrespective of political sway.

Human Capital

The conceptual relationship between human capital and self-employment choice is ambiguous following relevant literature on that topic (Dávila and Mora 2013).[4] Following this logic, on the one hand, it can be argued that education and other forms of human capital might make self-employment more attractive than paid employment, as this investment may lower credit access barriers, enhance the managerial ability, and increase awareness about available entrepreneurial opportunities. On the other hand, higher levels of human capital increase a worker's labor market value, leading to more job opportunities for the educated.

According to Table 8.3, higher levels of schooling and age (serving as a proxy for experience) enhance the likelihood of being self-employed for island-born and mainland-born Puerto Ricans, albeit age does so at a diminishing rate. Moreover, the results are not statistically different from those found for non-Hispanic whites. These findings suggest that the self-employment sector attracts relatively skilled workers.[5]

One difference worth noting between Puerto Ricans and non-Hispanic whites is the role of English-language fluency. English-language fluency enhanced the likelihood of being self-employed among mainland-born Puerto Ricans during our timeframe of study, further supporting the results for the other human capital variables. However, it did not play a significant role when accounting for other observable characteristics, among island-born Puerto Ricans. Dávila and Mora (2013) reported a significant decline in the role of English-language fluency as a predictor of Hispanic entrepreneurship during the first decade of the 2000s. This finding can be suggestive of the waning importance of English proficiency, as additional push factors among Hispanics overall were at work as the Great Recession got underway on the mainland. The results in Table 8.3 with respect to English fluency fit with the conceptualization of greater push factors among island-born Puerto Ricans than for their mainland-born counterparts. They are also consistent with the case where the growing numbers of Puerto Ricans (and of Hispanics in general) on the mainland created additional business opportunities for native Spanish speakers.

FEDERAL ELECTIONS AND PUERTO RICANS ON THE MAINLAND

In addition to shaping the business landscape, as noted earlier in this chapter, the rapidly growing Puerto Rican population on the mainland could result in an increasing role in shaping the political landscape. We have noted throughout this volume that Puerto Rican population growth has been particularly large in Florida. Population changes can inform the political discourse including through elections. Even though Trump was elected as U.S. president on November 8, 2016, the preliminary analyses of the 2016 presidential election results and exit polls (just underway as this book was nearing completion) indicate that Puerto Ricans overwhelmingly voted for the Democratic candidate, Hillary Clinton.

Florida voted Republican, but the number of Puerto Ricans in Florida is expected to soon surpass the number of Cubans (who as a group, tend to vote Republican) in the state. A recent Pew Research Center report by Jens Manuel Krogstad and Antonio Flores (2016) indicated that Puerto Ricans represented the second largest group of Hispanic eligible voters in Florida (28%), after Cubans (31%). While this report only disaggregated between "Non-Cubans" and "Cubans" with respect to votes cast, it reported that 71 percent of non-Cubans voted for Clinton, compared to 41 percent of Cubans. Pennsylvania also went Republican, but according to Israel Colón (2016), 92 percent of the Hispanic vote in Philadelphia went to Clinton, compared to 7 percent for Trump; more than two-thirds of Hispanics in Philadelphia are Puerto Rican. Mirroring such patterns, Angelo Falcón (2016) estimated that Hispanics, particularly Puerto Ricans and Dominicans, overwhelmingly voted for Clinton in New York City (albeit, New York was not a swing state).

Arguably, the importance of states such as Florida and Pennsylvania in the political landscape will continue in the federal elections of 2020 and beyond. It remains to be seen if the growing presence of Puerto Ricans on the mainland will shift the outcomes of these elections. Between the 2004 and 2012 Presidential elections, unpublished data from Mark López (2016), Director of Hispanic Research at the Pew Research Center, indicate that the number of Puerto Rican eligible voters (U.S. citizens aged eighteen years and above) on the mainland increased by 41.0 percent (from 2.2 million to 3.1 million individuals). Moreover, as Table 8.4 shows, the participation rate among Puerto Rican eligible voters rose from 47.0 percent in 2004 to 49.7 percent in 2008, and to 52.8 percent by 2012. Over this timeframe, this 5.8 percentage-point increase exceeded the increase among Cubans (3.2 percentage points, to

Table 8.4   Presidential Election Voter Turnout Rates of Stateside Puerto Ricans and Other Groups: 2004–2012

Characteristics	2004	2008	2012	Change: 2004–2012
All Puerto Ricans	47.0%	49.7%	52.8%	5.8 p.p.
Island-Born Puerto Ricans	46.0%	46.9%	52.4%	6.4 p.p.
Mainland-Born Puerto Ricans	48.0%	52.2%	53.4%	5.4 p.p.
Mexican Americans	43.0%	45.1%	42.2%	−0.8 p.p.
Cubans	64.0%	69.4%	67.2%	3.2 p.p.
Non-Hispanic Whites	67.2%	66.1%	64.1%	−3.1 p.p.

Source: López and Gonzalez-Barrera (2013), and for the breakdown of island-born and mainland-born Puerto Ricans, López (2016).

Notes: The "p.p." stands for percentage points. Voter turnout is measured by the share of the voting eligible population (persons aged eighteen and above who are U.S. citizens) who self-reported voting in the corresponding presidential election. According to López (2016), the total number of Puerto Rican eligible voters on the mainland was 2.2 million in 2004, 2.8 million in 2008, and 3.1 million; island-born Puerto Ricans among Puerto Rican eligible voters on the mainland represented 47.0 percent, 44.0 percent, and 41 percent of all Puerto Rican eligible voters on the mainland in 2004, 2008, and 2012.

67.2%), while the voter turnout rates fell for Mexican Americans (to 42.2%) and non-Hispanic whites (to 64.1%).

As a result, the increase in the number of estimated votes cast by Puerto Ricans in federal elections outstripped their growth in the number of eligible voters (58.3% vs. 41.0%) between 2004 and 2012. While small in absolute size, given the U.S. electoral college system, and given the large growth in the number of Puerto Ricans in key swing states, this is a considerable shift in such a short period of time, especially as their increased voter turnout went against the national trend (at least between 2004 and 2012).

This increase was not solely the result of an increase in the number of island-born Puerto Ricans on the mainland (as the island hosts a relatively high voter propensity), but also in an increase in voter turnout of mainland-born Puerto Ricans. As seen in Table 8.4, this latter group increased its voter turnout rate in Presidential elections by 5.4 percentage points from 2004 to 2012 (up to 53.4%). It rose by an even larger margin (6.4 percentage points) among island-born Puerto Ricans on the mainland (to 52.4%). That said, the voter participation of the stateside Puerto Rican population was still well below that of non-Hispanic whites and Cubans.

Table 8.4 further indicates that in 2012, little difference existed in the voter turnout rates between mainland-born and island-born Puerto Ricans in the federal elections. This implies that whether the driving force behind Puerto Rican population growth is continued net migration from the island or relatively high fertility rates of mainland-born Puerto Ricans, the political impact of Puerto Ricans may shape the political landscape in particular congressional districts and federal elections, especially if their voter participation rates rise. At the same time, in light of the socioeconomic disparities Puerto Ricans have encountered across states discussed in earlier chapters, geographic disparities likely existed (and will continue to exist) with respect to their engagement in the political process, and thus, their local and regional impacts.

Given the recent population trends that we have reported in this book, trends that resulted in significantly more Puerto Ricans in Florida, an important consideration is whether Puerto Ricans will narrow the voter-turnout-rate gap with Cubans in the 2020 presidential election. If so, the political clout of Puerto Ricans in elections in key areas in Florida is likely to rise. We already know that in the 2016 federal elections, the first Puerto Rican to represent Florida in Congress, Darren Soto, was elected.

However, future focus on Puerto Rican voter registration along with their turnout rates is warranted. Analyzing data from the recent federal elections will provide more insight into Puerto Ricans' political impact throughout the country, especially in some of the key battleground states. The extent of this impact will result from their increasing population growth combined with their participation in voting booths throughout the country.

SUMMARY AND CONCLUDING REMARKS

While the effects of the Puerto Rican diaspora on their political influence and access to resources will take years, if not decades, to determine, we have documented that Puerto Ricans, especially women, represented one of the fastest growing groups of business owners on the U.S. mainland in recent years. On the one hand, we would expect that their political clout has been increasing as well, in light of the work of Bates (2011) and others. On the other hand, much of the growth in Puerto Rican–owned businesses was driven by the large population growth of Puerto Ricans on the mainland rather than an intensification of entrepreneurial tendencies among this population. We also detected evidence of push factors into business formation during this time, especially among Puerto Rican women. As such, their increased presence in the business sector might not have translated into an equal gain in political impact. At the same time, it should be highlighted that Puerto Rican firm owners hired more than 122,300 workers in 2012 alone, representing a 26.0 percent increase in employment since 2007—a pattern not repeated in the overall labor market.

We also analyzed socioeconomic and demographic characteristics related to the likelihood of being self-employed. Our findings indicate that ethnic enclaves did not foster entrepreneurship among Puerto Ricans (at least between 2006 and 2014) as they have traditionally been reported for other Hispanic populations. In fact, we found the contrary for mainland-born Puerto Ricans, who had a significantly lower incidence of self-employment in Puerto Rican enclaves. One explanation is that many regions with large stateside concentrations of Puerto Ricans tend to be traditional settlement areas that have been characterized by high rates of impoverishment and limited access to capital. As the Puerto Rican population continues to grow in nontraditional areas, future studies should examine whether these new Puerto Rican enclaves begin to foment business formation opportunities.

Finally, we reported in this chapter that the numbers of Puerto Rican eligible voters increased between the 2004 and 2012 U.S. Presidential elections, as did their voting participation rates. While we do not know at the time of this writing the full impact this ethnic group had on shaping the results in the 2016 federal, state, and local elections, we argue that Puerto Rican voters in swing states like Florida and Pennsylvania will continue to be targeted by the major political parties as they become increasingly influential in these states. The political influence of Puerto Ricans will also likely become that much more important if their business power becomes more aligned with that of other Hispanic populations on the U.S. mainland, including in nontraditional settlement areas.

NOTES

1. Note that the sales and payroll figures reported in this table are expressed in nominal values, not real values.

2. The self-employment "push-pull" framework is discussed in more detail later in this chapter.

3. Also, as Dávila and Mora (2013) noted, the type of self-employment occupation matters: self-employed Hispanics in restaurant businesses might be better off in non-enclave settings where they do not have to compete with other Hispanic entrepreneurs compared to Hispanic plumbers in enclaves who can better relate to their community members than in nonenclave settings. To account for such possibilities, we control for occupations in our empirical analysis; these results can be obtained from the authors.

4. In Dávila and Mora's *empirical* work (e.g., 2013), they uncovered a positive relationship.

5. An alternative interpretation is that the relatively weak mainland economy during the period of our analysis led more skilled workers to move into the self-employment sector in light of tighter labor markets in the paid-employment sector, whereas less skilled workers dropped out of the labor force. Yet when testing whether the relationship between human capital and the likelihood of being self-employed changed from 2006–2010 to 2011–2014, we found that the role of human capital remained steady, thus failing to provide support for this alternative explanation.

Chapter 9

The Continued Evolution of Politics and Socioeconomic Processes and Policies

Puerto Rico in the Twenty-First Century

For 525 years, Puerto Rico has been under the economic and political dominance of Spain (1493–1898) and the United States (since 1898 as a result of the Spanish American War). Many historical observers, sociologists, economists, and political scientists, among others, concur that the island's subordinate dependence on these countries, and lack of sovereignty have had significant and long-lasting impacts and consequences for Puerto Rico's cultural, demographic, social, political, legal, and economic development. Throughout most of its history during the past half millennium, Puerto Rico has often been characterized as a colony with limited control over its destiny.[1] Despite having its first democratic elections in 1948 and its 1952 Constitution designating the Commonwealth of Puerto Rico (or Estado Libre Asociado (Free Associated State) as it is known on the island), Puerto Rico's economy and many political and legal processes remain under the direct jurisdiction and control of the United States.[2]

A sobering reminder of Puerto Rico's dependency status on the United States and its lack of sovereignty during La Crisis Boricua was the island's inability to enact its own bankruptcy law (due to its status as a territory) while also being ineligible to file for federal bankruptcy protection.[3] Because the federal bankruptcy code authorizes Congress, not territories, to enact bankruptcy legislation, Congress created the nonelected Oversight Board (which was not accountable to the island's residents) in June 2016 through the passage of Puerto Rico Oversight, Management and Economic Stability Act (PROMESA) (discussed in chapter 3) designed to restructure the island's debt.[4]

There is no doubt that during Puerto Rico's history, including as a U.S. territory, the island and its inhabitants experienced remarkable economic development at different times. However, as we have documented throughout this book, the island's economic progress has gone through periods of severe disruptions, with significant downturns and extensive deteriorations of Puerto Rico's economy that have had ramifications for multiple indicators of economic development (e.g., low labor force participation, high unemployment rates, and high poverty rates, among others). As a direct result of these economic crises, massive migration from the island to the mainland has ensued, including in the 1940s–1960s (a period known as the Great Migration), as Puerto Ricans sought employment opportunities and higher incomes on the mainland—essentially pursuing what for many has been the ever-elusive American dream.

Even in its period of most rapid economic development, Puerto Rico experienced significant setbacks resulting from multiple severe economic crises. For example, as discussed in chapter 2, Puerto Rico's most aggressive economic development initiative, *Operación Manos a la Obra* (Operation Bootstrap), could not create as many jobs in manufacturing as it lost in agriculture. Ironically, today, Puerto Ricans import about 82 percent of the food they consume. As has been stated by other observers, Puerto Rico currently produces what it does not consume and consumes what is does not produce. Mary Williams Walsh in the *New York Times* (2016) states: "Even America's big development push in the 1950s, Operation Bootstrap, is viewed as suspect. With tax incentives for United States manufacturers, it prompted Puerto Ricans to leave the hinterland by the thousands. As they flocked to San Juan to seek factory jobs, Washington responded with new public housing, paved roads and schools."

PUERTO RICO'S UNCERTAIN FUTURE

La Crisis Boricua (which entered its second decade as the final stages of this book were underway) arguably brought to the forefront the economic and political dependence of Puerto Rico on the United States and consequences for its inhabitants. This crisis was also a manifestation of decades of failed economic policies, mishandling of public funds, and the inability of government officials to effectively and efficiently ensure Puerto Rico's economic development. The long-term impact and outcomes of these policies and strategies resulted in a massive net outmigration of nearly 647,000 people between 2006 and 2016 (equivalent to 16.5 percent of the island's 2006 population—a scale not seen since the Great Migration);[5] exceedingly high levels of unemployment and poverty; a crippling and unsustainable debt with unfunded pensions; the imposition of a sales tax higher than in any of the states; a significant loss in public- and private-sector jobs; a deteriorating infrastructure; and the government's filing for bankruptcy protection in 2017.

The economic prosperity of mainland Puerto Ricans will probably also be hampered in the next decade as the migration trends during La Crisis Boricua have been characterized by less educated individuals leaving the island in search of better employment opportunities on the mainland. However, even among Puerto Rican migrants with higher levels of education, their employment rates remain relatively low (except in Texas), their wages tend to lag behind those of other stateside workers, and their poverty rates tend to be high, especially in the traditional destination states. It is ironic that a quarter of a century ago, Havidán Rodríguez (1992) stated: "The continued deteriorating economic conditions of Puerto Ricans suggest that either policy makers have not taken the problems of Puerto Ricans seriously or that Puerto Ricans have not been targeted or benefitted from the implementation of policies designed to increase employment and alleviate poverty among minorities." While significant progress has been made and many Puerto Ricans have experienced economic mobility, this statement remained true at the writing of this book as it was twenty-five years prior in certain traditional stateside settlement areas.

Except for recent migrants on the mainland, significant socioeconomic differences continued to exist between mainland and island Puerto Ricans during La Crisis Boricua. Island Puerto Ricans had significantly lower labor force participation rates, employment/population ratios, and earnings, and higher unemployment and poverty rates than their mainland counterparts. However, the massive net outmigration from the island served as a safety valve and kept joblessness in Puerto Rico at lower rates than would have been otherwise. Through this major population exodus, the island exported to the mainland a significant proportion of its unemployed. Puerto Rico's low labor force participation rate and its high unemployment and poverty rates have raised significant policy issues that will continue to impact the social and economic mobility of Puerto Ricans. Fiscal policy changes, including the imposition of the island's first sales tax in 2006 and its subsequent increase in 2016 (which resulted in the highest sales tax relative to any U.S. state), plus a decrease in public-sector employment, school closures, and underfunded healthcare systems exacerbated the already weakening and deteriorating socioeconomic conditions on this Caribbean island.

These issues were further compounded by the island's loss in credit ratings on municipal bonds in 2014 and the government's unprecedented $74 billion public debt (and an additional $49 billion in unfunded pension obligations). This fiscal deterioration resulted in a series of defaults on debt payments starting in August 2015, just weeks after then-governor Garcia Padilla described the debt ($72 billion at the time) as a "death spiral" and "not payable." Puerto Ricans have essentially been pushed out of Puerto Rico's rapidly deteriorating economy to the U.S. mainland. As noted in chapter 4, work-related issues (i.e., moving because of a job or seeking a job on the mainland) were the primary reasons why two-thirds of all migrants between the ages of twenty-five and sixty-four left the Island of Enchantment to relocate to the mainland.

The Puerto Rican migration has thus become a diaspora of Puerto Ricans distributed throughout the mainland, but the migration into major settlement areas was not skill neutral. Puerto Ricans with higher levels of education migrated to nontraditional areas, such as Florida (an "older new" destination area) and Texas, whereas those with lower schooling levels tended to move into traditional settlement areas, including New York, Massachusetts, and Pennsylvania. We show in this book that significant demographic and socioeconomic differences existed in terms of education, poverty, labor force status, and income, among other characteristics, between the island and mainland as well as across the major states where Puerto Ricans reside. Arguably, the upward socioeconomic mobility of stateside Puerto Ricans over time will vary widely depending on where they live. It is important, then, that researchers, policymakers, and social workers continue to focus their attention on the Puerto Rican diaspora and dispersion throughout the mainland to determine how differences in their demographic and socioeconomic characteristics not only impact their transition into their new locations, but their intergenerational socioeconomic mobility as well (particularly in the traditional settlement areas where they have been most vulnerable).

We note that La Crisis Boricua will—in all likelihood—continue to be exacerbated by massive outmigration for years to come, rapidly leading to an increasingly elderly population resulting from the demographic transition on the island. These changing demographics, along with a population characterized by long-term chronic illnesses (as with high-income nations), such as cardiovascular diseases, cancer, and diabetes, among others (Figueroa-Rodríguez 2013) will presumably challenge the healthcare system's already stretched capacity, especially in light of the outmigration of physicians and nurses (noted in chapter 3) and the government's financial crisis.

As discussed by Joanisabel González in *El Nuevo Día* (Puerto Rico's major or primary newspaper) on August 11, 2016, a reduction in the island's population translates into a reduction in its workers and economic activity, thus reducing tax revenue collected by the government, which will result in reduced investments in public services provided to the island's population. As we highlighted in chapter 2, Puerto Rico's demographic transition to low levels of fertility and mortality as well as the recent massive outmigration resulted in a rapidly aging population, and for the first time in its recorded history, negative population growth. We expect María to expedite such shifts.

Even though less educated individuals comprised the majority of the outmigration flow during the first decade of La Crisis Boricua, the healthcare issues facing an aging population were aggravated by a significant outmigration of physicians, nurses, and other healthcare professionals (equivalent to one doctor migrating per day in recent years), as noted in chapter 3. Already 92 percent of the island's *muncipios* have been categorized by the U.S. Health Resources and Services Administration as Medically Underserved Areas (Levis 2016). Unfortunately, independent of María, the population's health-care system will continue to deteriorate in the face of declining income and state funding along with, as *The New York Times* described in 2016 as "the graying of Puerto Rico's doctors." Moreover, while nearly two-thirds of the island's residents were covered by Medicaid or Medicare, the caps on these programs to Puerto Rico were at levels far below those which states received, and Medicare payments had been reduced in recent years (Allen 2016). As noted in the April 2017 *Harvard Law Review*, "In the wake of the island's financial crisis, its doctors have left in droves. This exodus has been blamed in part on low Medicare and Medicaid payments" (*Harvard Law Review* 2017a).

Puerto Rico not only confronts an economic crisis, but a humanitarian crisis as well. As this book went to press before Hurricane María struck, Puerto Rico faced a reportedly unpayable debt of $74 billion and $49 billion in pensions. Numerous reports in the popular press compared the island's economic crisis to the crisis that impacted Greece. Juan Dávila (2016) in The *Huffington Post* referred to Puerto Rico's debt as an "Odious Debt, in which citizens of the island have not benefitted from the borrowed money." As a direct result of this crisis, the Puerto Rican government encountered its inability to pay its debts, fulfill its pension obligations, and provide adequate health care, education, and other public services to the island's population. During La Crisis Boricua, the island's residents were confronted with regressive income taxes, increases in the cost of living, a lack of adequate jobs, falling housing prices, and the potential for reduced public pensions, which culminated in the mass exodus from the island to the mainland—the largest migration stream from Puerto Rico to the mainland since just after World War II in absolute terms, and the second largest in relative terms (which will only be magnified by Hurricane María).

PROMESA: THE FEDERAL GOVERNMENT'S RESPONSE TO LA CRISIS BORICUA

The U.S. government intervened to provide "assistance" with Puerto Rico's the then-decade's long crisis by preventing bondholders from suing Puerto Rico through PROMESA in June 2016, passed by both the U.S. Senate (with a vote of 68 to 30) and Congress (297 to 127), and signed into law by the then-president Obama on June 28, 2016.[6] Although this measure was led by a Republican Congress, it required strong bipartisan support, and the number of Democrats voting for this bill exceeded the number of Republicans voting for the same.

Also, as discussed in chapter 3, PROMESA established a Financial Oversight and Management Board (known in Puerto Rico as *Junta de Supervisión Fiscal*), which was essentially granted unilateral power over Puerto Rico's finances and the island's economic future. It is important to highlight that this was not a bailout, as the U.S. Congress refused a bailout for Puerto Rico, but created the process through PROMESA to restructure its debt while not allowing the bondholders to sue the Puerto Rican government to obtain payment. Ironically, in May 2017 the Oversight Board essentially agreed with the previous governor's assessment two years prior that the debt was not payable, and it concluded that "From current revenues, the Commonwealth and its instrumentalities cannot satisfy their collective $74 billion debt burden and $49 billion pension burden and pay their operating expenses." While its territory status prevented it from being eligible for federal protection under Chapter 9 of the Bankruptcy Code, following advice from the Board, on May 9, 2017 Puerto Rico filed for a form of bankruptcy protection under Title III of PROMESA, which was modeled after Chapter 9 (Law360 2017).

Until the May 2017 report, one of the most critical issues or criticisms regarding PROMESA was that the Oversight Board did not focus on addressing Puerto Rico's chronic socioeconomic issues, such as high unemployment rates, low labor force participation rates, a lack of robust employment opportunities, and widespread poverty; and it essentially had no obligation to the Puerto Rican people. Such concerns were affirmed earlier in 2017 when the Oversight Board ordered Puerto Rico to cut its public pension system by 10 percent and furlough tens of thousands of government workers, among other actions, if the government could not find alternatives to increase tax revenue and reduce spending (*Associated Press* 2017). A 10 percent cut in pensions would place additional financial burdens on retired workers (many of whom rely solely on their fixed pensions) who were already impacted by the relatively high Impuesto a las Ventas y Uso (IVU), a rising cost of living, a reduction of public services, and other burdens.

The Oversight Board's ten-year fiscal plan also called "for everyone on the U.S. territory of 3.4 million people to make sacrifices" (*Associated Press* 2017), which would be on top of those made during the previous eleven years and implicitly assumed the absence of devastating events, such as natural disasters. Moreover, economists estimated that such austerity measures by themselves (designed to address fiscal issues) would not solve Puerto Rico's economic crisis or promote economic development, and in fact, could lead to a further contraction of Puerto Rico's economy by an additional 4 percent (*Associated Press* 2017). Indeed, in a February 27, 2017 letter to the Editor of the *New York Times,* Joseph Stiglitz stated that the Oversight Board predicted its own proposals would "turn the island's recession into a depression, of a magnitude seldom seen around the world—a decline of 16.2 percent of gross national product in the next fiscal year, comparable to the experience of countries in civil wars."

PROMESA Minimum Wage Provisions

One of the most controversial items in PROMESA was the Board's power to allow Puerto Rico to reduce its minimum wage to $4.25 for island Puerto Ricans aged twenty-five and below. Concerns existed regarding potential adverse economic impacts this policy may have on this population group if implemented. While provisions were established to avoid potential abuse, concerns remained that industries/companies would establish mechanisms to lay off (or not replace) higher paid adults, thus further aggravating the economic crisis in Puerto Rico, at a time when nearly half (over 46%) of the population resided below the poverty line. Another concern was that Puerto Ricans on the island, although U.S. citizens, would be treated differently and unfairly relative to U.S. citizens on the mainland (which as these critics noted, was already the case with respect to other policies and laws, such as the lower Medicare and Medicaid caps mentioned above).

That said, there are four conceptual points to be made regarding this controversial proposed minimum wage differential between younger and older workers recommended by PROMESA. First, the decision of young adults to stay in Puerto Rico or migrate to the mainland might be altered; according to a human capital framework, the young would be more likely to move to the mainland given its higher wages. Consider that, as a consequence, this policy prescription would have the effect of magnifying the selective migratory patterns we discussed in chapter 4, where we note that migration from the island had been skewed during La Crisis Boricua toward the young and unskilled workers.

Second, the aforementioned incentive for Puerto Rican employers to substitute older workers for younger workers could result in lower labor costs that would conceptually lead to more profits, attracting other businesses into the sector. This dynamic could increase production, making the net demand change for older workers ambiguous. Third, the extent to which there is an increase in the employment of younger workers due to the decrease in the minimum wage for the young, those workers (presumably older workers) who complement younger workers (say, for example, their supervisors) would be more in demand. Fourth, a lower minimum wage reduces the opportunity cost of going to school. As such, young adults on the island may be more enticed to continue their education. The longer-term impact would depend on whether jobs would be available to support a more educated workforce (which already has relatively high schooling levels), or if this would further dampen their wages.

We should note that if this policy were to increase jobs in Puerto Rico by reducing labor costs in the island, the increased demand for labor in Puerto Rico could come not only from current employers but also from mainland (or international) employers who may be attracted to the island.

Reponses to PROMESA

Concerns with PROMESA were publicly discussed by U.S. Senators and Congressmen, Puerto Rico's elected officials, the mass media, as well as then-President Obama and the 2016 Democratic nominees for U.S. president, Hillary Rodham Clinton and Bernie Sanders. At the same time, it is noteworthy that a survey conducted by *El Nuevo Día* in October 2016 showed that 69 percent of island Puerto Ricans favored the creation of the Board, up from 46 percent from a similar poll in June 2016. Some viewed PROMESA as the only mechanism available at the time to avoid a humanitarian crisis. It was also argued that Puerto Rico's government had been unwilling or unable to deal with and resolve Puerto Rico's financial crisis, and that it actually played a critical role in its generation. That is, the economic and political decisions by island politicians contributed to and exacerbated the growing economic crisis, which had been in the making for decades, resulting in the creation of the "perfect storm." Under these circumstances, as noted in chapter 3, some said that PROMESA was not only inevitable and necessary, but the only viable alternative at the time it was implemented.

However, as we also mentioned in chapter 3, others argued at the time that a humanitarian crisis already existed and that the law would do little, if anything, to resolve it and address other critical socioeconomic issues directly affecting the island's residents, such as widespread unemployment and poverty as well as the deteriorating healthcare infrastructure and the delivery of other public services. Also, some critics argued that the background of the Oversight Board members reflected extensive experience in the financial sector, but not in economic reform (e.g., Furth 2016). Moreover, others have interpreted PROMESA as an indication that the island's status is essentially colonial in nature rather than a self-governing territory (e.g., see notes 1, 2, and 4 in this chapter).

The deliberations leading up to PROMESA and the expected outcomes may have had a significant impact on Puerto Rico's general election (beyond La Crisis Boricua itself), which took place on November 8, 2016. The gubernatorial elections resulted in the election of a new governor, Ricardo Rosselló, representing the Partido Nuevo Progresista (PNP, which favors statehood for Puerto Rico); the outgoing governor represented the Partido Popular Democrático (PPD, the pro-Commonwealth party).

Thus, the change in governors with contrasting political ideologies and political platforms for Puerto Rico will likely has significant implications for the island's economic development and its intersections with PROMESA and the Oversight Board. Initial insight into the work between the new governor and the Board came when Puerto Rico filed for bankruptcy protection under Title III of PROMESA in May 2017, following the Board's recommendation.

Moreover, on June 11, 2017, 97 percent of those who participated in a nonbinding statehood referendum endorsed Puerto Rico becoming the fifty-first state. However, three of Puerto Rico's political parties had called for a boycott of the referendum, which allegedly led to a low voter turnout (23%), and as reported in a plethora of news reports (e.g., Coto 2017b), cast doubt on the legitimacy of the vote. These events were unfolding as we finalized the writing of this book, such that it was too early to know the details and ramifications of these actions for the island's short- and long-term socioeconomic, fiscal, and humanitarian directions. This was only months before María.

A GLIMPSE INTO PUERTO RICO'S FUTURE UNDER THE TRUMP ADMINISTRATION

It is imperative that we, albeit briefly, discuss the potential impact of the 2016 U.S. presidential elections on Puerto Ricans generally, and the socioeconomic and political implications for the island of Puerto Rico. While Puerto Rico failed to become a sovereign nation and for 120 years, has been under U.S. jurisdiction, it was not clear that the election of President Donald J. Trump would immediately have much (if any) impact on the economic stability or growth of the Puerto Rican economy or on the socioeconomic well-being of island residents. Unfortunately, if historical trends and previous experience are indicators of future behavior, it is quite possible that Puerto Rico's political and economic future will continue to be lost in the halls of the U.S. Congress and Senate, with little or no attention being provided by the Trump Administration. The lack of political action or intervention on Puerto Rico's behalf will probably result in continued political isolation and economic deterioration of the island, and additional exodus of Puerto Rican migrants to the mainland. That said, the filing for bankruptcy protection in May 2017 along with devastating impacts of María in September 2017 might spur Congress into action sooner than expected.

In what can only be described as a hotly contested and aggressive presidential campaign, national polling pundits, the mass media, and other so-called political experts failed in their attempts to predict who would be the forty-fifth president of the United States. The outcome was unexpected for both presidential candidates, their campaign teams, the nation, and the world. This election further resulted in a Republican-controlled House, Senate, and Presidency, thus yielding what seemed at the time immense executive power to the newly elected federal government. The outcomes of the 2016 U.S.

Presidential elections left both parties and an entire nation scrambling, trying to answer many questions, including *Why? How come? What now?* These debates will keep current and future politicians fully occupied on issues, challenges, and opportunities of national priority, which may to a large extent exclude Puerto Rico.

At the time of this writing, we cannot determine the impact of the new Trump administration on La Crisis Boricua, but we offer the following. If President Trump follows his campaign promises, Puerto Rico will not be on his economic or political radar for years to come, barring a major natural or man-made disaster directly affecting the island.[7] While a number of his initiatives, if implemented, would directly or indirectly impact Puerto Rico, they were not focused on the island. One important unanswered question as this book went to press was what would happen to Puerto Rico after filing for bankruptcy protection. As a presidential candidate, Trump stated in May 2016 that Puerto Rico "had far far too much debt" and he "wouldn't bail them out" (Long 2016).

Moreover, even under the most optimistic conditions, La Crisis Boricua will probably continue to impact mainland labor markets for years to come through continued massive outmigration of Puerto Ricans as well as through their fertility rates in key (now) Republican states such as Florida and Pennsylvania. If nothing else, the Trump administration has vowed to create a positive labor climate for the "forgotten men" (mostly non-Hispanic white), including those who live in states receiving many incoming Puerto Rican migrants. From a practical perspective, the points made in this chapter regarding the attention the new administration might put on Puerto Rico *vis-à-vis* other issues is valid, but so is the possibility that continued Puerto Rican net migration and their relatively high fertility rates on the mainland will impact future elections as we discussed in chapter 8.

Related to these observations, it is also important to highlight that Puerto Rico's economic future may be inextricably linked to its sister country, Cuba. As highlighted by James Gibney (2016) in *Bloomberg*, future capital investments in that country, its opening of borders, and United States-Cuba relationships may indeed lead to economic development and growth in Cuba, especially in the area of tourism, at the expense of Puerto Rico. President Obama's executive actions to foster communication and collaborations between the United States and Cuba could play a critical role in this process. At the same time, the Center for a New Economy (2016) indicates that Puerto Rico may benefit from expanded United States-Cuba relations given Puerto Rico's geographic location, its bilingual skilled workforce, and knowledge of U.S. legal, financial, and regulatory requirements and systems.

With the election of a Republican House, Senate, and President in 2016, these relationships may soon take a turn for the worse, especially if government officials yield to a strong U.S.- Cuban, Republican and wealthy population, which tends to favor the cessation of United States-Cuba relationships. For example, in his campaign trail, now Vice President Mike Pence, indicated that "When Donald Trump and I take to the White House, we will reverse Barack Obama's executive orders on Cuba" (Weyl 2016). Again, what will happen in this context may take years to unfold, but either way, Puerto Rico will probably be impacted by the decisions made by President Trump and Congress as it relates to United States-Cuba relationships.

MOVING FORWARD

In light of the sheer and unrelenting magnitude of La Crisis Boricua, and the fact that the seeds were sown decades earlier, there is no easy solution or a "silver bullet" that will resolve the crisis anytime soon. As we finalized this book, the island faced little to no options to alleviate the current socioeconomic conditions without additional federal intervention. Civil unrest through massive protests and strikes (including the closure of the University of Puerto Rico campuses throughout the island, for an indefinite period of time, led by students in May 2017) was the order of the day as the economy and the standard of living continued to deteriorate. The meaning of the controversial statehood referendum was also under debate.

That said, social scientists, elected officials, civic and community leaders, and others have begun identifying potential (and practical) policy solutions and initiatives to address the socioeconomic and humanitarian aspects, and take initial steps to rebuild the island's social, political, and capital infrastructure. For example, the Center for Puerto Rican Studies at Hunter College under the directorship of Edwin Meléndez hosted two national Diaspora Summits (on April 22–23, 2016, and May 12–13, 2017) to raise awareness among stateside Puerto Ricans, and discuss policy issues and community responses to address Puerto Rico's socioeconomic and humanitarian crisis (Center for Puerto Rican Studies 2016, 2017).

Groups such as the National Hispanic Leadership Agenda (NHLA, a coalition of forty Hispanic/Latino civil rights organizations, which created a Puerto Rican working group), the Center for a New Economy (CNE, an independent, nonpartisan think-tank that advocates for the development of a new economy for Puerto Rico), the National Puerto Rican Agenda (NPRA, formed in 2016 as a nonpartisan alliance of 150 elected officials, community leaders, and activists on the mainland), VAMOS4PR Network (a stateside extension of Puerto Rico's VAMOS Network, which includes labor, community, cultural and human rights organizations and individuals), and others have been involved in mobilizing stakeholders and providing policy recommendations.

Stimulating Employment

Finding solutions to increase employment opportunities and slow the Puerto Rican exodus is imperative. Reducing production and shipping costs through targeted deregulation efforts (which should increase Puerto Rico's competitiveness in attracting and retaining business and stimulating business formation) is a place to start. For example, as the NHLA (2016), CNE (2016), the Federal Reserve Bank of New York (2012), and others have discussed, exempting Puerto Rico from the Merchant Marine Act of 1920 (also known as the 1920 Jones Act, which as noted in chapter 3, requires the use of U.S. ships to transport goods between mainland ports and Puerto Rico), should reduce shipping costs, and hence the prices of imports and exports to and from the island. The CNE (2016) further points out that this exemption would help Puerto Rico become a major maritime transportation and logistical hub in the region.

Restructuring and/or reorganizing the island's monopolies on utilities (e.g., PREPA) and as suggested by the CNE (2016) and the Federal Reserve Bank of New York (2014, 2012), increasing their management efficiency, should also reduce the costs of these services. Moreover, reducing barriers to business formation (such as simplifying licensing and permits, as recommended by the CNE [2016] and the Federal Reserve Bank of New York [2014, 2012]) should further stimulate growth. The lower production, shipping, and start-up costs resulting from such initiatives are expected to foster a more attractive business environment (leading to more employment) in Puerto Rico.

In addition, successfully implementing these recommendations should help alleviate financial burdens on households, as they would pay lower prices for goods and services; as such, they could use such savings to purchase other goods and services, increasing aggregate demand (and likely employment opportunities) on the island. Moreover, stimulating production and employment would conceivably alleviate some of Puerto Rico's current budgetary problems (e.g., Mora, Dávila, and Rodríguez 2017; Kaske and Faries 2015; Alaniz 2014; *The Economist* 2013), as higher employment rates should generate additional income tax revenue collected by the island's government.

Related to taxes, as we (and others) have noted (e.g., Mora, Dávila, and Rodríguez 2017; Meléndez 2016; CNE 2016; Enchautegui 2014; Enchautegui and Freeman 2006), the current income tax structure on the island, including the IVU (which serves as a regressive income tax) and the absence of the Earned Income Tax Credit (EITC) and Child Tax Credit (CTC), which do not apply to Puerto Rico, has placed disproportionate tax burdens on some of the most vulnerable residents of the island; the lack of the EITC is also likely disproportionately affecting work incentives. As such, implementing the EITC and other work-credit policies (such as those discussed by the CNE

(2016), Meléndez (2016), the NPRA (2016), Enchautegui (2014), and others) should increase labor force participation. But for these to translate into reducing the island's high rates of unemployment and impoverishment, such policies would need to be designed in conjunction with stimulating employment opportunities.

Additional policy recommendations pertaining to health care in particular include the federal government eliminating Medicare and Medicaid disparities between Puerto Rico and the mainland (NHLA 2016). Such changes may ease the financial burden on island residents, help offset the expected financial shortfall of the Affordable Care Act, and serve to retain physicians and other healthcare professionals.

As proposed by VAMOS4PR Network (2016) and the Federal Reserve Bank of New York (2014), another way to create more jobs would be to capitalize on Puerto Rico's natural competitive advantage through longer-term development initiatives in tourism, renewable energy, agriculture, and even aerospace. Similarly, the CNE (2016) points out that Puerto Rico's bilingual skilled workforce and its access to the legal and financial system of the United States provides it with additional competitive advantages through closer interactions with other Caribbean and Latin American countries, including Cuba. Regarding the latter, the CNE (2016) notes that the ongoing opening of United States-Cuba relations may present particular *opportunities* for Puerto Rican firms, many of which already understand U.S. legal and regulatory requirements beyond the language. Finally, given that the elimination of Section 936 of the Internal Revenue Code in 2006 contributed to the perfect storm that launched La Crisis Boricua (as discussed in chapter 3), the NHLA (2016) has called for the preservation of any remaining federal tax incentives to attract and retain businesses and investments in Puerto Rico.

Debt Restructuring

Many groups, including the NHLA (2016) and VAMOS4PR Network (2016), also called on Congress to extend Chapter 9 bankruptcy protection to Puerto Rico, to place it on par with the states and allow it to restructure its debt without further austerity measures and additional financial burdens on the island's residents. (These calls went out before Puerto Rico filed for bankruptcy protection in May 2017.) On a related point, the NHLA (2016) advocated for the federal government to purchase Puerto Rico's debt and/ or issue bond guarantees. The NHLA's rationale was that the downgrade in Puerto Rico's credit ratings forced the island to borrow at high interest rates, placing additional constraints on its ability to address the economic crisis. Extending bond guarantees to investment companies in Puerto Rico (a mechanism the NHLA noted was already used on the mainland) should also protect Puerto Ricans "who might unknowingly invest in mutual funds that are heavily stocked with public debt bonds that have dropped significantly in value due to Puerto Rico's debt problems" (NHLA 2016). Clearly, Puerto Rico's debt represents the island's most critical and complex economic and political situation, which if not resolved in the near future, will have severe impacts on the island and mainland, and its adverse consequences will reverberate for generations to come.

SUMMARY AND CONCLUDING REMARKS

For decades, federal elected officials, for the most part, sidetracked and ignored the social and economic issues confronted by Puerto Ricans, despite their U.S. citizenship. However, one of primary outcomes of La Crisis Boricua has been the realization of the increasingly critical need for both island and mainland policymakers to promote economic prosperity among Puerto Ricans. Indeed, their socioeconomic outcomes are important not only to the economic progress on the island but also in key geographic areas on the mainland, including in nontraditional settlement areas.

Policy and structural changes should be made that are well beyond the role and responsibilities of PROMESA and its Oversight Board. However, through collective action of the Commonwealth and federal governments, the investment of industries in the economic future of the island, and the collective will and active engagement of island Puerto Ricans, as well as the Puerto Rican diaspora distributed throughout the United States, this ship can be turned around. Such changes will need to be consistent, impactful, and sustainable, to have positive and long-lasting outcomes in alleviating the humanitarian crisis affecting communities and a population of American citizens in one of the wealthiest and most powerful nations in the world.

For this to happen, social scientists, social workers, community activists, government officials, and other policymakers should regularly monitor and analyze the emerging social, economic, and political changes in Puerto Rico. It is also important that we continue to conduct research on the demographic transition in Puerto Rico, migration flows between the island and the mainland, and the Puerto Rican diaspora. Furthermore, it is critical to continue studying the impacts of the changing political and economic landscape on the labor, educational, and healthcare infrastructures on both the island and mainland. While Puerto Ricans have made significant progress and experienced socioeconomic mobility on the U.S. mainland, they still experience relatively low levels of income and high poverty rates, especially when compared to non-Hispanic whites. The future of mainland Puerto Ricans is intertwined with the economic growth and development on the island, but island Puerto

Ricans are also impacted by the socioeconomic mobility of mainland Puerto Ricans.

The collective future of nearly nine million Puerto Ricans on the island and the mainland remains uncertain more than a decade after La Crisis Boricua escalated. As American citizens through birthright for a full century, as this book went to press, many Puerto Ricans have not achieved the American dream nor they do have all the rights, privileges, and outcomes associated with American citizenship but are bound to follow federal laws.[8] However, the Puerto Rican diaspora, on the island and the mainland, has persevered, achieving socioeconomic success and upward mobility and making numerous and important contributions to U.S. society. Puerto Ricans are a resilient population and they continue to rise and succeed in the midst of adversity and economic crises that prevail in their homeland.

Systematically and successfully addressing the issues and challenges tied to the economic and humanitarian crises that prevail in contemporary Puerto Rican society will involve a restructuring of Puerto Rico's debt, economic revitalization, a reinvestment in and restructuring of public and higher education, the transformation of the island's healthcare system, changes to the tax structure, and a major rebuilding of the island's infrastructure. These policy and structural changes, as well as the creation of new and prosperous jobs, are indispensable to grow the Puerto Rican economy and bring to a close the massive exodus of Puerto Ricans from the island to the mainland. If sustained, these initiatives may contribute to a reversal in these migration flows, thus further enhancing the long-term development and growth of the Puerto Rican economy. Puerto Rico has been lauded as the Island of Enchantment (*la Isla del Encanto*). Arguably, many Puerto Ricans on the island and the mainland are still waiting for the socioeconomic opportunities they have earned and need to achieve the American dream.

NOTES

1. Puerto Rico is technically a U.S. territory and was removed from the United Nation's (UN's) list of non-self-governing territories with the 1953 adoption of U.N. General Assembly Resolution 748. However, the U.N. Special Committee on Decolonization has listened to numerous testimonies and drafted resolutions in support of Puerto Rico's self-determination, most recently (at the time this book went to press) on June 20, 2016. Moreover, an April 2017 *Harvard Law Review* (HLR) issue argued that "the decision was ultimately mistaken—the United Nations misjudged the level of internal autonomy enjoyed by Puerto Rico—and that the gap between the label thrust upon the island has only grown, as measured by UN criteria" (*Harvard Law Review* 2017). This HLR section further noted that "Acknowledging the reality of Puerto Rico's current political status would ... open a legitimate path for the

island's decolonization by providing improved access to international legal fora, and may influence the way the United States handles Puerto Rico's public debts and its own international obligations." A recent succinct summary was also provided by Lyle Denniston, the constitution literacy adviser at the National Constitution Center, in 2015: "For much of Puerto Rico's history, Congress treated it very much as if it were a dependent colony, giving it self-governing authority only little by little, but always retaining a veto power over what the territory's government chose to do." Moreover, island residents cannot vote for the U.S. president nor do they have voting representation in Congress.

2. Despite the reference to "free associated state," in the 105th Congress, the House Committee on Resources concluded in a June 12, 1997 report (H. Report 105-131) that "the Commonwealth remains an unincorporated territory and does not have the status of 'free association' with the United States as that status is defined under United States law or international practice." The Commonwealth of Puerto Rico is technically a U.S. territory, which means that Congress has the constitutional authority to revise or revoke the powers of self-government currently exercised in Puerto Rico under Article IV, Section 3, Clause 2 of the U.S. Constitution: "Congress shall have the Power to dispose of and make all needful Rules and Regulations respecting the territory or other Property belonging to the United States." Moreover, the April 2017 *HLR* indicates states that "the U.S. territories remain bound to their essentially colonial status" (*Harvard Law Review* 2017, p. 1624).

3. Another contemporary example included the U.S. Supreme Court's determination on June 9, 2016 in *Puerto Rico versus Sanchez Valle* that the ultimate source of sovereignty in Puerto Rico was the federal government. In contrast, state governments have a level of sovereign choice in terms of public policy, including enacting and enforcing criminal laws (Denniston 2015).

4. Describing the enactment of PROMESA, in 2017 Nobel Laureate Joseph Stiglitz and Martin Guzman stated Puerto Rico was "*de facto* an American colony," and that this action reflected "the standard colonialist view that a colony cannot be trusted to make independent decisions." An echo of this view can be found in the April 2017 *Harvard Law Review*, which stated that "PROMESA is much closer to legislation envisioned within a colonial relationship than a federal one; the Puerto Rican people certainly seem to see it as such" (*Harvard Law Review* 2017a).

5. Recall from chapter 1, this figure includes individuals who did not identify themselves as Puerto Rican, as well as those who moved to other countries in addition to the U.S. mainland.

6. PROMESA was developed by the Committee on Natural Resources, which was chaired by Rob Bishop; see www.congress.gov/bill/114th-congress/house-bill/4900.

7. For example, according to the presidential campaign rhetoric, President Trump's immediate priorities would be filling the vacancy in the U.S. Supreme Court; "immediate rollbacks" of the Deferred Action for Childhood Arrivals and Deferred Action for Parents of Americans and Lawful Permanent Residents; eliminating the Environmental Protection Agency's Clean Power Plan; developing a plan for the deportation of millions of undocumented immigrants with criminal records; a Muslim ban or what the President later called "extreme vetting" and curbing or restricting immigration from "terrorism-prone" regions; securing the United States-Mexico border with the

construction of a border wall (although it now seems the President may "settle for a fence on part of the border" or an "all virtual" wall combined with drone surveillance); plans to renegotiate or retreat from The North American Free Trade Agreement (NAFTA) and withdraw the United States from the Trans-Pacific Partnership (TPP); make significant changes to the North Atlantic Treaty Organization (NATO); focus on deregulation; eliminate the Iran Nuclear Treaty; the eradication of ISIS; and repealing and replacing the Affordable Care Act (also known as Obamacare).

8. A poignant summary illustrating this point can be found in the 1 June 12, 1997, report of the House Committee on Resources (H. Report 105–131), under the "Additional Views" by Representatives George Miller, William Delahunt, Frank Pallone, Jr., Bruce F. Vento, Edward J. Markey, Eni Faleomavaega, Sam Farr, Maurice Hinchey, Donna Christian-Green, and Peter DeFazio:

> Many problems exist in Puerto Rico under today's Commonwealth relationship. Almost 4 million American citizens live on the island without access to all benefits received by those in the several states. Puerto Rico does not have a vote on the floor of the House of Representatives and has no representation at all in the U.S. Senate, but must abide by all laws passed by the Congress unless specifically exempted.

Appendix A

Major Datasets Employed and Details on Selected Variables: American Community Survey

The American Community Survey (ACS), a random nationally representative sample of the U.S. population, has been conducted annually by the U.S. Census Bureau since 2000. We focus on the 2006–2015 surveys contained in the Integrated Public Use Microdata Series (IPUMS, as described later in this appendix). During these years, the American Community Survey (ACS) samples contain approximately 1 percent of the U.S. population. To maintain the national representation of the samples, we employ the sampling weights (constructed by the U.S. Census Bureau) in all analyses. The vast majority of the analyses were conducted before the 2015 data became available (November 2016), which is why many focus on the 2006–2014 period.

Sample Selection Criteria

In our analyses of earnings, we further restrict the sample to civilians between the ages of twenty-five and sixty-four who worked in the twelve months prior to the survey. In the ACS, these earnings refer to the pretax amount the individual earned through wages, salaries, commissions, and tips during the past twelve months. Business income is excluded unless otherwise indicated.

Identification of Puerto Ricans and Other Specific Hispanic Groups

We identify the Hispanic ethnic subgroups using the self-reported Hispanic classifications provided in the Integrated Public Use Microdata Series (IPUMS). We identify immigrants as those individuals who were born outside of the United States and its territories. Consequently, a small share of Puerto Ricans in our sample are immigrants, as some individuals reported Puerto Rican ethnicity but were born outside of the United States, Puerto Rico, or another U.S. territory. As we note in the text, there are other individuals who were born in Puerto Rico but do not identify themselves as Puerto Rican.

Recent Migrants

We identify recent migrants as individuals who moved between Puerto Rico and the U.S. mainland, or in the case of interstate migrants, those who moved across state lines within twelve months of the survey. The sending area is based on where individuals resided twelve months before the survey; we cannot identify individuals who made multiple moves during the twelve months.

INTEGRATED PUBLIC USE MICRODATA SERIES (IPUMS)

The IPUMS, a project of the Minnesota Population Center at the University of Minnesota, collects and disseminates U.S. census data for social and economic research. The current version, provided by Steven Ruggles and his colleagues (2017), includes microdata from the ACS and the Puerto Rican Community Survey (PRCS) (both described in this Appendix); Public Use Microdata Samples (PUMS) from 1980 to 2000 decennial censuses (which also include Puerto Rico); other decennial census data going back to 1850 for the U.S. mainland; and decennial census data for 1910, 1920, and 1970 for Puerto Rico. These data can be downloaded free of charge from the IPUMS website at http://www.ipums.org.

PUERTO RICAN COMMUNITY SURVEY (PRCS)

The PRCS, a random nationally representative sample of the population in Puerto Rico, is part of the American Community Survey described earlier in this Appendix. It has been conducted since 2005. The questionnaire is produced in Spanish and English. We focus on the 2006–2015 surveys contained in the Integrated Public Use Microdata Series (IPUMS, as described earlier in this appendix). During these years, the PRCS samples contain approximately 1 percent of the population in Puerto Rico. To maintain the national representation of the samples, we employ the sampling weights (constructed by the U.S. Census Bureau) in all analyses. The vast majority of the analyses were conducted before the 2015 data became available (November 2016), which is why many focus on the 2006–2014 period. Also see the subsection on the ACS earlier in this appendix for additional details.

SURVEY OF BUSINESS OWNERS (SBO)

The U.S. Census Bureau conducts the SBO as part of its required Economic Census every five years. The Census Bureau combines data from the SBO with data from other surveys, censuses, and administrative records. The publicly available data (published on the Census Bureau's website at http://www.census.gov/econ/sbo/index.html) include summary statistics on the composition of businesses in the United States by demographic and economic characteristics, including ethnicity, race, gender, veteran status, among other traits. The SBO identifies Hispanic-owned firms as those in which more than 50 percent of the owners are Hispanic. We estimate the number of non-Hispanic-white-owned firms by subtracting the firms owned by white Hispanics from those owned by whites.

The 2007 SBO questionnaires were mailed to a random sample of businesses selected from a list of all firms in operation in 2007 with receipts of $1,000 or more. As it moved toward an electronic-data collection methodology, the Census Bureau initiated the corresponding 2012 SBO by implementing a letter-only initial mailing, which consisted of a single-page letter asking respondents to report electronically to the survey. The firms for both surveys were identified using a combination of business tax returns for all companies reporting business activities on certain Internal Revenue Service tax forms (including the 1040 Schedule C "Profit or Loss from Business;" 1065 "U.S. Return of Partnership Income;" any of the 1120 corporation tax forms; 941 "Employer's Quarterly Federal Tax Return;" 944 "Employer's Annual Federal Tax Return") as well as from data collected on other economic census reports. The list excluded the industries of Crop and Animal Production; Scheduled Passenger Air Transportation; Rail Transportation; the Postal Service; Funds, Trusts, and Other Financial Vehicles; Religious, Grantmaking, Civic, Professional, and Similar Organizations; Private Households; and Public Administration. For most firms with paid employees, the Census Bureau also collected employment, payroll, and other information. For the 2012 SBO, respondents could request a Spanish-language version of the forms; in 2007, there was no translation of the report form into Spanish.

TRAVELERS SURVEY

The FY2011 and FY2012 Travelers Survey (TS) data sets (*La Encuesta de Viajeros*, as are known in Spanish), contain a sample of passengers who were aged sixteen and above flying into or out of Luis Muñoz Marín International Airport (San Juan metropolitan area) and the Rafael Hernandez Airport (Aguadilla) as well as cruise ship passengers in fiscal years 2011 (July 1, 2010–June 30, 2011) and 2012 (July 1, 2011–June 30, 2012). The survey, available in both Spanish and English, was coordinated by various government agencies, specifically the Puerto Rico Planning Board (la Junta de Planificación), Puerto Rico Tourism Company (la Compañía de Turismo), Puerto Rico Public-Private Partnerships Authority (la Autoridad para las Alianzas Público Privadas), and the Institute of Statistics of Puerto Rico (Instituto de Estadísticas de Puerto Rico), to measure tourism and economic conditions in Puerto Rico.

This dataset can be obtained from the Institute of Statistics of Puerto Rico. The TS does not necessarily contain a nationally representative sample of Puerto Rican *residents*. Moreover, the sampling methodology was not necessarily designed with the goal of obtaining a representative of all travelers aged sixteen and above. In an attempt to approximate such a representative sample, the Institute of Statistics of Puerto Rico generated statistical weights to be employed with empirical analyses of the the microdata to account for the probability that an individual was in the sample, based on factors such as the number of passengers on his or her flight, the number of flights during the same day, and so forth. We employ these statistical weights throughout our TS analyses.

Among other items, the TS includes questions about the country of residence, the primary purpose of the trip, and for those who lived on the island, the *municipio* of residence. Among those reporting they were moving, the survey asked about the destination state (or country for non-U.S. destinations), and the reason for moving. We focus exclusively on the air passengers in our analyses. To maintain the representative nature of the samples, we employ the appropriate sampling weights in all analyses.

Construction of the Continuous Education Variable

The TS provides information about education in categories. When there was more than one year of schooling in a given category (e.g., 1–5 years of education), we used the 2010–2011 ACS for people aged sixteen and above who moved from Puerto Rico, to estimate the average schooling within the ranges. To illustrate, people in the ACS with one to five years of schooling had an average of 3.7 years; we therefore used the value of 3.7 years for the continuous education variable. We also went through the list of answers for people who reported "otro" for education and provided a specific response to the next question about which level (e.g., "masters"). We coded the continuous education variable accordingly (e.g., 18 years for masters, 20 years for PhD).

Construction of the Sending Regions

We constructed the sending regions in Puerto Rico on the basis of the *municipios* (similar to counties), as follows:

* *Central*—Adjuntas, Aguas Buenas, Aibonito, Barranquitas, Cayey, Ciales, Cidra, Comerío, Corozal, Jayuya, Lares, Morovis, Naranjito, Orocovis, and Utuado
* *Northeast*—Bayamón, Caguas, Canovanas, Carolina, Catano, Ceiba, Culebra, Dorado, Fajardo, Guaynabo, Gurabo, Juncos, Loiza, Luquillo, Naguabo, Río Grande, Toa Alta, Toa Baja, Trujillo Alto, and Vieques
* *Northwest*—Aguada, Aguadilla, Añasco, Arecibo, Barceloneta, Camuy, Florida, Hatillo, Isabela, Las Marías, Manatí, Moca, Quebradillas, Rincón, San Sebastián, Vega Alta, and Vega Baja
* *San Juan*—San Juan
* *Southeast*—Arroyo, Guayama, Humacao, Las Piedra, Maunabo, Patillas, Salinas, San Lorenzo, and Yabucoa
* *Southwest*—Cabo Roja, Coamo, Guánica, Guayanilla, Hormigueros, Juana Díaz, Lajas, Maricao, Mayagüez, Peñuelas, Ponce, Sabana Grande, San Germán, Santa Isabel, Villalba, and Yauco.

Appendix B

Empirical Methodology and Selected Estimation Details

CHAPTER 4

Observable Skills and the Likelihood of Migration to the Mainland

We employ probit regression analysis to analyze how education and age related to the likelihood that island-born Puerto Ricans migrated to the mainland during the crisis when holding constant other socioeconomic and demographic traits. Specifically, we used the 2006–2014 American Community Survey (ACS) and Puerto Rican Community Survey (PRCS) data to estimate the following for adults between the ages of twenty-five and sixty-four.

(1) *Recent Migrant from Island* = f (*Human Capital, Family, Interest Income, Occupation, Year$_{2011\_14}$*),

where *Recent Migrant from Island* is a binary variable equal to one for Puerto Ricans who migrated from the island to mainland within twelve months prior to the survey; it equals zero for those whom remained in Puerto Rico. Island-born Puerto Ricans who resided on the mainland and were not recent migrants were excluded from this analysis.

The vector *Human Capital* includes education, age, age-squared (to account for the nonlinear relationship between age and the likelihood of migration), and English-language fluency, while the vector *Family* contains a set of binary variables for marital status [married (base); single, never married; and divorced, widowed, or separated] as well as the number of children residing at home. *Interest Income* is a binary variable indicating whether the individual has interest or dividend income (as a proxy for wealth), while the vector *Occupation* contains a set of binary variables for occupations (professional, managerial, and executive; health and technical support; office and administrative support; sales; services [base]; agriculture; blue collar; and no occupation). Finally, the binary *Year 2011_14* equals one for individuals observed in the 2011–2014 surveys. Selected results are presented in the first column of table 4.3.

Changes in Unobservable Skills

When estimating unobservable skills and other characteristics among Puerto Ricans relative to non-Hispanic whites, we examined the unexplained earnings differential between the two groups. Consider that the total earnings differential is comprised of two components, one that can be explained by differences in skills and other observable characteristics, and one that such differences do not capture.

(2) $ln(Earnings)_{PR} - ln(Earnings)_{NHW}$ = *Explained Differential + Unexplained Differential,*

where *ln(Earnings)* denotes the natural logarithm of annual wages and salaries, with the subscripts "PR" and "NHW" indicating Puerto Ricans and non-Hispanic whites. The explained and unexplained components can be estimated using the "Oaxaca-type" wage decomposition method, based on the work of economist Ronald Oaxaca, such as in his 1973 study.

Specifically, using the ACS, we first estimate the following earnings function solely for mainland-born non-Hispanic whites between the ages of twenty-five and sixty-four who worked on the mainland to obtain the mainland structure of wages:

(3) $Ln(Earnings)_{NHW}$ = *(Human Capital)$_{NHW}$ β_1 + (Occupation)$_{NHW}$ β_2 + (Work Time)$_{NHW}$ β_3 + (Other)$_{NHW}$ β_4 +Year β_5 + e.*

The vectors *Human Capital* and *Occupation* include the same variables as in Equation (1), with the exception that *Occupation* excludes the category of no occupation. *Work Time* represents a vector of binary variables indicating the amount of weeks worked in the previous twelve months (less than 27 weeks (base), 27–39 weeks, 40–47 weeks, 48–49 weeks, and 50–51 weeks) plus a continuous variable for the amount of usual weekly work hours. The *Other* vector includes gender plus a binary variable equal to one for workers residing outside of metropolitan areas, while the *Year* vector includes binary variables for each year of the survey (with 2014 being the base). The purpose of including the latter is to account for structural changes in the mainland labor market, including the Great Recession that occurred over time. Because this specification pools workers from different time periods, the earnings are adjusted for inflation using the consumer price index (CPI), to be expressed in terms of 2014 dollars. The β_i terms represent vectors of coefficients to be estimated, while e denotes the normally distributed error tem.

Using the estimated coefficients from the β_i vectors, the wages of Puerto Ricans and other groups can be imputed to estimate how much they should have earned based on the mainland wage structure, given their characteristics. The difference between these predicted earnings [*Predicted ln(Earnings)*$_{PR}$] and the predicted earnings of non-Hispanic whites [*Predicted ln(Earnings)*$_{NHW}$] measures how much of the Puerto Rican/non-Hispanic-white wage differential stems from differences in observable facets. That is,

(4) *Explained Differential* = *Predicted* $ln(Earnings)_{PR}$ - [*Predicted* $ln(Earnings)_{NHW}$].

It follows that the gap between the actual earnings differential and the explained differential yields the component of the earnings differential that is not explained by differences in observable characteristics between the groups:

(5) *Unexplained Differential* = $[ln(Earnings)_{PR} - ln(Earnings)_{NHW}]$ - *Explained Differential.*

That is, the *Unexplained Differential* reflects the earnings differential that is determined by differences in unobserved skills and other characteristics, including structural factors such as discrimination, between Puerto Ricans and mainland-born non-Hispanic whites. These unexplained differentials are reported in figure 4.3.

Temporary versus Permanent Migration

We employ probit regression analysis to analyze how observable socioeconomic and demographic characteristics related to the likelihood that island-born Puerto Ricans migrated from the mainland to the island during the crisis. Using the 2006–2014 ACS and PRCS data, we estimate the following for adults between the ages of twenty-five and sixty-four.

(6) *Recent Return Migrant from Mainland* = f (*Human Capital, Family, X,* $Year_{2011\_14}$),

where *Recent Return Migrant from Mainland* is a binary variable equal to one for island-born Puerto Ricans who migrated from the mainland to island within twelve months prior to the survey; it equals zero for those whom remained on the mainland. Island-born Puerto Ricans who resided on the island and were not recent return migrants are excluded from this analysis. The remaining variables are the same as in Equation (1). These results are presented in the second column of table 4.3.

CHAPTER 5

Inverse of the Herfindahl Index

The Herfindahl index (IHI), which ranges from zero to one, represents one measure of the geographic concentration of a given population; the closer the index is to one, the greater the level of concentration. A value of one means that all members of the population reside in only one community. As noted in chapter 5, the inverse of IHI can be interpreted as the equivalent number of communities in which the population resides. If the population is evenly distributed across all communities, the inverse of the Herfindahl equals the actual number of communities. To construct this index, we first estimated the share of the total island-born Puerto Rican population that resided in each state or DC. We then squared these shares and summed them for all states. We repeated this exercise for each of the groups shown in table 5.4.

CHAPTER 6

Mainland Employment Opportunities after 2010

To test whether the employment/population ratios changed among island-born Puerto Rican civilians between the ages of twenty-five and sixty-four in the largest receiving states after 2010, we conducted F-tests on the difference in these ratios for the 2006–2010 and 2011–2014 time periods for each of the large receiving states as well as for all states combined. None of these tests revealed a statistically significant difference (at conventional levels) in the employment/ population ratios between the two time periods among island-born Puerto Ricans, with the exception of New Jersey. Using the same methodology, the employment/population ratios among mainland-born non-Hispanic white civilians in the same age range significantly fell overall as well as in each of the six largest receiving states.

Labor Force Status and Other Socioeconomic and Demographic Characteristics

To analyze how socioeconomic and demographic characteristics related to labor force status, we estimated the following probit regression model for civilians between the ages of twenty-five and sixty-four:

(7) *In Labor Force = f (Human Capital, Family, Female, Year, Recent Migrant, Geography),*

where *In Labor Force* is a binary variable equal to one for individuals in the labor force, and equal to zero for those outside of the labor force. *Human*

Capital, Family, and *Female* are the same vectors as in Equation (1) in this appendix *Year* contains binary variables for year fixed effects and *Recent Migrant* includes binary variables indicating whether the individual recently migrated from Puerto Rico to the mainland or migrated between states. Finally, *Geography* includes a series of binary variables indicating residence in each of the six largest receiving states of Puerto Ricans from the island (with New York representing the base category) plus a composite binary variable for the "other" states; this vector further includes a binary variable equal to one for individuals who resided outside of a metropolitan area. We estimated Equation (7) separately for island-born Puerto Ricans, mainland-born Puerto Ricans, and for mainland-born non-Hispanic whites. To determine the statistical significance of differences between states, we used χ^2-tests for the differences in the estimated coefficients.

Similarly, to analyze how these characteristics related to the likelihood of being employed, we estimated a bivariate probit regression model for civilians aged twenty-five to sixty-four who were in the labor force, in which we jointly estimated Equation (7) and the following:

(8) *Employed* = *f (Human Capital, Family, Female, Year, Recent Migrant, Geography, Occupation),*

where *Employed* equals one for individuals who were employed and zero for those who were unemployed. The vector *Occupation* includes the same as Equation (7) while controlling for occupations (the specific set is described in the *Occupation* vector from Equation [1]).

Unexplained Earnings and Poverty-Rate Differentials

Following the methodology described earlier in this appendix under the subheading "Changes in Unobservable Skills" for chapter 4, this analysis utilizes the Oaxaca-type decomposition method (e.g., Oaxaca, 1973) by first regressing each socioeconomic outcome (i.e., the natural logarithm of earnings and being impoverished [a binary variable equal to one for individuals residing below the poverty line, and equal to zero otherwise]) on the set of observable characteristics for non-Hispanic whites on the mainland, using ordinary least squares for the natural logarithm of earnings, and probit regression for the likelihood of being impoverished.

We then applied these regression estimates to Puerto Ricans (and Mexican Americans) to impute their socioeconomic outcomes, given their human capital and demographic characteristics. The difference between these predicted outcomes for Puerto Ricans and non-Hispanic whites yields the Puerto Rican/non-Hispanic-white differential explained by differences in their observable characteristics. The remainder of the differential estimates the portion that observable characteristics do not explain.

Specifically, these characteristics include education, age, age-squared, limited English proficiency, gender, residence outside of metropolitan areas, and binary variables identifying the year of the survey to account for structural conditions that changed over time. When analyzing earnings (table 6.1), we only consider individuals who reported wage or salary income, and further include the control variables of the number of weeks worked (less than 27 (base), 27–39 weeks, 48–49 weeks, and 50–52 weeks); the number of hours usually worked per week; and occupational categories (services [base]; managerial, professional, and executive; health technicians; office and administrative support; sales; agriculture; and blue collar). When analyzing the likelihood of being impoverished (table 6.2), we include in the "other" characteristics whether the person was an attached worker, marital status, single motherhood, and the number of the individual's children residing in the household.

CHAPTER 7

The empirical methodology to estimate the unexplained earnings differentials (table 7.3) and unexplained poverty-rate differentials (table 7.4) mirrors the methodology under the subheading "Unexplained Earnings and Poverty-Rate Differentials" for chapter 6 described earlier in this appendix, when further partitioning the samples between men and women. The base group of comparison is non-Hispanic white men.

CHAPTER 8

Analysis of Self-Employment Tendencies

Our analysis of factors affecting the likelihood of being self-employed (table 8.3) is based on probit regression analysis of the following probit model:

(9) *Self = f (Human Capital, Family, Female, Year, Macro, Occupation),*

where the dependent variable *Self* equals one for workers who were self-employed, and zero for nonself-employed workers. The variable *Macro* includes the percentage of Puerto Ricans (or Mexican Americans or Cubans, in the case of the analyses for these two groups) in the metropolitan area, as a measure of ethnic concentration. It also includes the local unemployment rate, defined as the unemployment rate in the metropolitan (or state nonmetro) areas which we estimated using the ACS. The remaining variables are the same as for Equation (8).

Appendix C

About the Book Cover

We created the photograph collage for the cover of this book out of literally nearly 450 photographs we took during our four-day collaborative research trip to Puerto Rico in April 2015 (mentioned in the Preface), when we visited 25 of the island's 78 *municipios*. We selected the ones that best represented what we observed and also provided (in our view) a visual aid to many of the points raised in this book. The figure below in this appendix provides the numeric key to these photographs.

1. Going to mass on Good Friday at *Iglesia San Miguel Arcangel*, Utuado, representing the importance of religion (particularly Catholicism) throughout the history of Puerto Rico for over half a millennium
2. The Capitol of Puerto Rico, home to the bicameral Legislative Assembly, San Juan, representing a government that is neither a state nor sovereign government
3. Spanish- and English-language banners protesting the sales tax (*Impuesto a las Ventas y Uso*, or IVU), San Juan. (The IVU, which was not implemented in Puerto Rico until 2006, was increased from 7.0 percent to 11.5 percent (higher than any state sales taxes) after this photograph was taken.)
4. Private mansion in a gated community in Dorado, illustrating that pockets of wealth still exist in Puerto Rico despite the unfolding humanitarian crisis
5. Brewing storm overlooking the barrio of La Perla
6. Chained doors painted as the *Grito de Lares* flag, in Lares, with ominous reflection in glass panes above and worn base
7. Street near the plaza in Arecibo, typical of many throughout the *municipios*
8. Dilapidated building in now abandoned neighborhood in Aguirre, once one of the nicest during the heyday of Puerto Rico's sugar cane industry

9. Margarita R. at her home in Arecibo, after a fantastic lunch of pasteles
10. Sunrise on a beach near Ponce, a typical view observed by tourists
11. A beach in Puerto Rico seen from inside a passenger aircraft, a typical view observed by tourists as well as the hundreds of thousands of migrants who left Puerto Rico during La Crisis Boricua
12. Outside the Aguirre thermoelectric power plant, one of only four on the island, and the location of the fire that allegedly caused Puerto Rico's September 2016 blackout
13. A casita in a typical neighborhood in Aguirre
14. Lajeño soldier monument in the plaza of Lajas, reflecting the honor, pride, and sacrifice Puerto Ricans have made as U.S. citizens. (Many of the *municipios* have erected such monuments in their plazas to honor veterans.)
15. One of many protest banners in San Juan in April 2015.
16. Another view of the Aguirre thermoelectric power plant (see #12), taken while standing on a deteriorating pier
17. The abandoned central Aguirre sugar cane mill. (Once a highly profitable industry, this mill was one of the last sugar cane mills to shut down in Puerto Rico.)
18. Typical street in the barrio of La Perla, a sight rarely seen by tourists despite being minutes away from the charming streets of Old San Juan
19. Typical street in Old San Juan, a sight often seen by tourists who might be unaware of the vast socioeconomic disparities that exist just minutes away.

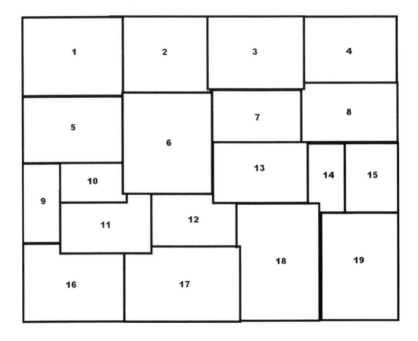

Bibliography

Acosta-Belén, Edna, and Carlos Enrique Santiago. 2006. *Puerto Ricans in the United States: A Contemporary Portrait*. Boulder, CO: Lynne Rienner Publishers.

Aguilera, Michael Bernabé. 2005. "The Impact of Social Capital on the Earnings of Puerto Rican Migrants." *The Sociological Quarterly* 46(4): 569–592.

Allen, Greg. 2016. "SOS: Puerto Rico Is Losing Doctors, Leaving Patients Stranded." *National Public Radio*, March 12, 2016, http://www.npr.org/sections/health-shots/2016/03/12/469974138/sos-puerto-rico-is-losing-doctors-leaving-patients-stranded, Access May 15, 2017.

Aranda, Elizabeth M. 2006. *Emotional Bridges to Puerto Rico: Migration, Return Migration, and the Struggles of Incorporation*. Lanham, MD: Rowman & Littlefield Publishers.

Associated Press. 2017. "Board Orders Furloughs, Pension Cuts, More for Puerto Rico." *NBC News*, http://www.nbcnews.com/news/latino/board-orders-furloughs-pension-cuts-more-puerto-rico-n732941. Accessed March 13, 2017.

Back, Kurt W., Reuben Hill, and J. Mayone Stycos. 1960. "Population Control in Puerto Rico: the Formal and Informal Framework." *Law & Contemporary Problems* 25: 558–576.

Bates, Timothy. 2011. "Minority Entrepreneurship." *Foundations and Trends in Entrepreneurship* 7: 151–311.

Birson, Kurt. 2013. "Puerto Rican Migration and the 21st Century: Is There a Brain Drain?" In Edwin Meléndez and Carlos Vargas-Ramos (Eds.), *The State of Puerto Ricans 2013*. New York, NY: Center for Puerto Rican Studies, pp. 27–31.

Birson, Kurt, and Edwin Meléndez. 2013. "The Economic Impact of the Great Recession on Puerto Ricans in the United States." In Edwin Meléndez and Carlos Vargas-Ramos (Eds.), *The State of Puerto Ricans 2013*. New York, NY: Center for Puerto Rican Studies, pp. 55–62.

Boden, Richard. 1996. "Gender and Self-Employment Selection: An Empirical Assessment." *Journal of Socio-Economics* 25: 671–682.

Borges-Méndez, Ramón. 2011. "Stateside Puerto Ricans and the Public Workforce Development System: New York City, Hartford, Springfield/Holyoke." *Centro Journal* 23, no. 2: 65–93.

Borjas, George J. 2008. "Labor Outflows and Labor Inflows to Puerto Rico." *Journal of Human Capital* 2: 32–68.

Bosworth, Barry P., and Susan M. Collins. 2006. "Economic Growth." In Susan M. Collins, Barry P. Bosworth, and Miguel A. Soto-Class (Eds.), *The Economy of Puerto Rico: Restoring Growth*. Washington, DC: Brookings Institution Press, pp. 17–81.

Bram, J., F.E. Martínez, and C. Steindel. 2008. "Trends and Development in the Economy of Puerto Rico." *Federal Reserve Bank of New York, Current Issues in Economics and Finance* 14, no. 2: 1–7.

Burgos, Giovani, and Fernando I. Rivera. 2012. "Residential Segregation, Socio-Economic Status, and Disability: A Multi-Level Study of Puerto Ricans in the United States." *Centro Journal* 24, no. 2: 14–47.

Burtless, Gary, and Orlando Sotomayor. 2006. "Labor Supply and Public Transfers." In Susan M. Collins, Barry P. Bosworth, and Miguel A. Soto-Class (Eds.), *The Economy of Puerto Rico: Restoring Growth*. Washington, DC: Brookings Institution Press, pp. 82–142.

Caraballo, José, and Juan Lara. 2016. "From Deindustrialization to Unsustainable Debt: The Case of Puerto Rico." Unpublished paper, University of Puerto Rico at Cayey, October 2016, https://www.researchgate.net/project/From-deindustrialization-to-unsustainable-debt-The-Case-of-Puerto-Rico. Accessed April 6, 2017.

Carr, Deborah. 1996. "Two Paths to Self-Employment? Women's and Men's Self-Employment in the United States, 1980." *Work and Occupations* 23: 26–53.

Carr, Raymond. 1984. *Puerto Rico: A Colonial Experiment*. New York: Vintage Books.

Center for a New Economy. 2016. *Policy Paper: Devising a Growth Strategy for Puerto Rico*. San Juan, PR: Center for a New Economy, file:///C:/Users/jdt810/AppData/Local/Microsoft/Windows/INetCache/IE/3UJ8GDEU/2016_18_DevisingAGrowthStrategyForPR.pdf. Accessed May 26, 2017.

Centro. 2017. *Puerto Rico in Crisis: Timeline*. New York: Centro, Center for Puerto Rican Studies, Hunter College.

Cohn, D'Vera, Eileen Patten, and Mark Hugo López. 2014. "Puerto Rican Population Declines on Island, Grows on U.S. Mainland." *Pew Research Center Hispanic Trends*, August 14.

CNN Money. 2016. *Cost of Living Calculator*, http://money.cnn.com/calculator/pf/cost-of-living/index.html. Accessed November 23, 2016.

Colegio de Médicos-Cirujanos de Puerto Rico. 2016. "Peligrosa Fuga de Miles de Médicos." *El Nuevo Día*, June 28, 2016. http://www.elnuevodia.com/noticias/locales/nota/peligrosafugademilesdemedicos-2225024/. Accessed May 28, 2017.

Collins, Susan M., Barry P. Bosworth, and Miguel A. Soto-Class (Editors). 2006. *The Economy of Puerto Rico: Restoring Growth*. Washington, DC: Brookings Institution Press.

Colón, Israel "Izzy". 2016. "Oye…It's Not Our Fault! The Latino Presidential Vote in Philadelphia, Guest Commentary." *NiLP Report on Latino Policy & Politics* (November 18, 2016). New York: National Institute for Latino Public Policy.

Coto, Danica. 2017a. "Report: Puerto Rico has Worse Drinking Water Violation Rate." *Associated Press*, May 10, 2017. http://www.apnewsarchive.com/2017/ An-environmental-group-says-Puerto-Rico-has-the-worst-rate-of-drinking-water-violations-of-any-U-S-jurisdiction-with-dangerous-contaminants-ranging-from-lead-to-disinfectants-to-colifo/id-810b149ccd47474aa41f0b368b67aace, Accessed May 27, 2017.

———. 2017b. "Puerto Rico Upholds Statehold Demand in Contentious Vote." *Associated Press*, June 12, 2017, https://www.yahoo.com/news/puerto-rico-gov-upholds-statehood-vote-hit-boycott-040136932.html. Accessed July 17, 2017.

———. 2013. "Doctors Flee Puerto Rico for U.S. Mainland." *Associated Press*, April 17, 2013, https://www.yahoo.com/news/doctors-flee-puerto-rico-us-mainland-165338626.html. Accessed May 27, 2017.

Dallas Independent School District. 2017. *The Time Is Now! The Place Is Dallas.* Website: http://www.dallasisd.org/puertorico, accessed May 14, 2017.

Dávila, Alberto, and Marie T. Mora. 2013. *Hispanic Entrepreneurs in the 2000s: An Economic Profile and Policy Implications.* Stanford, CA: Stanford University Press.

Dávila, Alberto, Marie T. Mora, and Havidán Rodríguez. 2017. "Education and Occupational Structures among Island-Born and Mainland-Born Puerto Ricans and Non-Hispanic Whites on the U.S. Mainland: 2006–2014." Paper presented at the Allied Social Science Association annual meetings, Chicago, IL: January 6, 2017.

Dávila, Juan C. 2016 (June 22). "PROMESA: Puerto Rico's 'Restructure' at $4.25 an Hour." *The Huffington Post*, http://www.huffingtonpost.com/juan-c-davila/promesa-puerto-ricos-rest_b_10615610.html, updated June 29, 2016. Accessed August 2, 2016.

Davis, Steven J., and Luis Rivera-Batiz. 2006. "The Climate for Business Development and Employment Growth in Puerto Rico." In Susan M. Collins, Barry P. Bosworth, and Miguel A. Soto-Class (Eds.), *The Economy of Puerto Rico: Restoring Growth.* Washington, DC: Brookings Institution Press, pp. 255–318.

Delerme, Simone. 2013. *The Latinization of Orlando: Race, Class, and the Politics of Place.* New Brunswick, NJ: Rutgers University (Anthropology).

Departamento de Salud. 2015. *Informe de Salud en Puerto Rico.* San Juan: Secretaría Auxiliar de Planificación y Desarrollo, Estado Libre Asociado de Puerto Rico.

Denniston, Lyle. 2015 (October 2). "Constitution Check: Is Puerto Rico Just a Colony under Congress's Control?" *Constitution Daily*, https://constitutioncenter. org/blog/constitution-check-is-puerto-rico-just-a-colony-under-congresss-control/. Accessed May 25, 2107.

Dietz, James L. 2003. *Puerto Rico: Negotiating Development and Change.* Boulder: Lynne Rienner Publishers.

Dietz, James, and E. Pantojas-Garcia. 1993. "Puerto Rico's New Role in the Caribbean: The High Finance/Maquiladora Strategy." In E. Meléndez and E. Meléndez (Eds.), *Colonial Dilemma: Critical Perspectives on Contemporary Puerto Rico.* Boston: South End Press, p. 104.

Disis, Jill. 2017. "Hurricane Maria could be a $95 billion storm for Puerto Rico." *CNN Money*, http://money.cnn.com/2017/09/28/news/economy/puerto-rico-hurricane-maria-damage-estimate/index.html. Accessed September 29, 2017.

Diversitydatakids.org. 2016. *Hispanic National Origin and Neighborhoods of Opportunity*. The Heller School for Social Policy and Management, Brandeis University, October 17, 2016. http://www.diversitydatakids.org/data/library/59/hispanic-national-origin-and-neighborhoods-of-opportunity, accessed October 19, 2016.

Duany, Jorge. 2002. "Mobile Livelihoods: the Sociocultural Practices of Circular Migrants between Puerto Rico and the United States." *International Migration Review* 36, no. 2: 355–388.

Dustmann, C., and J. Simon Gorlach. 2015. *The Economics of Temporary Migrations*. London: Center for Research & Analysis of Migration.

Enchautegui, Maria E. 2014. *A Work Tax Credit that Supports Puerto Rico's Working Families*. Washington, DC: The Urban Institute.

———. 2007. "Selectivity Patterns in Puerto Rico Migration." Economic Research Unit, University of Puerto Rico Río Piedras Campus, Working Paper Number 5.

———. 2003. *Reaping the Benefits of Work: A Tax Credit for Low-Income Working Families in Puerto Rico*. San Juan, PR: Center for the New Economy.

———. 1993. "Education, Location, and Labor Market Outcomes of Puerto Rican Men during the 1980s." *Eastern Economic Journal* 19, no. 3: 295–308.

———. 1992. "Geographical Differentials in the Socioeconomic Status of Puerto Ricans: Human Capital Variations and Labor Market Characteristics." *International Migration Review* 26, no. 4: 1267–1290.

Enchautegui, Maria E., and Richard B. Freeman. 2006. "Why Don't More Puerto Rican Men Work? The Rich Uncle (Sam) Hypothesis." In Susan M. Collins, Barry P. Bosworth, and Miguel A. Soto-Class (Eds.), *The Economy of Puerto Rico: Restoring Growth*. Washington, DC: Brookings Institution Press, pp. 152–188.

Estudio Técnicos, Inc. 2016. *Puerto Rico: 2016–2030*. San Juan, PR. Report submitted to the Puerto Rico Department of Economic Development and Commerce, October 2016. http://www.estudiostecnicos.com/projects/pr2030/PR-2030-Compendio-Nov-4–2016-Final.pdf. Accessed May 28, 2017.

Factfish.com. 2016a. *Puerto Rico: Infant Mortality Rate, under 1, per 1000 Live Births, Total*. http://www.factfish.com/statistic-country/puerto%20rico/infant%20mortality%20rate%20under%201%2C%20total. Accessed July 17, 2016.

Factfish.com. 2016b. *Puerto Rico: Life Expectancy at Birth, Total*. http://www.factfish.com/statistic-country/puerto%20rico/life%20expectancy%20at%20birth,%20total. Accessed July 17, 2016.

Factfish.com. 2016c. *Puerto Rico: Average Age*. http://www.factfish.com/statistic-country/puerto%20rico/average%20age. Accessed July 17, 2016.

Falcón, Angelo. 2004. *Atlas of Stateside Puerto Ricans*. Washington, DC: Puerto Rico Federal Affairs Administration.

Federal Reserve Bank of New York. 2012. *Report on the Competitiveness of Puerto Rico's Economy*. https://www.newyorkfed.org/regional/puertorico/index.html.

Federal Reserve Bank of New York. 2014. *An Update on the Competitiveness of Puerto Rico's Economy*. https://www.newyorkfed.org/medialibrary/media/outreach-and-education/puerto-rico/2014/Puerto-Rico-Report-2014.pdf. Accessed May 31, 2017.

Figueroa-Rodríguez, Raúl. 2013. *The Elders' Colony*. North Charleston, SC: Createspace.

Figueroa-Rodríguez, Raúl, Rivera-Negrón, Rosario, and Rodríguez-Figueroa, Judith. 2012. *Puerto Rico 2000–2010: Más Allá del Censo*. North Charleston, SC: Createspace.

Furth, Salim. 2016 (September 1). "Puerto Rico Oversight Board Members Specialize in Finance, Not Economic Reform." *The Heritage Foundation,* http://www.heritage.org/research/commentary/2016/8/puerto-rico-oversight-board-members-specialize-in-finance-not-economic-reform. Accessed October 9, 2016.

García-Ellín, Juan Carlos. 2013. "Internal Migration of Puerto Ricans in the United States." In Edwin Meléndez and Carlos Vargas-Ramos (Eds.), *The State of Puerto Ricans 2013*. New York, NY: Center for Puerto Rican Studies, pp. 33–37.

Gibney, James. 2016 (March 21). "As Cuba Rises, Puerto Rico Falls." *Bloomberg,* https://www.bloomberg.com/view/articles/2016–03–21/as-cuba-rises-puerto-rico-falls. Accessed November 15, 2016.

Godoy, Ricardo, Glenn P. Jenkins, and Karishma Patel. 2003. "Puerto Rican Migration: An Assessment of Quantitative Studies." *Centro Journal* 15, no. 2: 206–231.

González, Joanisabel. 2016 (August 11, 2016). "Economistas de la Fed Analizan la Ola Migratoria Boricua." *El Nuevo Día,* http://www.elnuevodia.com/negocios/economia/nota/economistasdelafedanalizanlaolamigratoriaboricua-2229528/. Accessed August 11, 2016.

Guadalupe, Patricia. 2016a (June 30). "Here's How PROMESA Aims to Tackle Puerto Rico's Debt." *NBC News Latino,* http://www.nbcnews.com/news/latino/here-s-how-promesa-aims-tackle-puerto-rico-s-debt-n601741. Accessed August 2, 2016.

———. 2016b (August 31). "Who Are the Members of the Puerto Rico Fiscal Control Board?" *NBC News Latino,* http://www.nbcnews.com/news/latino/five-members-puerto-rico-oversight-board-are-puerto-rican-n640811. Accessed October 9, 2016.

Hartmann, Betsy. 1987. *Reproductive Rights and Wrongs: The Global Politics of Population Control and Contraceptive Choice*. New York: Harper & Row, Publishers.

Harvard Law Review. 2017. "Developments in the Law – U.S. Territories." *Harvard Law Review* 130: 1617–1727.

Heredia Rodriguez, Carmen. 2017 (May 1). "Exodus of Puerto Rican Medical Students Deepens Island's Doctor Drain." *Kaiser Health News,* http://khn.org/news/exodus-by-puerto-rican-medical-students-deepens-islands-doctor-drain/. Accessed May 28, 2017.

House of Representatives Committee on Resources. 1997. *H. Report (105–131): United States – Puerto Rico Political Status Act, Report with Additional Views*. Washington, DC: 105th Congress. https://www.congress.gov/congressional-report/105th-congress/house-report/131. Accessed May 24, 2017.

Hundley, Greg. 2000. "Male/Female Earnings Differences in Self-Employment: The Effects of Marriage, Children, and the Household Division of Labor." *Industrial and Labor Relations Review* 54(1): 95–114.

Kneebone, Elizabeth, and Natalie Holmes. 2016. "U.S. Concentrated Poverty in the Wake of the Great Recession." *Brookings Report*, March 31. Accessed September 23, 2016. https://www.brookings.edu/research/u-s-concentrated-poverty-in-the-wake-of-the-great-recession/.

Krogstad, Jens Manuel. 2016. "Historic Population Losses Continue Across Puerto Rico." Washington, DC: Pew Research Center, http://www.pewresearch.org/fact-tank/2016/03/24/historic-population-losses-continue-across-puerto-rico/. Accessed June 28, 2016.

Krogstad, Jens Manuel, and Antonio Flores. 2016. "Unlike Other Latinos, about Half of Cuban Voters in Florida Backed Trump." Washington, DC: Pew Research Center, http://www.pewresearch.org/fact-tank/2016/11/15/unlike-other-latinos-about-half-of-cuban-voters-in-florida-backed-trump/. Accessed November 18, 2016.

Levis, Maria. 2016 (June 13). "Your Money Or Your Life: Federal Policies And Health Disparities In Puerto Rico." *Health Affairs Blog*, http://healthaffairs.org/blog/2016/06/13/your-money-or-your-life-federal-policies-and-health-disparities-in-puerto-rico/. Accessed May 26, 2017.

Long, Heather 2016a (February 21). "There's a Big Sale on Puerto Rican Homes." *CNN*, http://money.cnn.com/2016/02/21/investing/puerto-rico-foreclosure-crisis/?iid=EL. Accessed November 20, 2016.

Long, Heather. 2016b (June 30). "Puerto Rico to Hike Electricity Rates 26%." *CNN*, http://money.cnn.com/2016/06/30/investing/puerto-rico-crisis-electricity-price-hike/index.html. Accessed May 7, 2017.

López, Iris. 2005. "Borinkis and Chop Suey: Puerto Rican Identity in Hawai'i, 1900–2000." In Whalen, Carmen Teresa and Vázquez-Hernández, Víctor. (Eds.). (2005). *The Puerto Rican Diaspora: Historical Perspectives*. Philadelphia: Temple University Press, pp. 43–67.

López, Mark Hugo. 2016. Unpublished Data from the Current Population Survey, Voter and Registration Supplements, 2004, 2008, and 2012. Washington, DC: Hispanic Research, Pew Research Center. Shared with Marie T. Mora, via email, October 18, 2016.

López, Mark Hugo, and Ana Gonzalez-Barrera. 2013. *Inside the 2012 Latino Electorate*. Washington, DC: Pew Research Center.

Marazzi Santiago, Mario. 2017. "Some Partial Empirical Evidence from the Cost-of-Living Index (COLI)." Presentation in the American Society of Hispanic Economists' Session on *Puerto Rico: A Century of "Progress" under the Jones Act*, Western Economic Association International annual meetings. San Diego, CA: June 26, 2017.

Marzan, Gilbert. 2009. "Still Looking for that Elsewhere: Puerto Rican Poverty and Migration in the Northeast." *Centro Journal* 21, no. 1: 100–117.

Mass, Bonnie. 1977. "Puerto Rico: A Case Study of Population Control," *Latin American Perspectives* 15(4): 66–82.

Massey, Douglas S. 1990. "American Apartheid: Segregation and the Making of the Underclass." *American Journal of Sociology* 96, no. 2: 329–357.

Massey, Douglas S., and Nancy A. Denton. 1993. *American Apartheid: Segregation and the Making of the Underclass*. Cambridge, MA: Harvard University Press.

———. 1989. "Residential Segregation of Mexicans, Puerto Ricans, and Cubans in Selected U.S. Metropolitan Areas" *Sociology and Social Research* 73, no. 2: 73–83.

Massey, Douglas S., and Mitchell L. Eggers. 1990. "The Ecology of Inequality: Minorities and the Concentration of Poverty, 1970–1980." *American Journal of Sociology* 95: 1153–1188.

Massey, Douglas S., Andrew B. Gross, and Mitchell L. Eggers. 1991. "Segregation, the Concentration of Poverty, and the Life Chances of Individuals." *Social Science Research* 20, no. 4: 397–420.

Massey, Douglas S., Andrew B. Gross, and Kumiko Shibuya. 1994. "Migration, Segregation, and the Geographic Concentration of Poverty." *American Sociological Review* 59: 425–445.

Matos-Rodríguez, Félix, V. 2013. "Puerto Ricans in the United States: Past, Present and Future." Presented at the Regional Conference of the Council of State Governments. Fajardo, Puerto Rico, December 9, 2013.

Meléndez, Edwin, and Carlos Vargas-Ramos. 2013. Introduction to *The State of Puerto Ricans 2013*, Edwin Meléndez and Carlos Vargas-Ramos (Eds.). New York, NY: Center for Puerto Rican Studies, pp. 9–19.

Meléndez, Edwin, and M. Anne Visser. 2011. "Low-Wage Labor, Markets and Skills Selectivity among Puerto Rican Migrants." *Centro Journal* 23, no. 2: 39–62.

Mora, Marie T., and Alberto Dávila. 2014. "Gender and Business Outcomes of Black and Hispanic New Entrepreneurs in the United States." *American Economic Review Papers & Proceedings* 104(5): 245–249.

———. 2013. "An Overview of Hispanic Economic Outcomes in the First Decade of the 2000s." In Marie T. Mora & Alberto Dávila (Eds.), *The Economic Status of the Hispanic Population: Selected Essays*. Charlotte, NC: Information Age Publishing, pp. 1–21.

Mora, Marie T., Alberto Dávila, and Havidán Rodríguez. 2017. "Education, Migration, and the Earnings of Puerto Ricans on the Island and U.S. Mainland: Impact, Outcomes, and Consequences of an Economic Crisis." *Migration Studies* 5(2): 168–189.

Muschkin, Clara G. 1993. "Consequences of Return Migrant Status for Employment in Puerto Rico." *International Migration Review* 27, no. 1: 79–102.

National Hispanic Leadership Agenda. 2016. *2016 Hispanic Public Policy Agenda: Quadrennial Blueprint for Advancing the Latino Community*. Washington, DC: NHLA. https://nationalhispanicleadership.org/images/Agenda/NHLA_2016_Hispanic_Policy_Agenda.pdf. Accessed May 17, 2017.

Oaxaca, Ronald. 1973. "Male-Female Wage Differentials in Urban Labor Markets." *International Economic Review* 14: 693–709.

Ortiz, Vilma. 1986. "Changes in the Characteristics of Puerto Rican Migrants from 1955 to 1980." *International Migration Review* 20(3): 612–628.

Pantojas-Garcia, Emilio. 1990. *Development Strategies as Ideology: Puerto Rico's Export-Led Industrialization Experience*. Boulder, CO: Lynne Rienner Publishers.

Picó, Fernando. 1988. *Ediciones Huracán*. Puerto Rico: Rio Piedras.

Population Reference Bureau (2015). *World Population Data Sheet: Population, Health, and Environment Data and Estimates for the Countries and Regions of the World*. http://www.prb.org/pdf15/2015-world-population-data-sheet_eng.pdf.

Presser, Harriet B. 1973. *Sterilization and Fertility Decline in Puerto Rico*. Berkeley: Institute of International Studies, University of California.

Puerto Rico Department of Treasury. 2016. "IVU Loto General Merchant Guidelines." Accessed September 23. http://www.hacienda.gobierno.pr/pdf/prensa/ivu%20loto%20booklet_english.pdf

Puerto Rico Planning Board. 2016. "Economic Report to the Governor (Informe Económico al Gobernador): Puerto Rico 2015." Accessed September 23. http://gis.jp.pr.gov/Externo_Econ/Ap%C3%A9ndices%20Estad%C3%ADsticos/Ap%C3%A9ndice%20Estad%C3%ADstico%202015.pdf.

Ramírez de Arellano, Annette B., and Conrad Seipp. 1983. *Colonialism Catholicism and Contraception: a History of Birth Control in Puerto Rico*. Chapel Hill, NC: University of North Carolina Press.

Ramos, Fernando A. 1992. "Out-Migration and Return Migration of Puerto Ricans." In George J. Borjas & Richard B. Freeman (Eds.), *Immigration and the Work Force: Economic Consequences for the United States and Source Areas*. Chicago, IL: University of Chicago Press, pp. 49–66.

Reyes, Luis O., and Anna Rosofsky. 2013. "The Puerto Rican Education Pipeline: New York City, New York State, and the United States." In Edwin Meléndez and Carlos Vargas-Ramos (Eds.), *The State of Puerto Ricans 2013*. New York, NY: Center for Puerto Rican Studies, pp. 41–45.

Rivera-Batiz, Francisco, and Carlos E. Santiago. 1996. *Island Paradox: Puerto Rico in the 1990s*. New York: Russell Sage Foundation.

Rodriguez, Clara E. 1989. *Puerto Ricans: Born in the USA*. Boston, MA: Psychology Press.

Rodríguez, Havidán. 2004. "A "Long Walk to Freedom" and Democracy: Human Rights, Globalization, and Social Injustice." *Social Forces* 83, no. 1: 391–412.

———. 1992. "Household Composition, Employment Patterns, and Income Inequality: Puerto Ricans in New York and Other Areas of the U.S. Mainland." *Hispanic Journal of Behavioral Sciences* 14, no. 1: 52–75.

Rodríguez, Havidán, Sáenz, Rogelio, and Menjívar, Cecilia (Editors). 2008. *Latinas/os in the United States: Changing the Face of América*. New York: Springer.

Ruggles, Steven, Katie Genadek, Ronald Goeken, Josiah Grover, and Matthew Sobek. 2017. *Integrated Public Use Microdata Series: Version 6.0* [dataset]. Minneapolis: University of Minnesota, www.ipums.umn.

Sandis, Eva E. 1970. "Characteristics of Puerto Rican Migrants to, and from, the United States." *International Migration Review* 4, no. 2: 22–43.

Santiago-Rivera, A.I., and C.E. Santiago. 1999. "Puerto Rican Transnational Migration and Identity: Impact of English-Language Acquisition on Length of Stay in the United States." In L. Golden (Ed.), *Identities on the Move: Transnational Process in the Americas*. Austin: University of Texas Press, pp. 38–51.

Santos-Lozada, Alexis R and Velázquez-Estrada, Alberto R. "The Population Decline of Puerto Rico: An Application of Prospective Trends in Cohort-Component Projections." *Serie de Documentos de Trabajo, Working Paper Series*, Vol. 2015–1, October, 2015.

Scarano, Francisco, A. 2008. *Puerto Rico: Cinco Siglos de Historia*, Tercera Edición. New York: McGraw Hill.

Silver, Patricia. 2010. "'Culture Is More than Bingo and Salsa': Making Puertorriqueñidad in Central Florida." *Centro Journal* 22, no. 1: 57–83.

Silver, Patricia, and William Vélez. 2014. "From Great Migration to Great Dispersal: Puerto Ricans in New Destinations." Unpublished manuscript, University of Wisconsin, Milwaukee.

Sosa Pascual, Omaya. 2017. "Hurricane Maria's Death Toll in Puerto Rico Is Higher than Official Count, Experts Say." http://www.miamiherald.com/news/weather/hurricane/article175955031.html#storylink=cpy. Accessed September 29, 2017.

Sotomayor, Orlando. 2009. "Puerto Rican Migration Flows and the Theory of Migrant Self-Selection." *World Development* 37(3): 726–738.

Stanchich, Maritza. 2016 (September 26). "Dark Star: Puerto Rico Reels from 3-Day Blackout." *The Huffington Post Blog,* http://www.huffingtonpost.com/maritza-stanchich-phd/dark-star-puerto-rico-reels-from-3-day-blackout_b_12166262.html. Accessed November 12, 2016.

Stiglitz, Joseph. 2017 (February 27). "Letter to the Editor." *The New York Times, https://www.nytimes.com/2017/02/27/opinion/joseph-stiglitz-the-nobel-laureate-on-saving-puerto-rico.html?_r=2.* Accessed May 25, 2017.

Stiglitz, Joseph, and Martin Guzman. 2017 (February 28). "From Bad to Worse for Puerto Rico." *Project Syndicate – The World's Opinion Page,* https://www.project-syndicate.org/commentary/puerto-rico-debt-plan-deep-depression-by-joseph-e--stiglitz-and-martin-guzman-2017–02?barrier=accessreg. Accessed May 21, 2017.

Storey, D.J. 1991. "The Birth of New Firms: Does Unemployment Matter? A Review of the Literature." *Small Business Economics* 3: 167–178.

TheAtlantic.com. 2016. http://www.theatlantic.com/business/archive/2016/07/puerto-rico-promesa-debt/89797/. Accessed, August 3, 2016.

TheGlobalEconomy.com. 2016. www.TheGlobalEconomy.com. Accessed July 5, 2016.

The White House. 2016 (June 11). "Weekly Address: Addressing Puerto Rico's Economic Crisis." *Office of the Press Secretary, https://www.whitehouse.gov/the-press-office/2016/06/11/weekly-address-addressing-puerto-ricos-economic-crisis.* Accesses August 22, 2016.

Thurik, Roy, Martin Anthony Carree, Andre van Stel, and David B. Audretsch. 2008. "Does Self-Employment Reduce Unemployment?" *Journal of Business Venturing* 23(6): 673–686.

Turner, Tracy M., and Heather Luea. 2009. "Homeownership, Wealth Accumulation and Income Status." *Journal of Housing Economics* 18(2): 104–114.

United Nations. 2016 (June 20). "Special Committee on Decolonization Approves Text Calling upon United States Government to Expedite Self-Determination Process for Puerto Rico." Press Release, https://www.un.org/press/en/2016/gacol3296.doc.htm. Accessed May 25, 2017.

U.S. Bureau of the Census. 2016. *Annual Estimates of the Resident Population for the United States, Regions, States, and Puerto Rico* (various issues). Accessed September 23. http://www.census.gov/popest/data/historical/index.html.

———. 2015. Economic Census Shows Puerto Rico's Manufacturers Had Shipments of Nearly $77 Billion. Press release, http://www.prnewswire.com/news-releases/economic-census-shows-puerto-ricos-manufacturers-had-shipments-of-nearly-77-billion-300042825.html. Accessed July 15, 2017.

U.S. Bureau of Labor Statistics. 2014. *Local Area Unemployment Statistics.* Accessed June 21, 2014. http://www.bls.gov/lau/.

———. 2014. *Labor Force Statistics from the Current Population Survey.* Accessed June 21. http://www.bls.gov/cps/.

U.S. Government Accountability Office. 2006. *Puerto Rico: Fiscal Relations with the Federal Government and Economic Trends during the Phaseout of the Possessions Tax Credit.* Washington, DC: GAO Report to the Chairman and Ranking Minority Member, Committee on Finance, US Senate, GAO-06-541.

Valentín, Luis J. 2016 (September 30). "Puerto Rico Government and Public Corporations under Control of Fiscal Oversight Board." *Caribbean Business,* http://caribbean-business.com/promesas-fiscal-board-holds-first-meeting/. Accessed October 9, 2016

Vargas, Yaisha. 2005 (May 25). "Puerto Rico Watches Corporate Tax Breaks Finally Expire." *Puerto Rico Herald* http://www.puertorico-herald.org/issues2/2005/vol09n23/PRWatchCorpTax.html

Vargas-Ramos, Carlos and García-Ellín, Juan, C. 2013. "Demographic Transitions: Settlement and Distribution of the Puerto Rican Population in the United States." *Center for Puerto Rican Studies,* Hunter College, Issued July, 2013, Centro RB2013-05.

Vázquez-Calzada, José L. 1988. *La Población de Puerto Rico y su Trayectoria Histórica.* Raga Printing, Rio Piedras, Puerto Rico.

Vélez, William. 2015. "The Status of Puerto Ricans in New Destination: Towards a New Framework." Unpublished manuscript, University of Wisconsin, Milwaukee.

Vélez, William, and Giovani Burgos. 2010. "The Impact of Housing Segregation and Structural factors on the Socioeconomic Performance of Puerto Ricans in the United States." *Centro Journal* 22, no. 1: 174–198.

Venator-Santiago, Charles R., and Edgardo Meléndez (Guest Eds.). 2017. *CENTRO - Special Issue on U.S. Citizenship in Puerto Rico: One Hundred Years after the Jones Act,* 29(1).

Walsh, Mary Williams. 2016 (August 6). "A Surreal Life on the Precipice in Puerto Rico." *The New York Times,* http://www.nytimes.com/2016/08/07/business/dealbook/life-in-the-miasma-of-puerto-ricos-debt.html?smprod=nytcore-iphone&smid=nytcore-iphone-share&_r=3. Accessed August 7, 2016.

Warren, Charles W., Westoff, Charles F., Herald, Joan M., Rochat, Roger W., and Smith, Jack C. 1986. "Contraceptive Sterilization in Puerto Rico." *Demography* 23(3): 351–365.

Weyl, Ben. 2016 (October 14). "Pence: Cuba Executive Orders Will Be Overturned." *Politico,* See http://www.politico.com/story/2016/10/mike-pence-cuba-executive-orders-229827. Accessed November 15, 2016.

Whalen, Carmen, and Víctor Vázquez-Hernández (Editors). 2005. *The Puerto Rican Diaspora: Historical Perspectives.* Philadelphia, PA: Temple University Press.

Wilson Kenneth L., and Alejandro Portes. 1980. "Immigrant Enclaves: An Analysis of the Labor Market Experience of Cubans in Miami." *American Journal of Sociology* 86: 295–319.

World Bank. 2013. *Countries and Economies.* Accessed September 9. http://data.worldbank.org/country.

World Population Pyramid. 2017. http://www.worldpopulationpyramid.info/. Accessed July 17, 2017.

Zients, Jeffrey. 2016 (June 7). "Puerto Rico's Fiscal Crisis: What You Need To Know," *The White House Blog,* https://www.whitehouse.gov/blog/2016/06/07/puerto-ricos-fiscal-crisis-what-you-need-know. Accessed August 22, 2016.

Index

About the Authors

Alberto Dávila is professor of economics and associate dean for Administration, Graduate Studies and Research at the Robert C. Vackar College of Business & Entrepreneurship at The University of Texas Rio Grande Valley (UTRGV). Prior to this position, Dávila served as the department chair of Economics and Finance and professor at the University of Texas—Pan American from 1997 to 2015, and was a tenured faculty member at the University of New Mexico. He earned his PhD and MS degrees in Economics from Iowa State University and a BA degree in Economics from Pan American University.

Dávila's research interests include the economics of the U.S.-Mexico border, the economics of immigration, and Hispanic labor markets. Dávila has published extensively on these topics since 1982, first appearing in the *Federal Reserve Bank of Dallas' Economic Review*, and has a coedited book with Marie T. Mora, *Labor Market Issues along the U.S.-Mexico Border* (University of Arizona Press, 2009), and (also with Marie T. Mora) an award-winning book *Hispanic Entrepreneurs in the 2000s* (Stanford University Press, 2013). Moreover, he has received such professional honors as the *Small Business Administration District Research Advocate Award for the Lower Rio Grande Valley* (2003); the *Distinguished Alumnus Award* from the College of Business Administration at U.T.-Pan American's seventy-fifth anniversary (Fall 2002), and the *Academic Achievement Award* from the American Society of Hispanic Economists' (January 2014), among other research and teaching awards.

Marie T. Mora is professor of economics and associate vice provost for faculty diversity at the University of Texas Rio Grande Valley (UTRGV). Prior to this position, she was professor of economics and vice provost fellow for faculty affairs at the University of Texas—Pan American (which was consolidated to form UTRGV) after being a tenured faculty member at New Mexico State University. Mora earned her PhD in economics from Texas A&M University, and BA and MA degrees from the University of New Mexico (UNM) in her hometown of Albuquerque.

Mora is nationally recognized for her research on Hispanic socioeconomic outcomes, and has been invited to share her expertise with a variety of agencies and organizations across the country, including the White House Council of Economic Advisers; the White House Initiative for the Educational Excellence of Hispanics; the Board of Governors of the Federal Reserve System; the U.S. Department of Labor, and others. She is currently serving on the Data Users Advisory Committee of the Bureau of Labor Statistics (BLS). Her publications include over forty-five refereed authored/coauthored journal articles and book chapters, an award-winning coauthored book (*Hispanic Entrepreneurs in the 2000s: An Economic Profile and Policy Implications*, Stanford University Press, 2013) with Alberto Dávila, and two coedited volumes (*The Economic Status of the Hispanic Population*, Information Age Publishing, 2013; and *Labor Market Issues along the U.S.-Mexico Border*, University of Arizona Press, 2009), both with Alberto Dávila.

Mora's recent national honors include the *Inspiring Leaders in STEM Award* (*Insight into Diversity* magazine, 2017); *Outstanding Support of Hispanic Issues in Higher Education Award* (American Association for Hispanics in Higher Education, 2016); *Cesar Estrada Chavez Award* (American Association for Access, Equity, and Diversity, 2015); *Distinguished Alumnus Award* (UNM Department of Economics, 2015); and an invited published essay on the growing importance of Hispanics in the United States, commemorating the BLS *Monthly Labor Review*'s Centennial (September 2015); among others.

Dr. Havidán Rodríguez is president of the University of Albany, State University at New York. Prior to this position, he was professor of sociology and founding provost and executive vice president for academic affairs at the University of Texas Rio Grande Valley (UTRGV). Rodríguez previously served as professor and president, ad interim, at the University of Texas— Pan American (UTPA); provost and vice president for academic affairs at UTPA; and professor and deputy provost at the University of Delaware, among other positions. He earned his PhD in sociology from the University of Wisconsin-Madison.

Rodríguez has a significant number of publications in two major—and often overlapping—research areas: (1) social science aspects of disasters and (2) socioeconomic outcomes of Hispanics in the United States. He is the coeditor (with Enrico L. Quarantelli and Russell Dynes) of the *Handbook of Disaster Research* (Springer, 2006) and the coeditor (with Rogelio Sáenz and Cecilia Menjívar) of *Latinas/os in the United States: Changing the Face of América* (Springer, 2008). Rodríguez has led and participated in a number of field research projects, including trips to Honduras, following Hurricane Mitch; India and Sri Lanka, following the Indian Ocean Tsunami; and the Gulf Coast, following Hurricane Katrina. He has received funding from a variety of agencies, including NSF, the Ford Foundation, NIMH, FEMA, and others.

Throughout his career, Rodríguez has received numerous recognitions and awards, including the *Top Latino Leaders Award* (Council for Latino Workplace Equity, National Diversity Council, 2017); *Inspiring Leaders in STEM Award* (*Insight into Diversity* magazine, 2017); *Cesar Estrada Chavez Award* (American Association for Access, Equity and Diversity, 2016); being highlighted in *Bright Spots in Hispanic Education* by the White House Initiative on Educational Excellence for Hispanics (September 2015); being the June 2015 cover story of *The Hispanic Outlook in Higher Education*; the *Alfredo G. de los Santos, Jr. Distinguished Leadership Award* (American Association of Hispanics in Higher Education, 2015); *Hispanic of the Year* (2007) in Delaware for which he received a *Professional Achievement Award*; and the *National Disaster Medical System Outstanding Achievement Award* (FEMA, 2004); among others.